C000154176

Software Engineer's Pocket Book

Michael Tooley

Newnes
An imprint of Butterworth-Heinemann Ltd
Linacre House, Jordan Hill, Oxford OX2 8DP

A member of the Reed Elsevier plc group

OXFORD   LONDON   BOSTON
MUNICH   NEW DELHI   SINGAPORE   SYDNEY
TOKYO   TORONTO   WELLINGTON

First published 1994

British Library Cataloguing in Publication Data
A catalogue record for this book is available
from the British Library

ISBN 0 7506 0749 1

Typeset by *Steve Heath*
Printed and bound in Great Britain

Contents

Preface

Software engineering is primarily concerned with the specification, design, implementation and maintenance of fully optimized software systems. By definition, such 'optimized' systems should be both efficient and cost-effective. Furthermore, the 'software' should be supported by appropriate documentation and operating procedures.

Professionals involved with software engineering (i.e. software engineers) are responsible for the effective management of part (or all) of the software development process; they are not primarily computer scientists nor are they just programmers.

The practice of software engineering combines analytical skills with creativity in a disciplined approach to the specification, design, implementation and ongoing maintenance of a software product. Furthermore, since modern software products can be extremely complex, the process of software engineering is greatly assisted by the use of formal methods for design, testing and analysis.

The Software Engineer's Pocket Book is based on extracts from John McDermid's Software Engineer's Reference Book (Butterworth-Heinemann, ISBN 0-7506-0813-7). Further details of this book are included after the index. By virtue of its compact size, the Pocket Book is neither as exhaustive nor as comprehensive as the very much larger book on which it is based. For this reason, readers are advised to consult the Software Engineer's Reference Book for information on topics such as software development management, configuration management, metrics and measurements.

The Pocket Book is aimed at anyone who is involved with the specification, design, development, implementation, testing, maintenance and quality assurance of software. It provides an overview of current techniques and will thus appeal to newcomers and students as well as practising software engineers who need a handy reference book. The main aim has been that of giving the reader a broad appreciation of the subject, including an introduction to state of the art development techniques and formal methods.

The first chapter describes the process of software development and deals with requirements analysis, design methods, the software life cycle, process modelling, software testing, maintenance and quality management.

Programming languages are described in the second chapter. This chapter provides information on low and high-level languages and also outlines some modern techniques of program development. The third chapter deals with operating systems and with such important concepts as multiprogramming and multiprocessing.

The remaining chapters deal with discrete mathematics and numerical computation, data structures and algorithms. These three chapters include sections on logic, set theory, functions, relations, and computer arithmetic.

The book concludes with appendices which describe the standards relating to software development together with a comprehensive list of abbreviations used in software engineering.

Acknowledgments

The material in this book has been based extensively upon the Software Engineer's Reference Book (Butterworth-Heinemann ISBN 0-7506-0813-7) and the author wishes to acknowledge the work of a number of fellow authors and contributors including:

Chapter 1

Georgio Ausiello	La Sapienza University, Rome
Keith Bennett	University of Durham
John McDermid	University of York
John Buxton	Kings' College, London
Barry Cornelius	University of Durham
Darrel Ince	The Open University
Malcolm Munro	University of Durham
Martyn Ould	Praxis plc
Dave Robson	University of Durham
David Stokes	Praxis plc

Chapter 2

Roy Dowsing	University of East Anglia
Dorothy Graham	Grove Consultants
John Henderson	King's College, London
Brian Meek	Goldsmiths' College, London

Chapter 3

Laurie Keller	The Open University

Chapter 4

Tim Denvir	Praxis Systems and Brunel University
Brian Monahan	University of Manchester
Roger Shaw	Lloyd's Register of Shipping

Chapter 5

Peter Wallis	University of Bath

Chapter 6

Georgio Ausiello	La Sapienza University, Rome

Appendices

Patrick Hall	Brunel University
Maurice Resnick	EDS

Finally, special thanks are due to Janet Harper and Marylin Foster of the Computer Services Unit at Brooklands College.

Michael Tooley

Chapter 1

Software development

1.1 Introduction

As with any other engineering discipline, software development requires a purposeful, structured and methodical approach. Understanding, selecting and controlling the process of software development is fundamental to reducing and managing development risks.

This first chapter deals with the process of software development. It begins by describing the life cycle of software development from both technical and managerial viewpoints and continues by considering the stages, methods and approaches employed within software development projects.

The first technical activity within a software development project is crucial to the overall success of the project. This stage, requirements analysis, involves eliciting from potential users of the system their views on its intended functionality and other properties. Because of its importance, this activity is mentioned in some detail.

The definition of the system architecture forms a 'grand plan' which identifies the major system components and their inter-relationships. Like requirements analysis, architectural design is pivotal in the system development process and errors made at this stage, but not caught until implementation, are likely to be very expensive and very difficult to rectify. Architectural design methods (HOOD and MASCOT3) and structured methods (SA/SD, JSD and SSADM) are briefly considered within sections in this chapter.

In the normal process of software development, testing is the primary means for showing that the implementation has the requisite functionality and other (non-functional) properties. The chapter explains why testing should be considered to be an integral part of the software life cycle and how it should be performed.

Software maintenance can be perfective, adaptive, corrective or preventive and a number of tools for the maintenance of software projects are briefly described.

An ability to assess and control risks is essential if timescales and budgets are to be met. The next section explains the basic concepts of risk management within the software development process.

Finally, the chapter concludes with a section which deals with quality management systems and methods which can be used to control the quality of a software development project.

1.2   The software development life cycle

The software development 'life cycle' deals with the process of software development from initial concepts, through delivery and acceptance testing to ongoing maintenance. Life cycle models (LCMs) are abstract descriptions of the structured, methodical development and modification process, showing the main stages in specifying, producing and maintaining executable software. Although the target of the development process is the production of working software, the models have a much wider scope, being concerned with requirements, design specification, verification, and so on.

It is valuable to discuss life cycle models in order to understand the development process as a whole, to see relationships between different activities, and to understand the requirements for methods and tools to support each aspect of the life cycle.

Essentially, there are two main approaches to modelling the development of software; one treating the software life cycle from the technical point of view, the other taking a managerial viewpoint. These different approaches clearly relate to the same underlying process.

1.2.1   *Technical models*

Technical models are concerned with stages of development (i.e. technically related collections of activities such as the elicitation and validation activities in requirements analysis. Typical stages include requirements analysis, architectural design, detailed design and implementation. They are each characterised by being at a particular level of abstraction with respect to the executable software to be produced by the development project.

1.2.2   *Management models*

Management models are concerned with phases (i.e. temporarily related groups of activities). Typically, phases start and stop at well-defined points in time, and terminate with a review of some products. These products may relate to more than one stage. Some groups of activities, e.g. acceptance testing, might be referred to both as a technical stage and as a phase. However, in general there will be a complex relationships between the stages and phases which depends on the methods used for software development.

1.3   Selection of stages and methods

It is necessary for any development project to select, or design, its process, and both technical and managerial decisions have to be made. From a technical point of view the most important decisions are the choice of the set of stages, and the choice of methods to deal with each stage.

Note that there is a distinction between stages and levels of documentation. A project may decide to have an architectural design stage but, because of the size of the project, to have three levels of architectural design specification. The former is a technical decision and the latter is a managerial decision to do with the management of risk, setting of review points, and so on.

There is a set of development stages which are inherent in software development. However, structuring of these stages depends on the development paradigm chosen and, to some extent, the nature of the relationship with the customer for the system. These issues are briefly discussed below. Factors affecting each stage in the process are then considered, as are the choice of methods for each stage in the process.

1.3.1   Selection of stages

It should be stressed that the concern here is about the selection of constructive stages, i.e. those steps which produce descriptions, or specifications, of the system being developed. Thus, from the technical point of view, unit testing is part of the implementation stage even though, managerially, it may be a separate phase. This approach is adopted quite simply because different stages deal with different forms of risk.

Five development stages can be identified:

1.	Requirements analysis	⎫
2.	System specification	⎬ What
3.	Architectural design	⎫
4.	Detailed design	⎬ How
5.	Implementation (coding)	⎭

Maintenance, or evolution, may revisit any or all of the above stages.

The first two, requirements analysis and system specification, are in the domain of requirements, i.e. what the customer or user wants. The distinction between these two stages is that requirements are concerned with the operational environment for the system to be built, as well as the system itself, whereas the system specification is not. Indeed, the system specification can be thought of as the interface definition between the system to be built and its environment.

The remaining three stages are in the design domain, i.e. how the system developer intends to satisfy the requirements. The architecture represents the overall system structure and other important characteristics such as resource usage. The two further stages represent progressively greater levels of detail until one reaches the level of executable code. In practice there may well be multiple levels of detailed design and the number of levels will be dictated by the scale of the system being developed.

This set of stages and associated descriptions can be described as canonical as they each serve essential and different purposes.

Requirements analysis

The requirements are a primary communication vehicle between user and software engineer, and they identify the boundary between the system and its environment. This is an essential stage as one often does not know, ab initio, what functionality should be included in a system and which should not. This stage addresses the risk of specifying (and building) the wrong system.

System specification

The system specification defines precisely the interface at the system boundary to provide a basis for design and acceptance testing. This description addresses the (managerial and technical) risk that the system will be delivered and rejected as inappropriate. By contrast with the requirements, the system specification need not address the environment and it should be precise enough for acceptance testing against it to be unequivocal (the requirements need not).

Architectural design

The architecture shows how to satisfy the requirements, including the non-functional attributes, by defining the overall system structure and essential functionality and resource requirements. This is a key stage as the structure of the architecture may need to be different from the requirements to deal with non-functional attributes, e.g. performance, or fault-tolerance. This stage addresses the (technical) risk that the whole design will prove ill-founded because it is infeasible to satisfy the requirements given the basic design, i.e. tinkering with implementation won't overcome basic design faults. (Note: the results of many projects are never used, with basic architectural faults probably a major contributory cause.)

Detailed design

The detailed design adds enough detail to separate pieces of the architecture so that a software engineer can proceed to implement the programs which constitute the final system. This also addresses technical risk, albeit at a lower level.

Implementation

Implementation (or coding) consists of the production of the programs that implement the functionality of each module. This phase also involves the production of relevant module documentation.

Verification and validation (V & V)

Verification is concerned with demonstrating consistency and completeness within a description, and also that one description bears the correct relationship to another. Validation is concerned with demonstrating that the descriptions are consistent with initial system concepts, and high-level objectives.

Verification of consistency requires a demonstration that there are no contradictions in a particular description. Structured methods tend either to have well defined rules for transformation which obviate the need for explicit verification, or to be based on a much looser concept of correspondence between the descriptions. For these latter methods, verification implies production of informal arguments about the soundness of the transformation, or holding design reviews, structured walkthroughs, etc. These techniques have been shown to be very effective and are equally applicable to formal methods. When using structured techniques much verification is carried out by testing. It is also valuable with formal methods, although the role is rather different. With formal methods, mathematical analysis (proof) is used for verification, reducing the risk of error in development, but at increased cost.

Meeting the client's needs

In essence, descriptions associated with these canonical stages reflect interfaces between groups of individuals, e.g. users and requirements analysts, or analysts and designers. Thus they form a basis for intra-project communication as well as risk reduction or management. Clearly, therefore, the set of descriptions actually used will depend on the nature of the customer relationship.

If the developers are producing a unique system for a customer satisfying a 'new' need, e.g. automating some function which is currently carried out manually, then all stages are necessary. In particular, requirements analysis is essential to define the system boundary. However, if an existing system is to be replaced with, say, the same functionality but higher throughput, then it should be possible to proceed directly to system specification. Similar 'short cuts' will be possible in other circumstances, e.g. developing embedded systems where the design of the larger system has defined boundaries and requirements for the embedded system.

Innovative software products

A rather different situation occurs where a system is developed for a perceived market need, or opportunity. Here there is no customer to ask so it is not really feasible to produce a requirements specification (at least in the normal way). This is particularly true for innovative, 'market creating', products, e.g. spreadsheets when they were first developed. Here it may be possible to go directly to an architectural specification from the perception of market opportunity or need (probably via feasibility studies). Alternatively, requirements and system specification documents may be produced albeit as 'frames of reference' for the designers, rather than as documents for communication with a customer. The choice may well depend on the development approach adopted (contractual, incremental or prototyping, see below).

1.3.2 Choice of development approach

The stages identified clearly map most directly on to a contractual approach to software development. In such an *approach* there would be a one to one mapping between stages and (sets of) contractual specifications. A similar relationship will hold with an incremental *approach* (i.e. defining and developing only one part of a system at a time). Note, however, that within the framework of an overall development contract, each individual contractual specification will correspond to a single increment.

With *prototyping* (i.e. an approach based on successive investigations of feasibility as a project develops) the mapping is less clear. For example, in developing a product for the market one might use a prototype to investigate the 'problem' and the design space and also to serve as a system specification and architectural model. Thus a prototype, with supporting documentation, may fulfil the role of the description for more than one stage. Thus prototyping can blur the distinctions between stages identified above.

The choice of stages and development paradigms is a precursor to choosing methods. Each of the 'canonical' stages has a role to play in development. If a stage is omitted it should be made clear how that role is to be fulfilled.

Other considerations

A number of other issues should be considered during all stages of the life cycle. These include:

1. Specifications should be 'modularised' in order to be able to divide specification and implementation tasks among the members of a development team.

2. Different notations used throughout the life cycle should relate to one another. This means that they should not be wantonly different in linguistic form and, more significantly, that they should be based on compatible models of the system.

3. Languages should be tailored to particular application areas in order to promote greater efficiency in the development of specifications (for many applications, 4GLs should now be considered).

4. The specification of non-functional requirements and other facets of the design should be considered.

1.3.3   Choosing descriptions

In any development it is essential to have some form of a statement of requirements and an architecture. Without the requirements one has no way of knowing when the project has been (successfully) completed. Without the architecture one has no way of controlling the development process, as the architecture will form the basis for dividing the system up in to work packages, and for carrying out integration and integration testing prior to acceptance and delivery. The choice of other descriptions (levels) is governed by:

1. The size of the application. In general the larger the application, the more descriptions are needed to handle the complexity. (Note: this might mean having several levels of description within one stage of the process.)

2. Whether the application area is new or old. In new areas there is likely to be a need for more explicit documentation to counteract unfamiliarity.

3. Whether the system is being developed for a specific customer or it is being developed against a general requirement for a perceived marketplace.

4. The skill of the project staff. In general higher levels of skill imply that one can use fewer descriptions (although one should not forget the issue of maintenance).

These four factors are probably the most important for choice of 'levels' of description, but other issues are also relevant, such as the technical characteristics of the application. For example, for a safety critical system one would expect to produce far more descriptions, etc., than for a non-critical application, because of the cost of failure. However, these technical issues have more direct bearing on the choice of method.

Also as indicated above, one should seek to choose notations for descriptions that are modular, reflect non-functional characteristics, and perhaps are specific to the problem area. The notations chosen for each stage should be compatible. There are many circumstances where it is appropriate to take an eclectic approach to specification rather than to seek a ubiquitous notation, where each notation deals with a different facet of the system, e.g. timing, or functionality.

1.3.4   Choosing methods

The characteristics of each project that an organisation undertakes are different. Hence, in principle, methods should be selected for each project. This 'ideal' is constrained by training costs, availability of suitable tools, etc., but it is still helpful to consider this ideal. The STARTS Guide (DTI, 1987) gives some important and helpful criteria for choosing methods including maturity, level of tool support, etc.

Some methods are good at dealing with particular classes of system, e.g. real-time systems, and poor with other classes, e.g. database systems. The technical characteristics of an application and of the available methods should drive the choice of methods for the project to develop that application.

Many methods purport to span the full life cycle, but few, if any, effectively cover the life cycle in its entirety. Hence it is necessary to consider combinations of methods for particular development projects.

There are three primary technical factors which influence the selection of methods:

1. Technical characteristics of the application.

2. Technical characteristics of the methods.

3. Life cycle coverage.

In principle one needs to choose methods for each stage of the life cycle which are good at dealing with the technical characteristics of the application and which are technically compatible.

In selecting methods for a new application one should seek a set of methods which:

1. Covers all the life cycle stages chosen for the project.

2. Minimises the number of distinct methods.

3. Makes the best match of method and application characteristics.

4. Has compatible system models and similar notations.

In practice it is unlikely that a perfect match will be found. It will usually be necessary to 'strengthen' the chosen methods either by adding techniques from other methods, or by semi-managerial approaches such as instituting more thorough design reviews for critical projects.

Additionally, it is desirable to choose methods which give some guidelines for transformations and preferably give scope for automated transformation. However, care must be exercised to avoid getting caught in a 'straitjacket' by selecting a transformation tool which cannot be adopted to changing (non-functional) requirements.

A further criterion for selecting methods is that they should have well-defined rules and guidelines for V & V. An associated criterion is that they should deal adequately with consistency, completeness and quality.

For many projects a positive decision is made to undertake incremental development. Pragmatically, a lot of work is undertaken incrementally anyway. In other words, much development is concerned with changing existing specifications or programs, not with creating them anew. Thus an important criterion is to select methods which support incremental change, and incremental (re)verification and validation.

1.4 Software development from the project management viewpoint

The primary aim in software project management is to control the development process so that the resultant product is delivered:

1. On time.

2. Within budget.

3. Of acceptable quality and reliability.

4. Meeting customer's requirements and expectations.

5. Satisfying the specifications, etc.

Note that these latter two points are not equivalent and it is here that many of the problems of software development arise.

To achieve these objectives, it is necessary for project managers to prepare development plans, to monitor progress against the plans, to take remedial action if there are significant deviations from the plan, and so on. The 'technical' process models presented in the previous sections showed that iteration occurs in software development, for example, to correct errors or to satisfy the requirements for additional functionality in the system. Thus one of the most significant responsibilities, and major sources of difficulty, in project management is the achievement of control over the iterative nature of software development.

While management is thus strongly linked with technical activities, it is primarily concerned with:

1. Risk assessment, e.g. deciding whether or not a system is technically or economically feasible.

2. Planning and control, e.g. monitoring progress and replanning as necessary.

3. Decision making, e.g. selecting between alternative implementation strategies.

These issues are reflected in management-oriented models, which will be discussed from a semi-historical perspective, building up to the basis for the canonical life cycle model.

1.4.1   The waterfall model

The waterfall model (Figure 1.1) was derived from the thinking in the late 1960s. The intention is that the process remains under control if all rework needs only to go back one step for the team to retrieve the situation and then to have a basis for further progress. However, this is generally not easily achievable. Design iterations may not be confined to successive stages, leading to the sort of situation shown in Figure 1.2, with consequent problems in the cost of correcting the software and loss of control of the project.

This model of the process of working makes perfectly good sense when the software is developed by an individual, or by a team acting cohesively as an individual. In this case the management perception is limited primarily to 'started', 'working' and 'finished product'. When there is a larger organisation and more attempt to gain management insight and control of progress, then there is a significant problem in the meaning of the backwards arrows. Clearly the fact of rework is unarguable. But if the steps represent progress in time, then the backward arrows cannot represent reverse time. They must mean that any step can be revisited as required and anyone in the team can be working on any of the steps on any part of the product at any point in time. There is no control of such a software development team and management waits with bated breath until they have finished. This is the way many software projects were run, but by the late 1960s this was no longer acceptable and software development projects had to become better organised and more controllable.

1.4.2   Classical life cycle phases

The idea of a phase is based on the simple but fundamental principle that it ends at a specific point in time with a predefined set of items which undergo a thorough review.

The strongest early drive for definition of phases was based in the methods of working developed between the Department of Defense and its suppliers, and defined in American Military

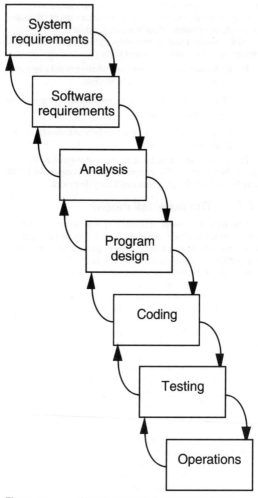

Figure 1.1   *Classical waterfall model of software development.*

Standards. The resulting philosophy of a method of working has been extensively documented. The example in Figure 1.3 is taken from a paper by Goldberg (1977) reporting work at TRW.

Deliverable sub-products should be reviewed against checklists at each phase. This naturally leads to thorough definitions of the form of the reviews, the standards and procedures and a whole method of working which can be understood and supported by management and the customer. Also, the staff on the software

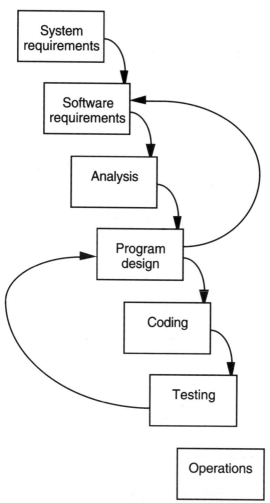

Figure 1.2   *Uncontrollable model - the unfortunate situation where design iterations are not confined to the successive stages.*

development team can clearly see a structure of what is expected of them, and when it is expected. Additionally, they can expect training in an explicit way of working.

The set of phases shown in Figure 1.3, or something similar, is what has become known as the classical life cycle. Organisations which work on these principles refer to the life cycle model. These organisations know how to interpret the model and concentrate on developing the model by refining and interpreting the

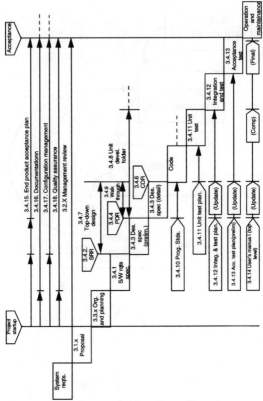

Figure 1.3   An example of a software life cycle.

definitions and standards for the phase deliverables. They also use the model, and by carrying out thorough reviews typically find errors early in the process so that the software development process is effective.

However, there are problems in trying to explain the process to management. These usually stem from relating the life cycle phases to the waterfall model and getting into complications and confusion with the idea of reworking based on 'iteration of phases'.

In the original waterfall model the team did indeed move a step (or more) back, as represented by the backward arrows, and rework before moving forward again. In Figure 1.3 the phases end at project milestones and the waterfall model is reinterpreted, as shown in Figure 1.4 (Boehm, 1976), with the backward arrows representing back references for V & V against baselines. There is now no 'iteration of phases' implied in this new version of the waterfall model, since the end of a phase is a point in time and no-one is suggesting time travel.

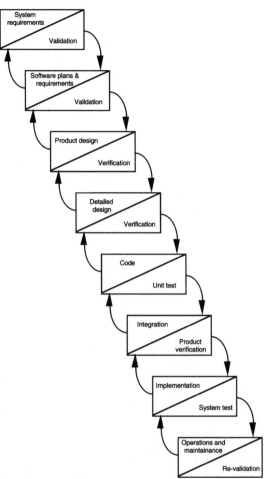

Figure 1.4 *Improved waterfall model incorporating stagewise V & V.*

Rework may be controlled within a phase when the phase-end review shows that the phase products are inadequate and further work must be done on them. The review is held again before the phase can be agreed to be finished. In fact, some organisations deliberately hold a series of informal reviews through which the work of completing the phase is really controlled. The product is then known to be acceptably complete and can be approved at a formal phase-end review.

Since staff on the project can relate to phases terminated with reviews as a helpful way of defining the software development process, the fact that there are management difficulties implies that understanding of the model is inadequate. It is therefore necessary to look at how the software development staff go about their work to find out how to improve the modelling of the process.

1.4.3   Software development activities

The activities which are the most important in each phase are defined, in principle, by the phase-end products. Thus, in the project initiation phase, the project manager must be concerned with sufficient analysis of requirements and design to be able to:

1. Plan the project.

2. Make decisions on methods, tools, procedures and standards.

3. Initiate strategies for configuration management, quality management, development facilities and testing.

In the requirements specification phase, although the major concern is with the capture and analysis of requirements and interface definitions, there is also considerable work required on updating the detail of the project plans. In the design phase, the emphasis must not only be on completing the design but also on the quality of the design for reliability, efficiency and maintainability with a major concentration on technical control.

Similar shifts in emphasis can be deduced for the subsequent phases. However, it must be clear that all activities continue across all phases of the project. Even if most of the attention of the project is concentrated on the major concern of a phase, there must be staff working on other activities during each phase.

An obvious example is architectural design. Not only must significant work be carried out on this during the requirement specification phase, it is the primary activity in the architectural design phase and there must also be a continuing strong design control to maintain design integrity during the phases following completion of the review, at the end of the architectural design phase.

Although coding of a module does not properly commence before completion of the detailed design of that module, there are still programming activities to be performed during the early phases. These include planning the coding methods and facilities, acquisition and testing of tools and, in some cases, there may be exploratory investigations into algorithms and operations to reduce perceived technical risks.

The primary activity of each of the phases should be thought of as continuing through the whole project; not as of fixed duration and stopping at the end of a phase. In a large software development, each activity should be staffed by a distinct group of people, whose numbers might grow and shrink, but whose existence is identifiable from project start to project end.

The following list is an example of a suitable set of representative activities for software development:

1. *Project management*: project level management functions. These include project level planning and control,

contract and subcontract management, customer interface, cost/schedule performance management, management reviews and audits, and includes acquisition of management tools.

2. *Technical control*: responsibility for the technical correctness and quality of the complete product and process. Covers responsibility for maintaining the integrity of the whole design during the detailed design, programming and testing phases. Specification, review and update of integration test and acceptance test plans and procedures. Acquisition of requirements and design verification and validation tools. Acquisition and support of test drivers, test tools and test data. Ensuring coherence of development process and tools.

3. *Requirements specification*: determination, specification, review and update of software functional, performance, interface and verification requirements, including acquisition of requirements analysis and specification tools. Development of requirement specification level documentation. A continuing responsibility for communication between customer requirements and the technical development staff.

4. *Architectural design:* determination, specification, review and update of hardware/software architecture, software design and database design, including acquisition of design tools. Development of structural design level documentation.

5. *Detailed design:* detailed design of individual computer program components. Development of detailed design-level documentation. When a significant number of staff is involved, includes team-level management functions.

6. *Code and unit test:* code, unit test and integration of individual computer program components, including tool acquisition. When a significant number of staff is involved, includes team-level management functions.

7. *Verification, validation and testing*: performance of independent requirements validation, design verification and validation, integration test and acceptance test, including production of test reports.

8. *Manuals production*: development and update of product support documentation: user manual, operations manual and maintenance manual.

9. *Configuration management:* product identification, operation of change control, status accounting, operation of program support library.

10. *Quality assurance*: consultancy on project standards and procedures, monitoring of project procedures in operation and quality audits of products.

Phase / Activity	Project initiation	Requirements specification	Architectural design	Detailed design
Project management	Project estimating, planning, scheduling, organisation, etc.	Project management, project planning, contracts, liaison, etc.	Project management, status monitoring, contracts, liaison, etc.	Project management, status monitoring, contracts, liaison, etc.
Technical control	Technical strategy, technical plans, technical standards	System models and risk analysis; acceptance test plan; acquire V & V tools for requirements and design Top level test plan	Design quality models and risk analysis; draft test plans; acquire test tools	Design integrity; detailed test plans; acquire test tools
Requirements specification	Analyse requirements; determine user needs	Analyse existing system;determine user needs; integrate document and iterate requirements	Update requirements	Update requirements
Architectural design	Design planning	Develop basic architecture, models, prototypes	Develop architecture, models, prototypes	Update design
Detailed design	Identify programming methods and resources	Prototypes of algorithms; team planning	Models, algorithms investigation, team planning	Detailed design; component documentation
Code and unit test	Identify programming methods and resources	Identify programming tools; team planning	Acquire programming tools and utilities; team planning	Integration planning
Verification, validation and test	V & V requirements	V & V specification	V & V structural design	V & V detailed design; V & V design changes
Manuals	Define user manual	Outline portions of user manual	Draft user and operator manuals; outline maintenance manual	Draft maintenance manual
Configuration management	CM plans and procedures	CM plans and procedures; identify CM tools	CM of requirements, design, acquire CM tools	CM of requirements design; detailed design; install CM tools; set up library
Quality assurance	QA Plans, project procedures and standards	Standards procedures; QA plans; identify QA tools	QA of requirements design, project standards, acquire QA tools	QA of requirements design, detailed design

Figure 1.5   *Software development task matrix.*

Code and unit test	Integration and test	Acceptance test	Maintenance
Project management, status monitoring, contracts, liaison, etc.	Project management, status monitoring, contracts, liaison, etc.	Project management, status monitoring, contracts, liaison, etc.	Support management, status monitoring, contracts, liaison, etc.
Design integrity; detailed test plans; install test tools	Design integrity; support test tools; monitor testing	Design integrity; support test tools; monitor acceptance	design integrity; risk analysis; test plans
Update requirements	Update requirements	Update requirements	Determine user needs and problems; update requirements
Update design	Update design	Update design	Update design
Update detailed design	Update detailed design	Update detailed design	Detailed design of changes and enhancements
Code and unit test	Integrate software; update code	Update code	Code and unit test of changes and enhancements
V & V top portions of code; V & V design changes	Perform product test; V & V design changes	Perform acceptance test; V & V design changes	V & V changes and enhancements
Full draft user and operator manuals	Final user and operator and maintenance manuals	Acceptance of manuals	Update manual
CM of requirements design, code, operate library	CM of requirements design, code, operate library	CM of requirements design, code, operate library	CM of all documentation; operate library
QA of requirements; design, code	QA of requirements; design, code, testing	QA of requirements; design, code, acceptance	QA of maintenance updates

Figure 1.5   Software development task matrix (cont)

1.4.4   Matrix of phases and activities

Using the activities defined above and the classical life cycle phases, a matrix can be drawn out, as shown in Figure 1.5, defining tasks for the teams corresponding to the specific work of an activity in a phase. The tasks can be subdivided, where relevant, to subsystems and modules of the product.

Note that this is only a simple basis for seeing the definition of the tasks, the standards and procedures that should be in use and the appropriate tools, etc. for every box in the matrix. Note that the matrix is not the life cycle model; it is only the outworking of the model for a particular set of phases and activities. The more precisely defined the phases and activities, the more precisely the process can be defined in the terms of a matrix.

1.4.5   Baselines, reviews and the V-diagram

Each development phase is defined in terms of its outputs, or products. The products of the phases represent the points along the development path where there is a clear change in emphasis: where one definition of the emerging product is established, reviewed and used as the basis for the next derived definition. As such, they are the natural milestones of the development progression and offer objective visibility of that progression.

To use this visibility for effective management control, a software development process based on the model uses the concept of baselines. A 'baseline' established at any stage in the development process is a set of information which defines the product at that stage.

The completion of each phase is determined by the satisfactory review of the defined products of that phase and the products placed under configuration management. These products then form the baseline for the work in the next phase. The products of the next phase are measured and verified against previous baselines before themselves forming a new baseline. In this way confidence in project progress is progressively built on successive baselines.

It should be noted that the phase boundaries represent discontinuities in the product development. Representations or descriptions differ between phases. For example, a requirements specification is very different from a design in terms of the viewpoint (*what* the system does versus *how* it does it) and hence the semantics and notation of the documentation. In a large project the staff involved in different phases are often different. Discontinuities are weak points in any process, so although phases provide the basis for managerial control points, extra care must be taken to avoid misunderstandings and undetected ambiguities. This is one area where technical control is essential.

A common representation of the phases of software development is the V-diagram, an example of which is shown in Figure 1.6. Here the rectangular boxes represent the phases and oval boxes represent the baselined phase products. The form of the diagram has the advantage of showing the symmetry between the

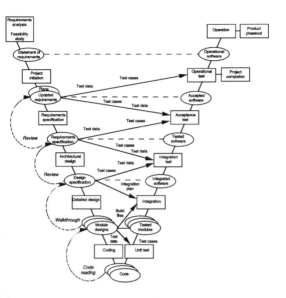

**Figure 1.6   V-diagram showing the software develop-
ment life cycle.**

successive decomposition of the design and the building of the
product by successive stages of integration and test. Figure 1.6
also shows the verification and testing relationships. The product
of each specification and design phase is verified against the
previous baseline. The product of each integration phase is tested
with data derived from the corresponding design or specification
baseline on the left-hand side of the diagram. Validation occurs at
many points in the process, particularly associated with reviews
and testing.

Formal reviews at baseline stages of development are the
most powerful determinant of the successful control of progress
of a project. The review team should include not only development personnel but also experts from other projects and disciplines and, whenever possible, customer and user personnel.

The involvement of the user cannot be over-emphasized. One
of the most frequent causes of unreliability or failure to achieve
the required performance of a product is associated with the
requirements and the users' expectations of their implementation
in the final product. Getting the requirements right is arguably
both the most essential and most difficult activity in a software
project, and close involvement of the customer/user throughout
the development process is essential, but nowhere is it more
effective than at project reviews.

It can be seen from the V-diagram that verification takes the
form of reviews when what is being reviewed refers to the product
as a whole. This applies to the earlier phases on the lefthand side

of the V-diagram, when prototypes, draft user manuals and test cases are very valuable in actualizing otherwise theoretical specifications.

Reviews are also used at the end of the phases of the righthand side of the V-diagram, but here they are not so much the vehicle for discovering problems as reviews of the status of problems shown up in the testing, which is the primary basis for checking the correctness of the products of the phases.

In the lower part of the V-diagram, verification is on parts of the product (modules or groups of modules). Then walkthroughs, code readings and unit test inspections are much more appropriate, involving only the few staff immediately involved. Reviews can take place at small and efficient meetings. Walkthroughs are not just small reviews. They have a quite different format. Walkthroughs and code readings are better at finding different sorts of errors than reviews and where they are used staff should be explicitly trained in how to run them.

As an illustration of the classical software development process, the V-diagram is useful in a number of ways. It shows the time sequence of the phases (they do not overlap — the end of one phase corresponds to the start of the next), the principles of baselines, verification and test relationships, and major review points. The structural relationships of the various parts of the development process are seen in the context of progression towards achieving the required product, without any confusion about iterating between phases which may arise from a misinterpretation of the waterfall diagram.

1.5 Requirements analysis

Requirements analysis is the first technical activity in software development and it is concerned with eliciting, clarifying and documenting the desired functionality of some system. This fact is recognised in most life cycle models, and requirements analysis typically either comes as the first stage in the models, or follows immediately after project initiation. Many studies have shown that errors or omissions made at the requirements stage are very costly (or even impossible) to rectify. Nonetheless, requirements are often neglected or only partially completed (sometimes because managers naively think that their staff are not 'getting on with the job' if they are not producing code), leading to problems later in development. Further, current requirements analysis techniques are far from perfect. Consequently, the aim of this section is to explain the fundamental principles of requirements analysis and to evaluate the current tools and techniques in order to clarify the role, content and value of a requirements specification.

First, however, it is important to explain a few terms and to consider a number of basic issues: what requirements are, why they are needed, who uses them, and what they are used for.

The term 'requirements analysis' (or requirements engineering) is a general term which refers to a collection of processes: elicitation, specification, verification and validation. The elicitation of requirements is an information-gathering exercise to ascertain exactly what it is that the customer or user requires. Specification is used to refer to both a process and the result of that process; it involves the presentation of the gathered information in a document referred to as the requirements specification. Verification is completed to ensure that this document does not contain any inconsistencies, and validation is carried out to ensure that the document describes accurately the artefact that the customer desires.

1.5.1 Requirers, facilitators and implementors

These processes involve a number of roles: the requirers, the facilitators, and the implementors. The requirers include customers and users, and represent the people that need or demand a system. The facilitators are analysts, and their role is to develop, through the application of appropriate elicitation, specification, verification and validation techniques, an accurate description of the system that the requirers want. Once the requirements specification has been produced, then the implementors, consisting of designers, engineers, and project managers (e.g. the contractors), build the system. Thus the facilitators write the specification for the implementors to build the system that the requirers need. Sometimes more than one role is filled by a given individual, or group of individuals, but requirements analysis is facilitated from both technical and managerial points of view if a clear distinction is made between these roles.

1.5.2 Requirements specification

The requirements are a collection of statements that should describe in a clear, concise, consistent and unambiguous manner all significant aspects of a proposed system. They should contain enough information to enable the designers and engineers to produce a system that will satisfy the customer and the users, and nothing more. Such a definition conveys the aim or purpose of requirements but gives little indication of exactly what information a requirements document should contain, nor to what level of detail and depth the requirements should be defined. Although it is clear from the definition that there must be some description of what the system should be capable of doing, the requirements usually have to include much more information.

There are six categories of information that are present in most requirements specifications:

1. *Functionality*. A set of statements describing the functionality of the system is always included. These requirements cover not only all externally observable behaviour, but may also define some internal functionality that is 'obviously' needed to support the external behaviour.

2. *Functional constraints*. In many applications, the results returned from any computation are only useful if they satisfy a number of constraints. These constraints should be included in the requirements specification, and they,

typically, include performance, response times, capacities, numbers of users, safety standards, security standards and quality issues. These requirements do not alter the overall functionality of the system, but they do restrict the engineer to a limited subset of the possible implementations.

3. *Design constraints*. It is quite frequently the case that in addition to the functional constraints, customers will also stipulate a number of design constraints. These can cover a great variety of different things: system compatibility, the choice of hardware, the choice of operating system, and may even be as specific as the size and layout of bit patterns. Such constraints should be included in the requirements document only where they are essential to customer satisfaction.

4. *Data and communication protocols*. Most systems will communicate in some way with 'the outside world', and the content (and also possibly the form) of this communication will need to be recorded in the requirements specification. This information is usually of a very high-level nature; for example, the major inputs and outputs of the system.

5. *Project management*. To ensure that the development of the project runs smoothly, and that the system is delivered to the customer's satisfaction, it is helpful to include in the requirements specification information such as deadlines, deliverables, assumptions, expected changes, life-cycle aspects, installation details, manual standards, and training information. The detail and extent of this 'managerial' information will depend upon the application and the customer/contractor agreements.

6. *Environmental description/system objectives*. Design and development of the system is likely to be more successful if the designers and engineers are aware of the reason a computer system is required, and of how the system should interact with its eventual environment. This contextual information can be provided by including in the requirements specification a description of the environment and a statement of the main system objectives. These two topics are linked as objectives are normally most readily stated in terms of the system's environment. In many ways these are the most fundamental aspects of requirements — and they are all too rarely articulated.

1.6 Methods for architectural design

Architectural design is the primary high-level design phase and many techniques deal with one or more facets of this process. Several of the available methods are briefly described in this section. HOOD is an object-oriented design composition method whilst MASCOT3 is a widely used real-time method. Structured methods, such as SA/SD and JSD are also intended for use in the (architectural) design phase. These are also briefly mentioned.

1.6.1 HOOD

HOOD (Hierarchical Object Oriented Design) is based on work on object-oriented design in relation to Ada carried out by Booch (1983 and 1986). In HOOD, objects are the basic unit of modularity. Each object is named and comprises a body that implements the provided operations and resources. HOOD enforces structuring of the objects according to three principles:

1. Abstraction, information hiding and encapsulation. Objects are defined by their external properties only (algebraic specification), and the internal structure is hidden from users of the objects.

2. Hierarchical decomposition and use:

   (a) *Composition hierarchy*. Objects may be composed from other objects, so that a system can be constructed as 'parent' objects including 'child' objects.

   (b) *Use hierarchy*. Objects may use operations provided by other objects, so that a system can be constructed with 'senior' objects using 'junior' objects in the hierarchy.

3. Control structuring:

   (a) *Passive objects*. Passive objects are invoked via a form of procedure call and are strongly analogous with the concept of monitors or MASCOT IDAs.

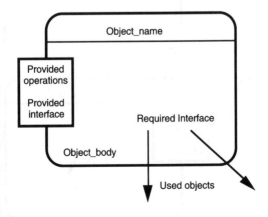

Figure 1.7   Basic HOOD object

(b) *Active objects*. Active objects may operate on behalf of several client (calling) objects simultaneously in response to external stimuli. In the terminology here, active objects may include processes.

An object binds together data and the operations working on the data. The basic object notation gives the object name and shows its 'incoming' and 'outgoing' interfaces. The interface falls into two parts (see Figure 1.7):

1. The provided interface defines the operations and resources provided by the object and their associated parameters and types.

2. The required interface defines the types and operations required from other objects.

The body implements the provided operations and resources (objects and types), as described in the interface, using external and internal operations and data, or using internal objects. As indicated earlier, objects can be passive or active, and this affects the control structure in the objects:

1. *Passive*. Control is transferred from the calling to the called object, and the operation is executed immediately. After completing the operation control is returned to the calling object. The flow of control is defined in an operation control structure (OPCS).

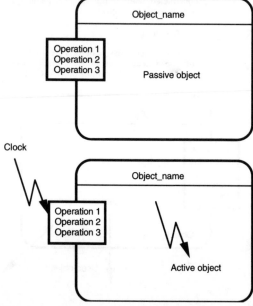

Figure 1.8   *HOOD active and passive objects.*

2. *Active.* Control is not transferred, and reaction to the stimulus will be serviced at a time determined by the internal state of the called object, as defined in a object control structure (OBCS).

The external influences on the top-level design object may 'trigger' an operation; to represent this case a 'zigzag arrow' is used. It may be annotated with the name of the associated (asynchronous) interrupt.

In either case, if the operation cannot be performed successfully, an exception can be raised and propagated to the user.

Figure 1.8 displays the graphical representations associated with active and passive objects.

The HOOD manual describes techniques for specifying object functionality based on an Ada-style pseudo-code. Thus HOOD deals with most facets of an architectural specification; the primary exception is the handling of resources and interfaces. The main methodological weaknesses are the absence of sufficient analysis techniques, and the concept of transactions for supporting such analyses.

1.6.2   MASCOT

MASCOT (Modular Approach to Software Construction Operation and Test) was initially developed in the 1970s, and has evolved to its current form, MASCOT3, as a result of feedback from practical use of earlier versions of the method in real-time embedded systems. MASCOT3 embodies the notion that software is constructed, operated and tested according to a single modular scheme. This means that, once the design structure is completed, the implementation team work entirely in terms of this design structure without the need to change concepts. Thus the testing and debugging of systems developed using MASCOT is always performed in terms of the design components and concepts.

MASCOT3 assumes that there are six basic stages to the development process, but it provides notation and guidelines only for stages 2, 3 and 4:

1. Requirements and constraints.

2. Design proposal.

3. Network decomposition.

4. Element decomposition.

5. Algorithm definition.

6. Integration and test.

The design proposal is presented as a data flow network diagram containing three categories of components: active, passive and servers.

Active components are like those in HOOD and can take responsibility for implementing a specific set of conditions and/ or handling a specified set of external interactions. Passive components can store data required for communication between the active components. They also have responsibility for maintaining the integrity of their data in spite of data being simultaneously accessed by (potentially many) active components. Servers are responsible for controlling the embedded hardware devices connected to the system, and can be either passive or active depending upon the nature of the devices controlled.

The passive components are inter-communication data areas (IDAs). These may be either channels or pools. In MASCOT3, there may be more general communication areas such as HOOD passive objects. MASCOT3 is different from HOOD in that the synchronisation requirements and mechanisms are well defined.

The active components may be either subsystems or activities. The former are composite components containing other (lower level) components within them. These lower level components can be subsystems, IDAs, activities or servers, thus achieving a hierarchical representation. IDAs and servers may also be composite, but they are not allowed to contain active components. A MASCOT3 design proposal (as illustrated in Figure 1.9) is generic and must be instantiated to form a particular network (architectural design). This allows common design components, e.g. terminal servers, to be replicated in a simple fashion.

The design proposal illustrated above shows three devices, D1, D2 and D3, controlled by three servers, sv1, sv2 and sv3. These servers are instantiated from templates known as st1, st2 and st3. The subsystem ss1 is instantiated from the template subsys_1, and the set of components is configured to make the system, sys_ex. Communication within the network occurs via access interfaces ai1-3, and connect windows (w) on servers to ports (p1-3) on subsystems.

The access interfaces define a set of operations provided at the window and required at the port. It is worth noting that it is only possible to connect a window to a port if the types match, so we are guaranteed type correct system construction. Also, it is possible to have multiple MASCOT3 components satisfying the same interface, e.g. a device driver which drives a local device could be replaced by one which sends output to a device across a network without need to change the interface or the rest of the system.

The network decomposition stage of the MASCOT3 method is concerned entirely with establishing the hierarchical representation of the design down to a level of detail where the network components are either activities or non-composite IDAs and servers. At this stage the data to be held by each IDA, and the access facilities it must provide, have been determined, and the functions required of each server and activity have been defined.

In terms of modelling hierarchy MASCOT3 is similar to the methods based on SA/SD. It deals comparatively well with issues such as synchronisation and control over communication, but is relatively weak in terms of function definition and representation of timing behaviour. However, the originators of MASCOT3 intended that it should be used with other notations, e.g. state machines for defining functionality, and MASCOT3 does provide a good framework for an architectural specification.

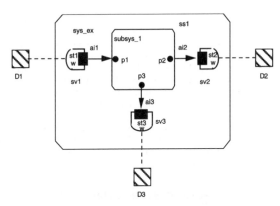

Figure 1.9   *MASCOT3 design proposal.*

Papers describing MASCOT3 in more detail can be found in a special issue of Software Engineering Journal (MASCOT, 1986) and an Official Handbook for MASCOT3 is available.

1.6.3   Structured analysis/structured design (SA/SD)

The techniques of structured analysis and structured design (SA/SD) were pioneered by De Marco (1978), and Yourdon and Constantine (1985). In applying the SA/SD (Yourdon) method, most of the process is concerned with producing and refining data flow diagrams. Initially a data flow diagram is produced which shows the whole system under consideration as a single process, with data flows going into and coming out of the system. This diagram is usually called the context diagram.

The context diagram is then refined or decomposed into a top-level data flow diagram, and this is subsequently decomposed into a number of further levels of design. As each level is produced, a number of additional data stores may be defined to hold data generated by the newly introduced functions or processes. This process stops when the individual functions or processes defined in the diagrams are believed to be small enough to be implemented simply from their specifications. These are usually referred to as primitive processes.

All the data flows and data stores in the diagram are included in a data dictionary. The data dictionary shows how the data elements are structured, or decomposed, into their component parts. There is a requirement that the flows should be consistent between the various levels of decomposition. Demonstrating consistency is usually referred to as achieving balance in the data flow diagrams.

The primitive processes are defined in more detail using the so-called mini-specs. These are usually textual specifications of the functionality expected of the process. It is common to use structured English or pseudo-code for these specifications.

These diagrams provide much of the basic structural information called for in the definition of an architectural specification. In particular, the techniques show quite well the process and inter-process communication structure. Since SA/SD represents a process structure, it has been fairly common for these techniques to be applied in real-time systems. However, SA/SD does not cover all the important issues in specifying real-time systems, so a number of developments of SA/SD have been produced dealing with timing and other issues.

One of the most commonly used extensions of SA/SD for real-time systems is that developed by Ward and Mellor (1985). More recently Hatley and Pirbhai (1987) have developed some fairly sophisticated extensions of SA/SD for dealing with real-time system specifications.

1.6.4 *Jackson System Development (JSD)*

JSD is another method that has evolved over many years of use. The original method had six steps, but JSD now comprises three basic stages: modelling, network and implementation. The notation used for JSD is conventional, and is similar to SA/SD.

The characteristic principle of JSD is that it focuses on modelling the problem which the system is intended to address, rather than addressing the detailed specification of functionality directly. This apparently simple shift in view has a fairly profound effect on the nature of the analysis process. This may imply that JSD is concerned with requirements, but it is more properly concerned with modelling those aspects of the organisation's behaviour that are going to be implemented in the system. Therefore it is properly an architectural design method rather than a requirements analysis method.

The modelling stage proceeds by looking for entities in the 'real world' and actions undertaken by those entities. An entity therefore represents some physical or logical object together with some associated actions which can modify the state of the object — in other words, it is closely analogous to the concept of object in object-oriented development. An example of such JSD entities might be a lift, which can be called, can move to a floor and so on.

The model of these entities is represented by a number of process structure diagrams (PSDs). These represent a process and its associated actions in a tree. The process is at the top of the tree and the individual actions are the leaves of the tree. With simple processes there will be only two levels in the tree — the process and the actions. For more complex processes, or entities, there will be an extended hierarchy where the intermediate nodes in the tree represent the groups of related actions.

Time ordering, alternatives, and iteration of actions are represented by simple diagrammatic conventions. More specifically, the events at the leaves form a regular grammar structure (albeit represented diagrammatically) which defines the allowable sequences of events. The state is represented by a data structure known as a state vector, and it must include enough information to support the actions and control over their ordering. Once the PSD is complete it is 'decorated' with actions and conditions, expressed as operations on the state vectors, which control selection and iteration in the regular grammar.

Determining suitable entities to form the basis of the model is an exercise which requires some skill and judgement. JSD gives some guidelines for finding suitable entities and particularly stresses the need to analyse the problem domain, rather than thinking about functionality that can be conveniently supported in a computer. However, the method recognises that this is an area where the skill of the analyst, or system architect, is most needed.

At the network stage, sometimes called the system specification stage, the architect produces system structure diagrams (SSDs). These diagrams represent the flow of data through the system. The data can be of two sorts: data streams and state vectors. The data streams are messages passing between processes, e.g. requests or commands to the processes, or reports produced as the result of a request. These are very strongly analogous to the data flows in MASCOT3. State vectors represent the internal values held by the entities, e.g. the values stored in some database. Again, some skill is required in determining the distinction between data streams and state vectors, but, typically, data streams represent transient information and state vectors represent persistent information which is held over a long period of time by the system. Perhaps more importantly, the state vectors can be written only by the process with which they are associated, but read (inspected in JSD terms) by any process.

The first part of the network stage, known as the initial model phase, primarily adds information about data flows relating to the entities identified in the previous stage. The initial model phase provides one process per instance of a model entity. Not surprisingly, this may yield more processes than are readily implementable. The issue of multiplicity of processes is dealt with in implementation. In addition, JSD provides ways of merging data flows between processes. The rules for merging give semantics for data access which are very similar to those for MASCOT channels and pools respectively.

The second part of this stage, known as the elaboration phase, may add new functions and processes to the system description. A number of new functions may be added to the entities or processes. Typically, these represent additional elementary operations which are needed to implement the existing model processes. These are often referred to as embedded functions.

The initial model phase identifies inputs and outputs to the system, but does not deal with any processing necessary to support input and output operations. As part of the elaboration phase, these additional functions, usually referred to as imposed functions, are added to the system model. Typical imposed functions include 'filters' on inputs which remove erroneous or invalid input from the user, and ensure that only valid inputs go through to the primary functions of the system which were identified at the entity modelling stage.

As part of the elaboration phase additional information is added about timing and synchronisation of the system processes. A novel feature of JSD is that it has the concept of time grain markers (TGMs) which effectively represents periodic synchronisation information. These TGMs are used to control the synchronisation and interaction of processes to ensure that data integrity is preserved.

The third stage of JSD is concerned with implementation. Whilst this is strictly outside the remit of a study of architectural design methods, it is central to JSD, so it is worthwhile briefly discussing this stage. In theory, all JSD processes can run concurrently, assuming that there are enough processor resources to support concurrent operation. In practice, there will usually be fewer processors than processes, and it is usually necessary to multiplex several processes onto one processor. JSD approaches this issue by developing an explicit schedule for execution of the system processes. It also includes a number of devices, e.g. process inversion, which are intended to optimise the process structure. Inversion eliminates some of the overhead caused by communication between concurrent processes. For example, if two processes communicate only by passing an iterated data stream, there will be a context switch every time a data item is passed. Inversion with respect to this data stream would mean that one process called the other, passing the data item as a parameter of the call. Thus a pair of communicating processes has been reduced to a single process communicating internally by procedure call, and this eliminates a good deal of scheduling and context switching overhead.

Like other methods described in this section, JSD addresses certain aspects of the architectural specification. In particular, it deals with the process structure, process communication, synchronisation and control, together with certain resource information, particularly timing. It is unusual in that it deals well with the 'protocol' aspect of architecture, determining the allowable order of events through the regular grammars. It does not directly address issues such as modularity, nor other aspects of resources such as space usage.

Once the basic entities have been identified, the method in JSD is essentially mechanistic and the proponents of JSD say that one of the great strengths is that no matter who uses the method, the same design should result, once the basic entities have been determined. This means that JSD can be very effective in certain circumstances but, if non-functional information is critical to the development, it is often very difficult to produce a satisfactory design. This is because there is no way of taking into account this information purely within the method as defined. Thus JSD is effective in many circumstances, but can become ineffective or unwieldy in other situations.

For further information, readers are referred to Jackson Systems Development (Sutcliffe, 1988). This book provides a readable and up-to-date account of the method.

1.6.5 Structured System Analysis and Design Method (SSADM)

SSADM (Nicholls, 1987) has been developed by the Central Computing and Telecommunications Agency (CCTA) of the UK government for use in data processing applications. It was originally based on a proprietary method developed by Learmonth and Burchett Management Systems (LBMS). The method is widely used in government circles in the UK and also has a considerable degree of use in commerce.

The method falls into two major phases: analysis and design. Roughly speaking, analysis corresponds to the requirements phase, and design corresponds to the architectural phase that we

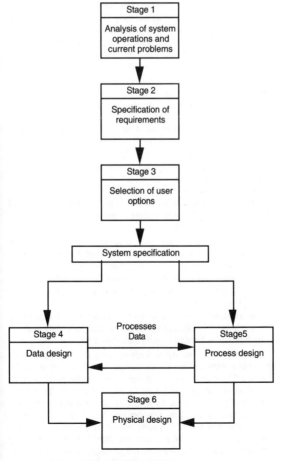

Figure 1.10   Basic SSADM structure.

are concerned with in this chapter. The method comprises six stages, three in each phase, and the interface between the two phases is the system specification. This method structure is illustrated in Figure 1.10.

In the analysis phase, the first stage looks at the current operational system, whether it is manual or automated, and investigates the problems of the system. The second stage determines the requirements for the system, and the third stage is concerned with selecting technical options for the system. That is, the third stage identifies priorities for the design and development process, and may determine major technical strategies based on results of a separate feasibility study.

In the design phase, the detailed design of the data structures and of the individual processes can be carried out in parallel. After the logical design of the data and the processes, physical design, which gives a structure for implementation in some particular hardware/software environment, is carried out. In particular, physical design is concerned with ensuring that performance requirements for the system are satisfied.

SSADM employs fairly conventional notation for modelling entity relationship structures. It also employs fairly conventional notation for dealing with process decomposition, and more abstract data structures. SSADM is frequently employed where the data requirements are large and complex. Consequently, SSADM depends very heavily on standard database analysis techniques.

SSADM provides detailed guidance on the steps that must be carried out within each stage in the method. However, the repertoire of basic techniques used in each of these stages is relatively limited. It should also be noted that SSADM is very much a data-driven method, and that one of the unique features of the method is the fact that it takes three different, but complementary, views of the data in the system.

SSADM employs data flow diagrams, strongly analogous with those used in SA/SD. The notation employed in SSADM is slightly different from that employed in SA/SD, but the structure and content of the diagrams are essentially equivalent.

SSADM supports the idea of logical data structures, which are stylised forms of entity-relationship diagrams. Those diagrams are used at a number of stages in the software development life cycle, and are the basis for third normal form data analysis which provides logically sound data structures.

SSADM also has the concept of entity life histories, which provide a view of how the data is generated or evolves in the system. These are conceptually very similar to the process structure diagrams in JSD, and show the order of events which affect some entity or data item. As with JSD, iteration and alternatives are shown in the diagrams, together with basic ordering of events.

These three sets of diagrams represent different facets of the data and processing in the system and should be viewed as being complementary, rather than isolated, descriptions of system functionality. The data flow diagram shows how processes and system maintained data fit together, as well as how the system interfaces with processes in the real world. The logical data structure then shows the structure and inter-relationships of the data in the system, and also ways in which the data can be accessed. The entity life history shows the dynamics of the system operation in the sense that it indicates how the entity changes over time. The developers of SSADM believe that this complementary approach to modelling the data gives SSADM its strength in modelling and specifying systems.

The detailed definitions of each stage of SSADM draw upon these techniques and other standard techniques in data processing such as third normal form analysis. They also stress the role of reviews in the development process and explicitly include QA activities in the stage descriptions.

SSADM is widely used, but there have been several criticisms of the method, mostly to do with the volume of paperwork generated when applying the method. Some refinement of the techniques have already taken place and there is an SSADM 'fast path' which is a much less onerous way of using the method for fairly simple and small systems. However, SSADM has been used for a much shorter period of time than other techniques such as JSD and SA/SD. Consequently it is to be expected that the method will evolve further over time and as experience of use of the method increases.

1.7 Testing and the software life cycle

The aim of this section is to outline the testing tasks that should occur during the various phases of the software life cycle. These tasks are technical — for example, deriving acceptance tests — or managerial — for example, planning for a test activity. In the description that follows it is assumed that the developer has one member of staff or a group of staff responsible for quality assurance. In large organisations such a function will be independent of the software project, while in smaller organisations the task will be delegated to project team members or the project manager.

1.7.1 Testing and requirements analysis

The major developmental activities that take place during requirements analysis are the elicitation and clarification of requirements and the subsequent construction of the system specification. The major testing activity that occurs during this phase is the derivation of the verification requirements. These are requirements which, during the latter stages of the project, are converted into the system and acceptance tests: tests which determine whether a system meets user requirements.

The expansion of the verification requirements usually takes place during the system design and detailed design phases. Normally most customers are happy to be presented with a system specification which is at a high level of abstraction and where there is a tacit understanding that phrases such as 'time period' covers a multitude of cases.

Although the verification requirements can be established as late as the final stages of system design, it is important that they be established as early as possible during the requirements analysis stage. The reason for this is that requirements analysis is such a difficult task that the presence of a member of staff continually asking 'How do I test that?' can be an excellent check on the quality of a requirements specification.

1.7.2   *Test planning*

During the testing phase a detailed test plan should be developed. The test plan should, eventually, be a very bulky document. However, at this stage it will only exist in outline. Often the outline test plan forms part of the contract for a software system and, occasionally, is used by a tendering board to judge the competence of competing developers.

The test plan should eventually contain:

1. The organisational responsibilities for the various tasks in the testing program. In a large company this section differentiates those activities which are carried out by the development team and those carried out by an independent quality assurance organisation, or by development staff in a project designated as having quality assurance functions.

2. The methods that are to be used to review documents associated with the test process. This includes:

    (a) When they are reviewed.

    (b) The staff who should carry out the review.

    (c) How unsatisfactory outcomes from a review are reported and follow-up actions taken.

    (d) How the execution of follow-up actions are checked.

    (e) How the conduct of reviews is checked.

    (f) What documents are associated with a review, i.e. which documents act as input to a review and which act as output.

    (g) The skills of the reviewers.

    (h) A description of any involvement of staff external to a project.

3. How the outcome of tests will be checked and monitored, and how discrepancies associated with tests will be acted on. This section will differentiate between tasks which are carried out by the developmental team and tasks carried out by an independent quality assurance function.

4. A description of the categories and levels of testing that will occur during the project. This chapter will describe a whole panorama of testing activities ranging from unit testing (testing individual program units) up to acceptance testing (the testing of a system to ensure that it meets user requirements). The test plan should detail these together with any standards that are to be applied.

5. The test schedule. This lists the tests that are to be carried out, together with the expected times that they will be executed. This test schedule should be presented in the standard form as an activity network such as a PERT chart. As with other project schedules, activities which are prone to delay should be marked, and alternative strategies to cope with possible delays should be outlined. For example, a developer might require a special test tool that needs to be built by a sub-contractor to a stringent timetable. The project plan should describe how the developer would cope with the late delivery of such a tool.

6. The various hardware configurations that are to be used when a test is executed. This is vitally important. One of the major reasons for project over-run is that developers underestimate the amount of hardware resource required for testing, particularly during the system and acceptance phase.

7. A description of each test that is to be carried out; and for each test a statement of the software configurations that will be needed to support the test together with the software tools required for the test. Normally simple software tools such as test harnesses are used. However, specialised tools such as simulators will occasionally be required.

8. A list of the verification requirements. This document will be in outline, since much of this information will be unavailable at this stage of the software project. However, it is important that this document be created during this phase of the project, even if it largely contains section headings.

1.7.3 Testing and system design

There are a number of activities that are carried out during system (or architectural) design which are relevant to testing. First, the verification requirements will be expanded out so that they correspond more closely to individual tests. For example, the verification requirement:

4.3 When the DISPLAY command is typed with an invalid user identification, then an error message will be displayed on the originating console. A valid user identification is a sequence of four alphabetic characters, ranging from AAAA to ZZZZ which has been allocated to the user of a system. This verification requirement might be expanded to:

V4.3/1 When the DISPLAY command is typed, with a user identification A, then an error message will be displayed on the originating console.

V4.3/2 When the DISPLAY command is typed, with a user identification Z, then an error message will be displayed on the originating console.

V4.3/3 When the DISPLAY command is typed with a user identification which does not match a currently logged on user, then an error message will be displayed on the originating console.

V4.3/4 When the DISPLAY command is typed with a user identification which differs from a logged-on user identification by one character step in the first position, then an error message will be displayed on the originating console. For example, if a logged-on user had the identification ASFR the test should check that the user identification BSFR was incorrect.

V4.3/5 When the DISPLAY command is typed with a user identification which differs from a logged-on user identification by one character step in the fourth position then an error message will be displayed on the originating console. For example, if a logged-on user had the identification FRED the test should check that the user identification FREE was incorrect.

In general, staff assigned to testing will generate tests which not only explore the normal behaviour of the system but will also check for extreme values. During this phase the verification requirements are considerably expanded. A second testing-related activity which should occur during this phase is to develop the test coverage matrix. This is a matrix which relates the expanded verification requirements to the modules which implement the requirements. An example of such a matrix, taken from a spreadsheet display, is shown in Figure 1.11. Each row in this matrix relates the verification requirement to the program units that should be executed when a test corresponding to the verification requirement are carried out. For example, when a test corresponding to verification requirement 2.3 is carried out the program units Update and Check are executed.

There are a number of reasons for developing this matrix. It checks that:

1. The completed software system is an adequate reflection of customer requirements. Occasionally the result of such a test will be coincidentally correct, i.e. the correct result will be given, but the wrong program units will be

	A	B	C	D	E	F	G
2					Program units		
3							
4	Verification						
5	reqts		Update	Find x	Find y	Newest	Check
6							
7	1.1		x	x			x
8	1.2			x		x	
9	1.3				x	x	
10	2.1			x			
11	2.2				x		
12	2.3		x				x
13	2.4				x	x	x
14	2.5		x		x		
15	3.1			x			
16	3.2		x				

Figure 1.11   *Example of a test coverage matrix.*

executed. By inserting print statements into simple program units, which type the name of the unit being executed, the staff carrying out system testing will be able to check, by referring to the test coverage matrix, whether the correct program units have been executed.

2. The thoroughness of the system and acceptance testing. By examining those verification requirements which are selected for acceptance testing and system testing, quality assurance staff will be able to calculate the total number of program units which would be executed and whether any program units have been omitted.

3. The system design has been correctly developed. By tracing verification requirements against program units, staff charged with quality assurance are rapidly able to discover inconsistencies and omissions in the system design.

4. The verification requirements which have been processed and expanded during system design have been expanded to the right level of detail. For example, a verification requirement may have been expanded to the point where one of two program units may be executed if certain items of data are input to the system. This

cannot be expressed in the test coverage matrix; it assumes that each test corresponds to the execution of a particular, fixed set of program units.

5. The process of system modification has been adequately recorded. A software system is a dynamic entity; requirements change during project execution, and certainly change after release of the system. Such change is manifested in modifications to program code.

When the program code, in a specific unit or units, is changed the developer wants to know what other functions may be affected by that change. The usual reason for this is that he or she wishes to run a series of tests to ensure that a modification due to a requirements change has not affected other functions of the system. The test coverage matrix gives this information. For example, the test coverage matrix shown in Figure 1.11 shows that verification requirement 1.3 involves the execution of the program unit 'Findy'. If that requirement is changed and leads to a modification to Findy, then the developer should run tests that check that verification requirements 2.2, 2.4 and 2.5 are unaffected by the change.

A third activity that should be carried out during systems design is the development of the integration test strategy. This involves specifying the order in which the program units are added to the system which is being built up. There are essentially two strategies which are possible: a bottom-up strategy or a top-down strategy. In the latter the system is built from the topmost program units in a system, with the former the bottom level units are added first. The strategies are shown below for the simple system design described by Figure 1.12. A top-down strategy would involve the order of integration:

A AB ABC ABCD ABCDE

while a typical bottom-up strategy would involve the sequence of integration:

D DE BDE BDEC BDECA

In general, the major advantage of a top down approach is that it allows an early demonstration of a system and boosts morale. The major disadvantage is that stubs (dummy program units which replace program units which have not yet been programmed) have to be developed, whilst conceptually, it often seems easy to write such stubs, in practice it is often quite a difficult task.

The major advantage of a bottom-up strategy is that it is easy to detect flaws that occur towards the bottom of a design. The major disadvantage is that it requires scaffold software. This is software which encloses a program unit and provides test data and prints out test results. In general a top-down strategy is to be preferred because of the importance of having an early version of

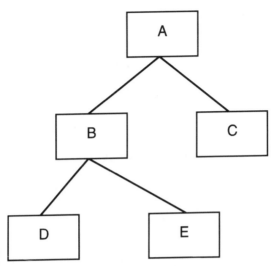

Figure 1.12   A simple system design.

a system which can be shown to a customer and which can enable the customer to detect any inconsistencies in the developers' perception of requirements. In practice the integration test plan needs to be defined taking into account the technical and schedule difficulties of integrating the product.

An integration test plan should include the order in which integration takes place and the tests that should be carried out. It is a fallacy to assume that the main function of the integration test should be to test that the interfaces between program units are correct. While this type of test is important, a number of other tests should be carried out. First, preliminary tests from the verification requirements should be executed. If, after integrating a set of program units, a verification requirement (or more accurately, software which can be checked by a specific verification requirement) has been implemented then a test should be carried out that the implementation has been correct. The reason, of course, is that it is a good principle in software development to check, as early as possible, that requirements have been implemented correctly. Carrying out such a test during integration, and discovering a fault, will save resources when compared with discovering the error during the final stages of testing.

Another type of test that should be carried out is a design function test. After the integration of a number of program units into system, a number of design functions (functions expressed in software terms), will have been implemented. A typical design function is:

When the program unit MOD-X is executed with a plane position, the position will be written into the flight database and the parameter FULL set to false. However, if the database is full then the parameter FULL is set to true.

Another important activity that should be carried out during integration testing is the testing of the response time of a real-time system. It is exceptionally difficult to predict the response time of a system during system design. Integration testing gives the first chance for the developer to check that real-time requirements have been met. This will only be a rough check because a partial system will only be executed and, hence, the full system will not be memory-resident. However, integration testing for response time does give the developer the confidence to assume that nothing has gone badly wrong with the real-time response of the system being constructed.

1.7.4   Testing and detailed design

The next phase of the software project is detailed design. The main testing activity that occurs during this phase is the construction of the test procedures. A test procedure is a detailed step-by-step set of instructions for the staff who carry out the final stages of testing. A test procedure contains details of the software configuration used, the hardware configuration, the location of the job control language commands necessary for carrying out the test, the files containing test data, the expected outcomes of the tests and the location of the files which contain the test outcome. A typical test procedure is:

TP1/23 (Verification test V1.24)

> Execute the test JCL commands stored in the file TP1/ 23.COM. This sets the test up. Connect the file TP1/ 23.FIL to the program held in the file TP1/23.PAS. The program should then be executed. During execution the program will halt four times with the prompt TEST>. Each time that the prompt is shown, type in an employee number between 1200 and 3200. When the execution has terminated, run the program FILEMONITOR.OBJ. This will print out the employee database state after the employee numbers have been added. Check that the employee numbers are contained in the database.

Test procedures should be developed for both the system tests and the integration tests.

1.7.5   Testing and programming

The first, or primary, activity in this phase is programming or coding the individual units or modules. Work may also be carried out on producing test harnesses or stubs. A second activity is the testing of the program units after they have been programmed. This process, normally called unit testing, is an informal process. The word 'informal' does not imply disorganised or unstructured. It means that the testing process is not under the control of a quality assurance organisation; it is normally carried out by the software engineer who produced the unit.

The aim of unit testing is to check that a program unit matches the specification produced for it during system design. Unit testing is a structural testing activity, the aim being to ensure some degree of test thoroughness with respect to some measure of structural coverage. A typical measure is that the test data generated should ensure that 100% of the statements in a unit are executed. Although this is a common metric it is beginning to be regarded as inadequate, and the better metric of 100% statement coverage and 85% branch coverage is being gradually adopted in industry.

An important concept, which is relevant to unit testing, is the directed graph. This is graphic description of the flow of control in a program or program unit. Nodes in a directed graph represent conditions or the destination of jumps, while lines represent flow of control. The directed graph for the Pascal procedure shown below is given in Figure 1.13.

```
Procedure Init (iter-times:integer; Check:Boolean;
a:arrayint); var i:integer;
begin
if Check then
        begin
        i: = 0;
        repeat
                i:=i+ I; a[i] := 0
        until i = iter_times
end;
```

a, b, c and d are decision points of destinations of flow control. d is the exit point, b is the decision in the if statement, c is the decision in the repeat statement and b is the destination of the jump implied in the repeat statement.

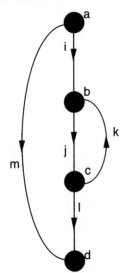

Figure 1.13   *Directed graph of the procedure Init.*

An important concept in program testing is the program path. This is a trace of the flow of control through a program or program unit. One path through Init is m which occurs when the condition in the if statement evaluates to false. Another path is ijl, which occurs when the if condition evaluates to true and the repeat loop is only executed once. A further path is ijkjkjkjkjl, which occurs when the condition in the if statement is true and the repeat loop is executed four times. In general, a program or program unit contains an extremely high, if not infinite, number of paths and a high structural coverage during testing is usually the only practical test metric that can be aimed for.

1.7.6   Testing and integration

Testing during the integration phase will follow the plans set out in system, or architectural, design. The primary aim of the testing activity is to verify the design, but a subsidiary aim is to begin to verify requirements functions. During coding individual, tested program units will have been produced. These are then progressively integrated according to the agreed strategy, e.g. top-down or bottom-up. A number of specific facets of the design are tested, leading up to the testing of full design and requirements functions. The first step is to check interface compatibility, i.e. that functions in units are correctly called by functions in the units that use them. This involves testing the validity of the parameters on all calls to functions, and the appropriateness of the response. As a minimum, parameter validity tests will ascertain that each parameter is of correct type and legal values.

The notion of coverage extends to the invocation of function in the called unit, or module. The aim should be to ensure that the use, and operation, of the called function is valid for every possible call from the calling unit, i.e. there should be 100% call coverage. This, coupled with unit testing, should give high confidence in the interworking of the units if the programs are well structured.

If a given design function implements a requirements function in its entirety, then it will be possible to follow design function testing with preliminary evaluation using acceptance tests. With a more complex relationship between design and requirements functions, testing of requirements functions will only be possible later in the integration phase. The non-functional properties should be re-tested as more design functions are integrated.

To carry out integration testing, it will be necessary to build 'scaffolding' to exercise the partially integrated software. Producing the scaffolding, e.g. test harnesses and stubs, is expensive, especially as this software is likely to be of only temporary utility. One of the aims of test planning is to reduce the amount of scaffolding required. Another is to bring forward the times at which design and requirements functions can be tested.

Integration testing is a precursor to system and acceptance testing. If integration testing has been carried out effectively (and the necessary remedial work carried out) then the next phase should be relatively trouble-free.

1.7.7 **System and acceptance testing**

After programming and integration have been completed the (in some senses) most important testing activities occur. These are system testing and acceptance testing. In contrast to unit testing both these activities are black-box activities. System testing is the process of executing the test procedures associated with the verification tests. Acceptance testing is the process of executing the test procedures associated with a subset of the verification requirements which are agreed by both the customer and the developer as being an adequate representation of user requirements. The major difference between system and acceptance testing is the fact that the former takes place in a simulated environment. It is usually carried out at the developer's premises, with items of equipment, or external sources or sinks of data, replaced by such tools as simulators or by stored data files.

System testing is a set of preliminary tests which are run to give the developer a high degree of confidence that the acceptance testing will be successful. They are executed for two reasons. First, it is very embarrassing when an acceptance test fails. Second, and more importantly, if an acceptance test fails the customer has every right to ask the developer to rerun all the acceptance tests after the error in a system has been remedied. The reason for this is that in modifying the system in response to an acceptance test error, the developer could have adversely affected some other part of the system and caused a further error which would only have been detected by an acceptance test that had already been executed. Thus, a failed acceptance test can cause the developer a large amount of expense.

1.7.8 **Testing and maintenance**

The final testing activity associated with the software life cycle is regression testing. This occurs during maintenance when a system has been modified. Regression testing is the execution of a series of tests which check that a modification, applied during maintenance, has not affected the code corresponding to those functions of the system which should be unaffected by the maintenance modification that had been carried out. A major item of documentation which is important during regression testing is the test coverage matrix described earlier. In practice it is also useful to carry out regression testing in earlier stages, e.g. when testing and rectifying faults in the programming phase.

1.8 **Software maintenance**

Software maintenance is the post-delivery modification of a software product to correct faults, improve performance (or other attributes), or to adapt the product for a changing environment. Maintenance can be categorized as perfective, adaptive, corrective ('bug fixing'), and preventive.

Unlike other types of software maintenance, preventive maintenance is not derived from a user change request. The objective of preventive maintenance is to alter software so that one or both of the following is met:

1. The altered software is of higher quality (e.g. in terms of detected defect rate). A system may exhibit so-called 'hot spots' where, statistically, the defect rate is poor and has remained so after modifications have been undertaken.

2. The altered software is more maintainable.

The terminology used in preventive maintenance is interpreted in different ways by different authors. The following definitions of preventive maintenance processes are used:

1. *Inverse engineering.* The process of discovering the requirements specification for a software system or component, and then reimplementing using modern software engineering methods.

2. *Reverse engineering.* The process of redesigning parts or all of a software system, to improve its quality, and then reimplementing the design.

3. *Re-engineering* (also called rejuvenation). The modification of source code items (code, data structures, documentation etc.) based on modern software engineering principles to improve the maintainability of software.

It is important to note that, in an hierarchical system, the design at one level is a specification for the next less abstract level of implementation. Hence the above terms need to be interpreted carefully in the context in which they are being used.

1.8.1 Program comprehension

Program comprehension is a vital part of the maintenance process. A software maintainer has to be able to understand the system to be modified before designing the modification. The system may not have any associated documentation, or if it has, it may not have been updated to include recent changes. Even worse, the documentation may also be incorrect. Relying on the availability of the developers of the system is also not always possible as there is high turnover of staff in the industry. Thus the maintainer may only have the latest version of the source code as the only reliable authority on how the system is constructed. From the source code the maintainer needs to obtain an understanding of the various components of the system and their interaction.

1.9 Tools and workbenches

There are a number of tools designed specifically for use in the software maintenance work environment. In general, the tools tend to be aimed at specific tasks and lack an ability to integrate with other tools or with existing project support environments.

1.9.1 GSA Programmer's Workbench

The GSA identified eleven categories of tools for software maintenance and brought them together in what is termed a Programmers Workbench (PWB). It should be noted that the GSA did not develop any of the tools described below; the tool categories were identified and third party tools were then bought in. The PWB sits on top of the Rand Development Center (RDC), although it should be noted that each tool can be used alone. The PWB was established specifically to deal with applications written in COBOL on IBM architectures. Since the PWB described below uses COBOL terminology, it is appropriate to provide very brief details of salient language features. COBOL programs are divided into four divisions: identification, environment, data, and procedure divisions. The data division contain declarations, in a highly formatted form in which some substructures and storage attributes (such as local working storage) are indicated by associated two-digit level numbers. Data type and initial values are indicated in such declarations by key words USAGE, PIC, VALUE.

The procedure division contains executable statements. COBOL has a primitive procedure mechanism known as CALL, and an iteration construct called PERFORM. Control transfers are provided by IF and ALTER constructs.

The categories of tools identified by the GSA were:

1. Test coverage monitor.

2. Source compare.

3. File compare.

4. Translator.

5. Reformatter.

6. Data standardization tool.

7. Restructuring tool.

8. Code analyser.

9. Cross-referencer.

10. Documentation and metric analyser.

11. Data manipulation tool.

1.9.2   *Test coverage monitor*

The test coverage monitor is a tool to address the following important aspects of program testing:

(a) Preparation of test data.

(b) Measurement of test data coverage.

The tool should:

(a) Compile and run programs with all available test data.

(b) Identify and report any logical decision path or executable statements within the program that the test data fails to exercise.

With the information from this type of tool programmers can evaluate areas of a program that require further testing and software quality assurance personnel can make more accurate and reliable judgements of a program's readiness for production implementation.

1.9.3   Source compare tools

The source compare tool can be used to compare:

(a) New software releases to previous releases for debugging and documentation purposes.

(b) Source code versions to provide audit trails.

(c) Database files against backups to ensure integrity of the data.

(d) Output files to ensure the results of source changes are installed as requested.

1.9.4   File compare tools

File compare tools are intended to compare object and load modules.

1.9.5   Translator tools

Translator tools perform the translation of one language to another or one dialect of a language to another.

1.9.6   Reformatter tools

Reformatter tools are also known as pretty-printers, and as such will layout source code in a standard format. They transform old, large, or poorly written or documented programs into standardized formats that are more readily and easily maintained. Key words are aligned in the DATA and PROCEDURE divisions, including level numbers and compound and nested IF statements.

1.9.7   Data name standardiser tool

The data name standardiser tool standardises data and paragraph names to:

(a) Improve the overall readability of source programs.

(b) Automatically enforce an installation style standard.

(c) Provide all the necessary spacing and indentation in support of an installation's structured programming requirements.

Within a DATA division, the tool will:

(a) Replace selected data names with more meaningful names.

(b) Insert user-specified record prefixes.

(c) Produce alphabetic sequencing of all working storage entries.

(d) Convert USAGE, PICTURE, VALUE, and other specified clauses to standard forms and pre-defined positions.

Standardization within a PROCEDURE division can provide:

(a) Sequencing, resequencing, or unsequencing of paragraph names.

(b) Insertion and deletion of EJECT and SKIP statements, or of blank lines.

(c) Multi-line indentation and alignment of COBOL reserved word pairs.

1.9.8 Restructuring tools

The restructuring tool transforms an unstructured program into a structured program. It takes unstructured COBOL code and replaces it with logically equivalent software consistent in style, format and structure. The transformations on the code include:

(a) Reduction of GOTO logic.

(b) Elimination of fall through confusion.

(c) Increased use of the PERFORM construct.

(d) Elimination of PERFORM THRU constructs and ALTER statements.

(e) Conversion of NOTEs to comments.

(f) Elimination of all unentered procedures ('dead code').

1.9.9 Source code analyser

The source code analyser analyses programs to detect program structure, identify data usage and relationships, and trace data usage and logic flow. It is a tool that will greatly help in the understanding of how a program works. This interactive tool assists the most difficult aspect of the software maintenance process — the evaluation and analysis of a program and program modifications. Through the use of this tool the following essential steps in the maintenance process are fully automated:

(a) *Task estimation*. Achieved by isolating program functions, allowing analysts to focus on program and I/O structures, control and data flow, and interaction between program modules.

(b) *Analysis*. Achieved by highlighting complex and subtle logic and data relationships, and by predicting the outcome of changes proposed by the programmer prior to actual production tests.

(c) *Testing*. Changes can be made and tested online.

(d) *Documentation*. Automatically produced.

(e) *Quality assurance*. Commands can be tailored to specific data processing environments, thus allowing the quality assurance analyst to determine standards compliance.

1.9.10 Cross-reference tool

The cross-reference tool identifies all occurrences of data names, words or literals within a program. It is a useful tool for navigating around source code. The tool will:

(a) Identify and trace data element modification, branch logic, program CALLs, and performed paragraph reference patterns.

(b) Generate graphic record layouts to visually communicate data structures and formats.

1.9.11 Documentation and metrics analyser

The documentation and metrics analyser analyses source code and produces documentation reports of the results of the analysis.

The tool evaluates the logic paths of a program without executing it and stores metric information about the program before or after a modification, for later reporting. It applies pre-established algorithms to compare the standards maintained in its summary statistics file to the various structural characteristics of programs. These algorithms are also used to derive practical metrics of a program's relative complexity and architecture.

The tool produces detailed and summary reports. These reports combine the measurements to assess overall asset quality at the system and program library levels.

1.9.12 Data manipulation tool

The data manipulation tool allows data within records to be examined, modified, extracted, and printed for various file and record structures. The tool is an interactive, full-screen data manipulation system designed to edit, browse, extract, reformat, and print VSAM, ISAM, PDS and sequential files. It checks the validity of data for each field in a record and identifies data that does not match related COBOL PICTURE and USAGE clauses.

1.10 Configuration management

Configuration management is the discipline of identifying the components of a continually evolving system for the purposes of controlling changes to those components and maintaining integrity and traceability throughout the life cycle (BSI, 1994).

Software configuration management is a formal engineering discipline which provides software developers and users with the methods and tools to identify the software developed, establish baselines, control changes to these baselines, record and track status, and audit the product. Software configuration management is the means through which the integrity and continuity of the software products are recorded, communicated and controlled (ANSI/IEEE, 1983a). The software product is not just software but also the documentation necessary to define, develop and maintain that software (Bersoff, 1984).

Software configuration management is not always distinguished from hardware configuration management, which is the older discipline. This has led to the use of inappropriate definitions and procedures in some cases. The two disciplines do share many common aspects, but they are different not least in that hardware has a physical existence. Each copy of a piece of hardware is potentially different because the physical fabrication process can introduce variations.

Configuration management benefits all phases of the life cycle of a system, and touches on all aspects of a project. Project control is concerned with planning what the components of a system should be, when they should be delivered, and providing the resources to produce the components. Quality control ensures that the components are fit for their purpose and of the required quality. Configuration management provides stable instances of those components which can be tested and have their quality assessed. Tests and test software themselves should be subject to configuration management. Configuration management interacts with contractual concerns; the contract is usually based around the supply of specified components. Delivery requires goods in/out procedures that are based on the components. Maintenance is concerned with evolving the components in response to requested changes.

Configuration management is sometimes only thought to be a concern in large projects. However, the basic techniques of configuration management apply to projects of all sizes and kinds; the application can differ considerably between projects, and between different stages of the life cycle.

Configuration management should begin when the first document of the system is written, continue throughout the life cycle, and terminate only when that last release of the system has been decommissioned. Without configuration management the reliability and quality of the software cannot be assured. The consequences of failure of configuration management can be economically and technically severe, and can lead to the complete failure of a project.

Configuration management of documents has generally been considered as another separate discipline. However, the advent of sophisticated text and word processing packages has allowed documents and software to be treated in a uniform manner. Software and related electronically created documents may be treated as members of a more general class specifications to which software configuration management is applicable. A piece of software is an executable specification written in a computer language; a document is a human-processable specification written in a natural language.

1.11 Quality

Quality is the totality of features and characteristics of a product, process or service that bear on its ability to satisfy stated or implied needs. Quality attributes are ideally defined in a quantitative fashion and certainly in a way that allows compliance to be checked.

Quality assurance is that aspect of the overall management function that determines and implements the overall quality intentions and objectives of the organisation as formally expressed by senior management. The corporate quality assurance policy sets the framework within which each software development team defines and carries out quality control activities. The policy is generally implemented in the form of a quality management system (QMS) and is normally described in a corporate quality manual. Perhaps the most important general standard for QMSs is ISO 9001.

Quality control is made up of all the operational techniques and activities that are used to satisfy the quality requirements of any product. One can view quality control in the general case as a five-step process:

1. Define the quality attribute(s) and level(s).

2. Define the attribute check procedure.

3. Carry out the check procedure.

4. Record the result.

5. Take and record any corrective action taken.

Techniques which specifically support quality control are generally those that are more formal in nature since that formality means that the semantics of the product are well defined and hence properties of the product can be more easily checked for. Many quality control checks can be automated if the meaning, i.e. semantics, of the representation we are using is well defined. In other situations we have to fall back on more general, less formal and hence less powerful quality control actions, such as structured walkthroughs and Fagan Inspections.

Each development project should have its own quality plan identifying how each of the (final and intermediate) products of the project will be checked for quality. The quality plan will often call upon existing standards in the organisations quality manual.

1.11.1 Quality assurance

Quality assurance covers first, determination of a quality policy, and second, checking that predetermined quality control activities are being properly undertaken.

Policy determination takes place at the corporate level of organisation, and it sets the framework within which the software development team defines and carries out quality control activities. The policy defined by the organisation is normally described in a document (typically a corporate quality manual) and is generally implemented in the form of a quality management system.

1.11.2 Quality management systems (QMSs)

ISO 8402 defines a quality system as the organisational structure, responsibilities, procedures, activities, capabilities and resources that together aim to ensure that products, processes or services will satisfy stated or implied needs'. A QMS is something that is set up by an organisation to cover a group of projects or departments, on one or more of its sites. It is a statement by management of the strategy and tactics that will be used across the organisation to achieve the required quality in whatever is produced.

A great deal of work has been done in industry in general and in the software engineering industry in particular in defining what constitutes a QMS and this has culminated in national and international standards for them. They are of increasing importance to software engineering organisations as many purchasers of software are starting to realise the benefits of requiring that some form of accredited QMS has been used in the development of the software they are buying.

Perhaps the most important general standard for QMSs is ISO 9001 (which is identical to BS 5750 (1987) and the proposed European standard EN29000). Because of its importance we look at it in some detail. (It is important to note that ISO 9001 covers any QMS in any industry, so its requirements need to be carefully interpreted for the software engineering industry. In the UK this interpretation is provided in part by British Standards Institution Quality Assessment Schedules which are covered below.)

ISO 9001 defines 20 major requirements of a QMS:

1. *Management responsibility.* The organisation must 'define and document management policy and objectives for and commitment to quality' and must 'ensure that this policy is understood, implemented and maintained at all levels in the organisation'. In particular the responsibilities of all staff who perform and verify work affecting quality have to be defined, and the senior management must systematically review the operation of the QMS to ensure it remains suitable and effective. Again, there is this emphasis on the need for quality to be addressed from the top of the organisation down.

2. *A documented quality system.* This system must cover quality control of all activities in development, and documentation of all the procedures. The documentation will generally take the form of a corporate quality manual (see later).

3. *Contract review.* This is included to ensure that a contract (in this case to produce a software system) starts out with a mutually agreed set of requirements for the system and that the developer is capable of delivering it to the purchaser. Without these safeguards, all else is futile!

4. *Design control.* The standard requires that the developer has, and uses, procedures to control and verify the quality of the design of the system to ensure that it meets its requirements. These procedures should cover planning, identification of the inputs to the design process, identifying what form the design should take and what properties it should have, the verification of the design against the requirements, and how changes in the design will be handled.

5. *Documentation and change control.* This is an especially important area for software development where so much of what is produced takes the form of documents or data in some form: specifications, designs, code, test data, etc. Control of all these generally comes under the heading of configuration management, change management/control, and version control. ISO 9001 calls for procedures for document approval and issue, and for the handling of changes.

6. *Purchasing.* If you plan to incorporate someone else's work in your own system it is clearly important that you satisfy yourself of its quality in some way, and the standard requires, for instance, the assessment of subcontractors' ability to meet quality requirements, what records should be kept about purchased items, and the verification that bought-in items satisfy the requirements on them.

7. *Purchaser supplied product.* This section of the standard requires procedures for the verification, storage and maintenance of bought-in items. At first sight this has little relevance to software engineering, but it is increasingly common for third-party software to be included in a delivered system, and for that third party to issue a stream of new versions, part updates, patches and the like — you need to ensure that you have ways of handling these properly so that the right version is included in the system you release to your client.

8. *Product identification and traceability.* This has always been an important issue for software developers who, like other engineers, build their systems from many small components. Configuration management/control and build control procedures are once more required.

9. *Process control.* This is a general requirement that the production process itself be planned and monitored.

10. *Inspection and testing.* The standard requires that inspection and testing should take place during the development process, once the system has been completed and before it is delivered for use, and on bought-in-items before they are incorporated. It also requires here, as in most other areas, that records be kept of the results of tests.

11. *Inspection, measuring and test equipment.* Equipment can here be taken to mean software tools in particular. These must themselves be properly controlled with respect to quality, version, etc.

12. *Inspection and test status.* So that the quality of all items at all stages of their development should be clearly known, the standard requires that their test status should

be shown in some way at all times. As examples, the design specification of a system should say whether or not it has been reviewed or is only at draft status; a code module should say whether it has been successfully compiled, has passed its tests successfully, or has been frozen as definitive for integration purposes; and so on.

13. *Control of nonconforming products.* This is a requirement that items that do not meet their requirements cannot be inadvertently used.

14. *Corrective action.* If an error is found in an item when a quality control check is carried out on it there are two things that must be done. First, the error must be removed from the item, and second, the processes involved in its production need to be checked to see if they should be changed to avoid such an error appearing in future items of that type.

15. *Handling, storage, packaging and delivery.* Again, this is not obviously of concern to the software engineer but an organisation that makes and sells a software product will need to consider its procedures for replicating the software reliably, for ensuring that the correct versions are reaching the correct buyers, that magnetic media — especially those with the product on them — are correctly stored to prevent corruption, and so on.

16. *Quality records.* Here the standard requires the developer to ensure that sufficient records are maintained to demonstrate that the required quality has been achieved and that the QMS is itself operating effectively. The first requirement effectively says that — as far as the purchaser is concerned — unrecorded quality actions never took place; the second requirement ensures that a poor QMS is not followed, lest it become a potential cause of poor quality itself.

17. *Internal quality audits.* This continues the theme that the QMS itself must be subjected to review to maintain its effectiveness, and requires a system of quality audits whose findings are followed up and reported to management.

18. *Training.* If staff are not adequately trained to do their jobs it is unlikely that their work will be of the necessary quality. This requirement covers the identification of training needs and the training itself.

19. *Servicing.* This is an area that must be subject to the same care as production itself.

20. *Statistical techniques.* The developer is required to 'establish, where appropriate, procedures for identifying adequate statistical techniques required for verifying the acceptability of product characteristics'.

It should be clear from this short coverage of the ISO 9001 standard for QMSs that, taken this seriously, quality requires considerable investment and commitment from the software developer and management.

1.11.3   Quality control

Quality control is 'the operational techniques and activities that are used to satisfy the quality requirements.' Quality control is best carried out on products (things produced during software development) rather than on processes. It would be possible to define the quality of processes: one could check that predefined actions had actually been taken and had been taken in the right order, but this would only say that the 'rule-book' had been followed, so to speak. Checking the quality of the product of those actions is likely to be far more efficient in bringing to our notice any errors introduced by the process.

For each product — say, a Pascal module — one will want to apply quality control. What does this mean in practice? It can be viewed in the general case as a five-step process:

1.   Define the attribute(s) and level(s).

2.   Define the attribute check procedure.

3.   Carry out the check procedure.

4.   Record the result.

5.   Take and record any corrective action taken.

Steps 1 and 2 are planning steps that would be carried out before the product was ready for quality control operations on it — they say what will be done. In step 3 the planned actions are carried out and in step 4 they are recorded. Step 5 is vital: it closes the loop by ensuring that, if the product fails the check, the error is traced, corrected and the corrective action recorded as having been taken. It is all too easy to spot problems and then never quite get round to solving them and correcting the errors. Step 5 ensures that they are solved and that a trace is left to that effect.

1.11.4   Structured walkthroughs

A structured walkthrough is an organised event at which a particular item — a design, a code module, a chapter of a user guide, a test plan, or whatever — is scrutinised by a group of people looking at it from different perspectives and trying to find as many errors as they can in the item. The action centres on the producer of the item who presents it to the other participants who jointly look for errors. Any errors — or possible errors — found are recorded by a co-ordinator. The group concentrates on error detection rather than error correction, as it is the producer's responsibility after the walkthrough to take the record of errors found and make sure each is corrected in the item.

Yourdon identifies the following roles as appropriate in a structured walkthrough:

1. The presenter — the 'owner' of the item and probably the person who produced it.

2. The coordinator — someone to organise the walkthrough and chair it.

3. The secretary — who will ensure that the material is issued beforehand and that the records are taken and presented to the presenter.

4. The maintenance oracle — who represents the people who will one day be responsible for maintaining the item.

5. The standards bearer — who scrutinises the item for adherence to the local standards that apply to items of that sort.

6. The user representative — who checks that the item conforms to the views of its user (who might be the final user of the system or, in the case of a specification say, the 'user' of that specification, namely the designer).

7. Any outsiders who can contribute to the scrutiny.

Crucial to the success of a walkthrough is the prior preparation done by the participants. It is the presenter's responsibility to choose the other participants who could most usefully contribute, to nominate a co-ordinator who will be able to run the walkthrough effectively, and to choose a time and place. Copies of the item to be reviewed are given to all participants sufficiently in advance for them each to do their own scrutiny of the item. The more individual work done by participants the more productive the walkthrough will be. Participants will take their comments and queries to the walkthrough and, with the guidance of the co-ordinator, will present these and discuss them sufficiently to decide whether there is an error or likelihood of an error that demands further analysis by the producer of the item.

At the review, the item is scrutinised in whatever way makes most sense; a piece of text can be taken page by page, code procedure by procedure, design diagram by diagram. These are the 'natural' and obvious ways of tackling the problem.

Unfortunately, this serial approach to the walkthrough can lead people towards scrutinising what is there, and hence away from what is not. In other words, it makes it difficult to see deficiencies and gaps. This can in part be handled by the use of checklists. Many users of walkthroughs and related techniques maintain lists of specific questions that are always asked at such reviews (or better, by participants during their preparation). Such checklist will generally be specific to particular products: system specifications, module code, test plans, etc. For instance, a checklist used to check the completeness of the coverage of a system specification might contain the following questions:

1. Have all inputs to the system been defined?

2. Have their sources been identified? (human agent, other machine, communications lines, peripheral types . . .)

3. Have their types been specified? (analogue, digital, electrical, acoustical, optical etc.)

4. Have the range, scaling, format, byte layout etc. been specified?

5. Have validity checks been specified?

6. Have the accuracy levels been defined?

7. Have all outputs from the system been defined?

8. Have all aspects of system performance been defined?

9. What is the throughput of the system under different loads?

10. What are the response times in different circumstances?

11. What must be the system's response to failures of software hardware, power etc?

1.11.5 *Refining the QMS*

An important aspect of a good QMS is that it is constantly refined by looking to see how it has failed to find errors in past items. This feedback loop helps to reduce the likelihood that similar errors will creep through in the same way in the future. Thus, you might discover as development proceeds that an interface with another system does not operate as expected — this could happen as late as system integration when correction will be expensive. On investigation you find that the error lay originally with the system specification which failed to specify the period for which data on an interface remained valid, and that this was not noticed when the system specification was originally reviewed. This would lead you to add to your checklist a new check for completeness:

12. For how long does the data on the input channel remain valid?

1.11.6 *Fagan Inspections*

Fagan Inspections (Fagan, 1976) are based on general inspection techniques developed within IBM. The overall principles are similar to those of a Yourdon walkthrough, but Fagan set his inspections in the wider context of planning, measurement and control. They serve two purposes: to find errors in a product, and to give greater control over error detection through the collection of error statistics. As with walkthroughs, the aim is detection and not correction, but errors are now classified in the record by type and severity so that profiles can be maintained to show up the more common types of error and to suggest how they can be avoided in the future. The emphasis, as so often in this area, is on feedback into the development process — learning from mistakes.

A number of 'checkpoints' are defined during the development path. A checkpoint corresponds to the completion of some product or other: a design, some code, a test plan, and so on. For each checkpoint, 'exit criteria' are defined. These are quality levels that need to be reached by the product before it can pass the checkpoint. The inspection (a four-phase process) is the activity where the quality control check is made.

Suppose that an inspection is to be carried out on a piece of design. The procedure would then be as follows:

1. The designer presents the entire inspection team with an overview of the product and distributes the design documentation and any other relevant material.

2. The participants do their own preparation using the material supplied. Besides bringing their own knowledge to bear on their analysis of the design, they use the accumulated experience of past inspections of designs in their part of the organisation — in the form of inspection guidelines to concentrate on looking in the areas where errors have most frequently been found in the past. This is designed to optimise the effectiveness of the inspection by concentrating on 'high-yield' problem areas.

3. The inspection itself now takes place. Someone nominated by the moderator walks through the product as for a structured walkthrough, and errors or potential errors are pointed out by the participants. Detection rather than correction being the order of the day, the moderator simply notes things found, and, importantly, assigns it a severity and classifies it by type. As in walkthroughs, strong moderation is necessary if the inspection is not to waste effort and temper on the solution of problems, on issues of style, and so on.

4. After the inspection, the moderator produces the inspection report which then goes back to the item's producer for action. All these issues raised in the report must be resolved, and the moderator has the job of checking that their resolution is complete and satisfactory. Fagan recommends that if the level of reworking involves more than 5% of the item, then the moderator should require another inspection of the item.

The notion of feedback is important. The records of errors found, together with their severity and type, allow the organisation to refine the inspection guidelines used at step 2 above.

Like walkthroughs, inspections have a number of beneficial side-effects that do not concern us directly here but that are worth noting as part of the justification for installing one of these techniques in your quality control system:

1. They spread understanding and knowledge around the team.

2. They allow easier transfer of ownership should staff leave or change responsibility.

3. They build team strength at the emotional level (if properly managed!).

4. They increase the level of shared ownership of the system by the team, without removing personal responsibility for the individual products.

Organisations often take the good points of Yourdon's and Fagan's techniques and combine the social aspects of the first with the feedback aspects of the second. As always this is an area where an organisation can set its own quality control procedural standards.

1.12 Risk management and choice of process

The software development process is inherently subject to risks, the consequences of which are manifested as financial failures (timescale overrun. budget overrun) and technical failures (failure to meet required functionality, reliability or maintainability). The objectives of risk management are to identify, analyse and give priorities to risk items before they become either threats to successful operation or major sources of expensive software rework, to establish a balanced and integrated strategy for eliminating or reducing the various sources of risk, and to monitor and control the execution of this strategy.

The practice of software risk management involves two primary steps: risk assessment and risk control. Each of these primary step has a number of subsidiary steps (e.g. risk identification, risk analysis, risk prioritization, etc).

Risk identification checklists can be used by managers and technical staff on a new project to help identity, and suggest resolution techniques for, the most likely serious risks on the project. However, they should be backed up as soon as possible by checklists derived from local experience.

When risk assessment has determined the major risk items for a project and their relative priorities, the next step is to establish risk control. There are two categories of risks to be distinguished: project specific risks and generic risks.

Project specific risks are those which only apply to a particular project, such as:

1. Personnel shortfalls.

2. Unrealistic schedules and budgets.

3. Inappropriate requirements.

4. Shortfalls in externally supplied components and services.

5. Technology shortfalls, unknowns and reliance on advances in the state of the art.

6. User-interface uncertainties.

7. Ambitious performance requirements.

Generic risks are those which are common to the generality of software development projects, such as:

1. Costly, late fixes, addressed by early requirements and design verification and validation.

2. Error-prone products, addressed by testing, verification and validation through the life cycle.

3. Uncontrollable process, addressed by planning and control.

4. Uncontrollable product, addressed by configuration management and quality assurance.

5. Poor communication, addressed by documentation, reviews. The degree to which these are expected to be significant for the particular software development determines the choice of the method of working and the process for the project.

1.13   References and bibliography

ANSI (1983a) *IEEE Standard for Software Configuration Management Plans*, ANSI/IEEE

ANSI (1983b) *IEEE Standard Glossary for Software Engineering Terminology*, ANSI/IEEE

Backhouse, R. (1986) *Program Construction and Verification*, Prentice- Hall

Bate, D. G. (1986) MASCOT3: an informal introductory tutorial. *Software Engineering Journal*, 1, 3

Bersoff, E. H. (1984) Elements of software configuration management. *IEEE Transactions on Software Engineering*, SE-10, 79-87

Boehm, B. W. (1976) Software engineering. *IEEE Transactions on Computers*, 1226-1241

Boehm, B. W. (1981) *Software Engineering Economics*, Prentice-Hall

Boehm, B. W. (1988) *A spiral model of software development and enhancement. IEEE Computer, May, 61-72*. Reprinted in Thayer, R. H. (ed.) (1988) *IEEE Tutorial on Software Engineering Project Management*

Boehm, B. W. (1989) Software risk management. *IEEE Tutorial* EH 0291-5

Booch, G. (1986) Object-oriented development. *IEEE Transactions on Software Engineering* SE-12.

Booch, G. (1987) *Software Engineering with Ada, 2nd edn*, Benjamin Cummings

BSI (1984) *Configuration management of computer-based systems*, British Standards Institution

Buckle, J. K. (1982) *Software Configuration Management,* The McMillan Press

Cohen, B. (1982) Justification of formal methods for system specification. *IEE Software and Microsystems*, 5

Coleman, D. and Gallimore, R. M. (1987) *Software Engineering Using Executable Specifications*, Macmillan Computer Science Series

DeMarco, T. (1978) *Structured Analysis and System Specification*, Prentice-Hall

DeMarco, T. (1981) *Controlling Software Projects*, Yourdon Press

DTI (1987) *The STARTS Guide*, Second Edition, Department of Trade and Industry. Available from the National Computing Centre, Manchester

DTI (1989) *STARTS Purchasers' Handbook*, 2nd edn., Department of Trade and Industry

Fagan, M. (1976) Design and code inspections to reduce errors in program development. *IBM Systems Journal*, 15, 3, 182-211

Fagan, M. (1986) Advances in software inspection. *IEEE Transactions on Software Engineering*, 744-751

Freedman, D. P. and Weinberg, G. M. (1982) *Handbook of Walkthroughs, Inspections and Technical Reviews. Evaluating Programs, Projects and Products*, 3rd edn., Little, Brown and Company, Boston, Mass, USA

Goldberg, E. A. (1977) *Applying Corporate Software Development Policy*, TRW Defense and Space Systems Group (December). Reprinted in Thayer, R. H. (ed.) (1988) *IEEE Tutorial on Software Engineering Project Management*

Hayes, I (ed.) (1986) *Specification Case Studies*, Prentice-Hall

HOOD (1989) *HOOD Manual* (revised P. J. Robinson), CISI Ingenerie

Humphrey, W. S. (1989) Managing the Software Process, Addison-Wesley

Jackson, M. A. (1983) *System Development*, Prentice-Hall

Jones, C. B. (1986) *Systematic Software Development using VDM*, Prentice-Hall

Kitchenham. B. A. and Walker, J. G. (1986) *The meaning of quality. Software Engineering 86* (ed. P. J. Brown and D. J. Barnes) Peter Peregrinus

MASCOT (1980) *The Official Handbook of MASCOT*, MASCOT Suppliers Association

MASCOT (1986) *Software Engineering Journal*, 1 (No 3: Special Issue on MASCOT3)

McClure, C. and Martin, J. (1988) *Structured Techniques: the Basis for CASE,* (revised edn), Prentice-Hall International

McDermid, J. A. (1990) Issues in developing software for safety critical systems. *In Reliability Engineering and System Safety*

McDermid, J. A. (1990) *The Theory and Practice of Refinement: Formal Approaches to the Development of Large Scale Software Systems,* Butterworths

MOD (1985) *Configuration Management Policy and Procedures for Defence Material*, Ministry of Defence

Myers, G. J. (1975) *Reliable Software Through Composite Design*, Van Nostrand Reinhold

Nicholls, D. *Introducing SSADM — The NCC Guide*, NCC Publications, Manchester

Stark, S. (1980) General object-oriented software development. NASA Software Engineering Laboratory Series, SEL-86-002

Sutcliffe, A. (1988) *Jackson System Development*, Prentice-Hall

Thayer, R. H. (1988) Software Engineering Project Management. *IEEE Tutorial* EH 0263-4

Ward, P. T. and Mellor, S. J. (1985) *Structured Development for Real-Time Systems*, Prentice Hall

Wirth, N. (1976) *Algorithms + Data Structures = Programs*, Prentice Hall

Yourdon, E. and Constantine, L. L. (1985) *Structured Design: Fundamentals of a Discipline of Computer Program and Design*, Prentice Hall

Chapter 2
Programming languages

2.1 Introduction

This chapter describes the use of programming languages and their relationship with the architecture of modern computer systems. The chapter begins by describing the characteristics of the basic von-Neuman computer and the central processing units which form the heart of such a machine. The internal representation of data is described together with the concepts of logical and physical addressing, instruction sets and data types.

High and low-level languages are described in detail. However, rather than devote a large amount of much space to any particular language, the aim has been to introduce the reader to a number of important programming concepts and discuss their application in a wide variety of languages. Such concepts include important control constructs; functions, subroutines and procedures.

At the outset it is important note that, whilst a software engineer may not be concerned with the intimate details of the hardware platform on which his or her software is mounted, he or she does need to know what the machine 'looks like' at the machine code level. As a consequence, this chapter begins by exploring some of the common elements of the architecture of modern computer systems.

2.2 Computer architecture

The low-level details of a machine are usually well hidden from the user by layers of support software, especially high-level language compilers and operating systems. These are intended to allow a programmer to ignore the details of a particular processor and its input/output (I/O) structure. In practice this goal is only partially achieved and it is often necessary to write some additional code to overcome a shortfall in the support software specification or implementation.

Examples of this include the writing of a driver to control some new type of peripheral device or to write 'interlude' (interface) routines to stand between the outputs of compilers for two languages and to convert between their different conventions for parameter passing.

It is unusual today for a complete suite of programs to be written in assembly language. The advantages of high-level languages outweigh the benefits that can be achieved by writing at a low level. For example, programmer productivity on a large project, measured in terms of the number of source instructions produced, appears to be independent of the language used. Since a high-level language program to solve a given problem will contain fewer instructions than the same program written in assembler, it is obviously quicker, and therefore cheaper, to use a high-level language.

In the past it has often been argued that a program written in a low-level language is much more efficient in terms of memory usage and execution time than the equivalent program written in a high-level language. Whilst this may have been true in the past it is only true now for specialised applications. This is due to a number of features, such as improvements to computer architecture, compiler technology and execution environments. Another reason why high-level languages have gained dominance is that the users of such languages need not be so expert at the low-level details of the particular computer architecture being used.

In order to use low-level programming effectively the programmer has to understand thoroughly the machine architecture, which is why an understanding of the low-level details of hardware and software are important.

2.2.1 *Basic von-Neuman machine*

The basic von-Neuman machine is the model for the overwhelming majority of computers in use today. This computer comprises a processor which executes instructions and a memory which holds instructions and data. One of the fundamental ideas of the von-Neuman concept is that there is no distinction in memory between instructions and data; they are only distinguished by their use.

The processor and memory represent the absolute minimum components to constitute a computer. With very few exceptions, computers are connected to external devices, traditionally called "peripherals".

In addition to the main memory, there are usually a number of extra storage locations, known as registers, many of which reside in the processor. Registers are used to hold intermediate values, a variety of state indicators known as flags, and data necessary to the operation of the processor such as the program counter (that is, the address of the current instruction) and the processor state. The program counter is usually referred to as the PC.

The main memory is likely to be constructed from separate random access memory (RAM) components while the registers are likely to be implemented as part of the central processing unit (CPU).

Main memory can range in size from only a few bytes to many megabytes (millions of bytes). A typical personal computer today will have one or two megabytes of main memory. The number of registers in the system can vary from a few to several hundred, but typical modern processors have between ten and fifty.

Registers are much faster to access than main memory, often because they are implemented using intrinsically faster methods and because they are intimately bound up in the processor implementation and so avoid the overheads of memory access. Registers are used to hold the results of operations on data and to assist in the addressing of memory. Flags are used to indicate conditions caused by operations and to indicate aspects of machine state. These flags can be used to choose various paths through the program code.

2.2.2 Execution cycle

An important machine register is the instruction address register or program counter. This register contains the address of the next instruction to be executed. The basic machine cycle comprises two operations which are continually executed in sequence:

Read/Fetch Next Instruction (RNI)
Execute Instruction (EI)

During the read/fetch operation the CPU fetches from memory the next instruction word and decodes it. This is the process of deciding which operation from the instruction set to perform. The CPU then takes the necessary steps to execute the instruction. This may well involve reading further bytes that are parts of the instruction, and then reading data from the memory or storing data into the memory.

2.2.3 Instruction sets

The collection of instructions which the processor is capable of executing is known as the order code or instruction set. Compatible ranges (families) of processors all share to a greater or lesser extent the same instruction set. 'Compatible' processors may differ in the range of addressing options supported, and some may offer a wider repertoire of instructions. Increasingly, a more advanced member of a family may support the instruction set of an earlier family member as a subset. For example, the Motorola 68030 contains the 68000 instruction set as a subset of its instructions. Incompatibilities sometimes arise because apparently identical instructions are implemented differently and thus have different side effects. Incompatible processors (i.e. from different families) have order codes which, while performing much the same basic operations, are quite different at a detailed level. These differences will include the number of instructions, addressing mechanisms, data types supported, number of registers and the organisation of the more complex instructions, i.e. those which combine several basic operations. These differences occur because of the different applications fields of the processors and because of the different ways in which designers perceive the 'best' way to construct the processor.

2.2.4 CISC and RISC

Computers (or, more strictly, processors) are often classified according to the complexity (richness) of their instruction sets. The two major classifications are Complex Instruction Set Computer (CISC) and Reduced Instruction Set Computer (RISC).

CISC is used to describe computers with a rich and diverse order code. On the face of it the more instructions the better as there is a possibility of the availability of an instruction that will perform exactly what the programmer wants. However, the design of all computers is a compromise and the price to be paid for such an instruction set is in speed of execution and in the complexity of the hardware implementation.

Moreover, the more abstruse instructions may never be used, certainly in the code generated by compilers, because of the difficulty of recognising the circumstances which would make the use of such an instruction appropriate.

It is the intention of the order code designer to simplify the work of the low-level programmer by providing only generally useful instructions. This aim is not always met. Research into actual programs has shown that the designers sometimes provide features which are hardly ever used. The trend in evolving architectures is for the instruction set to become larger and more complex.

In direct contrast to the CISC, a RISC instruction set is designed to be rapid in execution. The instruction set is not intended to be used in low-level programming but to be generated by a compiler from a high-level language program.

The proponents of such systems argue that the reduced complexity of the hardware and the intrinsic speed of the relatively simple instructions provide the way forward in processor design. It follows that for most programs a RISC program will use more instructions than the same algorithm implemented on a CISC system. There are now several RISC based computers on the market, all of them with different order codes.

2.3   CPU characteristics

This section briefly describes those aspects of CPUs which characterise them from the point of view of the low-level programmer. Once programmers understand these characteristics they are in a good position to appreciate the primary constraints on program design.

2.3.1   *Variable length versus fixed length*

There are two conflicting requirements in order code design; making the order code easy for the programmer to use by including the facilities he or she requires and the production of an order code which is both cheap and easy to implement. The job of the designer consists of a number of tasks. First, there is the need to allocate bits in an instruction word. Second, there is the problem of making the circuits to perform the functions.

It is necessary to have instructions which read data from memory and instructions to write data into memory. The transfers take place into and out of registers. It will be seen that there is a need to define:

(a) The operation to be performed.

(b) The source address.

(c) The destination address.

If there is a large address space, many registers and many instruction types, then the instruction word needs to be large. Word machines, as opposed to byte machines, traditionally hold a complete instruction in a single word. In the case where the instruction length is fixed, say a word, there is a trade-off. More instructions implies less address ability, while more registers mean fewer of the other features. The compromise is because the total number of bits to specify the required instruction, select the appropriate register and to address the memory is fixed. Suppose the number of registers is doubled. Then an extra bit is needed in the register select field. This must be 'stolen' from another field, thus halving the address ability or the instruction repertoire. Many instructions may well not need to address the memory and so mechanisms are developed to avoid wasting the bits reserved for the address and use them instead to extend the order code repertoire. For word machines with fixed length instructions many mechanisms are introduced to minimise the adverse effects of these compromises.

Another technique is to make the instruction length variable. In this case, if there is a need for an address part of the instruction, then it is tagged on the end as extra bytes. The instructions then are of variable length dependent on the address mode. This has implications for execution time as additional memory references need to be made before the complete instruction can be decoded. The programmer need not be aware of the length of the instruction generated, because the assembler will handle that level of complexity. There are problems associated with short skip (jump) instructions, which if used carelessly may 'skip' (jump) into the middle of an instruction and thus start executing data. It is also more difficult to use a low-level debugger. The advantages seem in practice to be overwhelming as most CISC order codes now implement variable length instructions.

2.3.2   Co-processors

If the facility is included in the original design, the instruction set can be extended by the use of a co-processor (e.g. 80x87). This technique is used most often to supply additional arithmetic capabilities especially floating point. Many order codes do not implement floating-point operations in hardware, but require a software emulation to be used. Often the CPU will trap the missing instructions and automatically invoke a manufacturer supplied software package. The programmer must be aware of the performance differences and of the possibility that the software may not emulate the hardware exactly.

2.3.3   User/supervisor modes

Many machines implement at least two distinct states or modes. One, the 'user', mode is most frequently in use. This mode has restrictions built into it, preventing a user either inadvertently or deliberately interfering with the integrity of the system. Typically in user mode I/O instructions are unavailable and it is impossible to execute the 'halt' instruction. In addition, depending on the processor design, other facilities are denied to a user program.

In 'supervisor', privileged or system mode, it is possible to manipulate all the machine facilities. The supervisor or operating system can then perform I/O, allocate storage and modify the page registers which are used in complex processors to control the allocation and use of physical memory and so control the entire system.

2.4 Instruction classification

The processor instruction set is generally divided into four main groups; arithmetic, logical, program flow control, and machine control and I/O instructions.

2.4.1 Arithmetic instructions

Instructions within this group are implemented to handle addition, subtraction and the testing of values. Associated with the arithmetic unit are the 'carry' and 'overflow' bits. These are necessary to detect certain possible error conditions associated with finite accuracy arithmetic and to implement arbitrary precision arithmetic. Some processors implement condition codes. Condition codes are a set of testable bits which in addition to 'carry' and 'overflow' include 'zero' and 'sign' flags. These flags are set as the result of performing certain instructions. They are not always implemented consistently and it is necessary to check each instruction individually to see whether or not the relevant flags will be altered. Where condition codes are not set as the automatic result of operations there are instructions provided explicitly to test for, and take selective action on, various possible conditions. Multiple register machines usually use a condition code design; it reduces the number of instructions that need to be specified.

2.4.2 Logical instructions

Logical instructions allow the manipulation of byte fields as bits. Typically such instructions include and, or, exclusive or and not. A variety of logical and arithmetic shift and rotate instructions are usually supplied. These instructions may use the 'carry' bit. They are used for manipulating packed fields and for fast multiplication by manifest constants. Care must be taken when using such instructions to be very clear exactly what happens because there is a wide range of possible outcomes, including sign extension and the use of the carry bit. Some word machines contain byte swap instructions to interchange the bytes in a word, which may make certain operations easier especially in word addressable machines.

2.4.3 Program flow control instructions

Control instructions. These are used to alter the sequence of instruction execution. They include 'jumps', which are both conditional and unconditional, and 'calls' and 'returns', which are used for procedure invocation.

2.4.4 Machine control and I/O instructions

The final group of instructions is used for controlling the state of the machine and for performing I/O. The sort of internal state flags that can be manipulated are ones for turning the interrupt system off or setting instruction trapping. I/O instructions send and receive control information and data to external devices. Because these instructions can interfere with the basic operation of the processor, they are the ones restricted to the system user, where such a facility is provided. These are typically used by the operating system.

2.5   Processor hardware design

The internal hardware design of a processor can have a very significant effect on its operation (though the process of low-level programming is usually not directly affected by the implementation technology). It is, however, worth noting that the hardware techniques employed within the instruction decoder and execution unit of the processor are particularly crucial in determining how instructions are decoded and acted upon. The two principal methods are hard-wiring and microcoding.

2.5.1   Hard-wiring

The traditional implementation method is to design a circuit whose function is directly to execute the defined order code. This is known as 'hard-wiring' (i.e. the processor is said to be 'hard-wired'). The advocates of this method emphasise that it leads to the quickest execution. Unfortunately, processor design errors can only be corrected by redesigning the internal circuit of the processor.

2.5.2   Microcoding

Increasingly the implementation is achieved by means of microcoding. The hardware is designed to execute very quickly a highly restricted instruction set. A program is then written in 'micro' instructions to implement the target or visible instruction code being supported. Micro coding is a relatively arcane art as the micro-instructions operate at a very low level and each instruction may perform several operations at the same time. One approach to microcode implementation is the so called bit-sliced processor. In this case the target processor uses standard chips which support a limited instruction set. These chips operate in parallel and require a microcode program to control them. By using a standard chip the designer does not then have to build all the basic circuits, such as adders, from even simpler circuits himself.

The micro-program itself must be stored in a memory. If that memory is read-only it is described as hard microprogrammed; otherwise, it is known as soft microprogrammed and can in principle be written. Thus the visible instruction set being 'emulated' can be changed. There are systems which allow a choice of which of several micro-programs is to be used. This allows execution or hardware emulation of different order codes. A system which depends entirely on a soft micro-program has certain problems in starting itself up and needs appropriate hardware for its initial bootstrapping.

2.6 Data types and internal representation

There have been machines where the data held in memory has associated descriptors for identifying the type of data stored. For the vast majority of processors in common use the interpretation of data is conventional and at the machine language level there is no type checking, so the types of the operand are assumed by the instructions operating on them. A knowledge of the data types available is critical to low-level program design.

Five types of data are usually supported by modern computers; bytes/characters, integers, addresses, logical variables, and floating point/real numbers.

2.6.1 Bytes/characters

Bytes are usually eight bits and can therefore store 256 unique values. These are used to store characters. Two conventions are in common use. These are ASCII (American Standard Code for Information Interchange) and EBCDIC (Extended Binary Coded Decimal Interchange Code). ASCII is used in many different manufacturers' machines. EBCDIC is largely in use by IBM, although the PC range uses the ASCII character code. ASCII defines 128 7-bit characters, which means that the eighth bit is available for use in a variety of non-standard ways.

2.6.2 Integers

Fixed-length integers are the basic arithmetic unit. There are two conventions for negative integers: two's complement and one's complement. With one's complement representation zero is represented both by all zeros and by all ones; this latter is known as 'negative zero' and can give rise to programming problems.

Integers are stored as 8, 12, 16, 18, 24, 32 or even 64-bit quantities. With the increasing acceptance of the 8-bit byte as a standard storage unit the most common sizes are 8, 16 or 32 bits. In the case of the two smaller sizes, there is often a need to implement in software multi-length arithmetic to handle values greater than can be held in the basic integer. It is, of course, possible to implement arithmetic of arbitrary precision on any machine with the basic arithmetic facilities.

2.6.3 Addresses

It is necessary to be able to manipulate addresses. Memory addresses are unsigned integers and it is necessary to be able to perform operations on them and test the results.

2.6.4   *Logical variables*

Logical variables can be implemented as single bits in words or bytes. Such 'flags' can usually be conveniently set, reset or tested using the logical instructions.

2.6.5   *Floating point/real numbers*

A number of computers have the additional facility of hardware floating point. While there is an international standard for all aspects of floating-point manipulation there exists a wide range of formats between different manufacturers. These differences, often of both magnitude and accuracy, can lead to inconsistent results if applications programs using such arithmetic are not written with care and insight into their particular problem domain.

2.6.6   *General data structures*

Low-level programming can use these basic facilities to construct more complex data structures. What the programmer constructs is limited only by his or her ability to manipulate the basic data types available. The most complex structures offered by high-level languages must be mapped by the compiler onto the facilities available for low-level programming. Indeed, the programmer may well be able to use the machine code to implement even more complex structures appropriate to his application.

2.7   Addressing

Instructions that perform operations on data need to know where to find the data. The data address is sometimes implicit in the instruction, as when the operation can only be applied to the single accumulator. Many instructions involve at least two operands, e.g. addition (of the form $i := i + j$), loading and storing (though the distinction is historical and both are sometimes called moving). In this case the operation will be one of three possible types:

(a) *Register/register*

   The operation takes one register as a source operand and another as a destination.

(b) *Memory/memory*

   Both operands are in memory.

(c) *Register/memory*

   The operation takes place between a register and memory.

Not all instruction sets offer all three types of addressing mode. Memory-to-memory operations are the least common because they require longer instructions to specify the addresses and so both machine designers and programmers have become used to register-based designs. Some processors have relatively few registers, making register/register instructions relatively useless. All processors which use registers for data manipulation and nearly all modern order codes do must at least be able to load from and store to memory.

Processors are seldom consistent or symmetrical in their order codes. There are usually good implementation-dependent reasons why some instructions that might be expected are not provided. Nevertheless, it is essential in all cases to find out exactly what has been provided.

2.7.1 *Logical versus physical addressing*

A distinction must be made between logical and physical addressing. With modern architectures, there is no longer a direct relationship between logical and physical addresses and systems are invariably designed to cope with addresses which are greater than those that the hardware supports. The programmer must be aware of the effect of using addresses in such ranges, i.e. of the effect of logical to physical mapping.

2.8 Logical addressing

One of the biggest problems with producing low-level programs results from difficulties in structuring and accessing data. It is therefore important for the programmer to understand the range of addressing modes that are likely to be available. Other important considerations involve the ability of a processor to cope with various types of 'jump' amd 'call' and to suppprt code which is 're-entrant'. This section explores these concepts.

2.8.1 *Logical addressing methods*

The following summarises the principal logical addressing methods (not all of which will be available for use with any particular processor type):

(a) *Direct addressing*

The most obvious form of addressing is where the instruction contains a bit pattern which is the address of a storage location. Such an address is called a direct address.

(b) *Indirect addressing*

In this form of addressing, the address of the storage location is contained in another location (typically a CPU register) which acts as a 'pointer' to the main memory location in question. A common use of register-based indirection is the implementation of a stack. Some machines implement a single hardware stack using only one particular register which therefore can be implied rather than explicitly specified in the instruction. Other order codes combine this register indirect addressing with auto-incrementation and auto-decrementation. This can be used to implement a last-in, first-out (LIFO) stack or scan sequentially through an array of characters (a string) or a table of integers. It is also possible to specify memory indirection, in this case a memory location holds the address of the operand. Some processors implement 'multiple indirection', in this case the top bit of the address word indicates whether or not to take the next address as further indirection or not.

(c) *Addressing based on special areas of the address space*

The growth in the size of memories fuelled both by the availability of inexpensive memory chips and the inevitable tendency of programs to get bigger, has made it impracticable to design an order code where each instruction can contain within itself a full memory address. Accordingly a variety of techniques are in use so that the abbreviated address that can be held in an instruction is useful:

(i) *Base page.*

The idea is that a certain area of memory, starting at location zero, can be addressed by all instructions. This base page can then be used conventionally to allow access to all the address space using some form of indirect addressing.

(ii) *Current page.*

In addition to the base page an instruction can also address the current page. One bit in the address field is used to designate either base or current page. The reference, depending on the machine, may be relative to the current PC value or it may be generated by ignoring the bottom bits of the PC and then adding the displacement. This effectively divides the address space into 'pages' starting on fixed regular boundaries. It must be noted that it is only possible to give references to this restricted area of the address space when using basic instructions. Some architectures provide an escape mechanism to use a second word and so generate a double-length instruction. Even when this option is available it uses additional memory space and takes extra cycles to execute. The programmer has to organise the data so that most references can be to these easily accessible areas. To access other parts of the address space it is necessary to store in the directly addressable locations pointers to those other areas. This can prove a considerable restriction in practice.

(iii) *I/O addresses.*

In some computers I/O is handled by designating a portion of the address space as I/O registers. Memory addressing instructions can then be used to handle I/O. This reduces the number of instructions to be implemented at the price of losing some address ability. With the large addressing space of modern processors this is rarely a problem.

(iv) *Registers as memory addresses.*

Some processors 'map' the registers onto store addresses. This means that some apparent storage references are in fact referring to registers. These register addresses may be low memory or in the I/O address space. Mapping registers to store addresses allows for a faster context switch mechanism as only the pointer to the registers in memory has to be changed. (vi) Base/base and limits. Relocation and protection are provided in some processors by the provision of hardware base registers and, sometimes, limit registers. This means that the base register is set to the low address in the real address space and all references, while in user mode, are automatically relocated by this value. A limit register contains the highest address that the program may validly reference. These registers are usually used by the operating system to provide an area of memory for an application program and/or to confine it within limits to prevent interference with other programs co-existing within the memory.

(d) *Indexed addressing.*

An extremely powerful addressing mechanism built into most order codes is indexing. In this case the address contained in the instruction is modified by (added to) the value contained in an index register. The number of index registers varies from only one to as many as 128. The more there are, the more bits are needed in the instruction to specify which one is needed. Typical uses of index registers are for the register to contain the base address of a data structure such as an array and for the elements of that structure to be addressed via offsets. Alternatively the register can be used to contain the offset of a location which is an element in an array or string.

(e) *Hardware stacks.*

Some architectures implement a hardware stack which is used implicit in the execution of some instructions. In particular, it is used by the procedure call-and-return mechanism. The same stack may also be used by the interrupt mechanism. It is essential that the stack pointer should be set to a suitable area of memory and that the appropriate disciplines are used if the same stack is used for data storage.

(f) *Based addressing.*

Another technique for constructing addresses dynamically is 'based' addressing. All addresses are constructed by adding the contents of the specified base register to the offset in the instruction. This technique may be combined with indexing, in which case three values are added to produce the effective address.

(g) *Segmented addressing.*

When segmentation is implemented the total possible address space is regarded as a collection of segments, which are often 64K (words or bytes) in size. An address is then constructed as a displacement within a segment. Additional segment registers are used to indicate within which segment the displacement is to be interpreted. Mechanisms vary as to how the segment is specified. There may be fixed boundaries at segment-sized intervals, or a segment register may contain an address which is the start of the particular segment. One common characteristic of segment-addressing systems is that addresses 'wrap round' within a segment. Thus if a data structure crosses a segment boundary, the program must detect this and change, as appropriate, the relevant segment register. This problem makes the manipulation of large arrays bigger than a segment quite complex.

2.8.2   Modes

The ability of a processor to support user and system modes has been mentioned previously. Processors can also support modes in a way that changes the order code in use and so can be used to support hardware emulation of previous order codes. Some processors support a trace mode in which the processor traps after each instruction execution. This allows the implementation of single stepping for debugging purposes, under program control. Programmers need to understand the effect of modes because they may well affect the environment in which their program is to run, or their program may need to manipulate the modes to achieve its goals.

2.8.3   Long/short jumps and calls

Because most programs do not contain many jumps but, in practice, proceed in a progressive fashion through the code, many machines provide skips and 'short' jumps and calls. This can give rise to problems when a large program is loaded from a number of separately compiled procedures, each of which is small enough not to exceed segment boundaries, as jumps may need to be converted from short to long form. Long jumps are necessarily slower, requiring more memory accesses, and taking up more space. Thus there is often a mixture of long and short forms of jump in the same program.

The ability to force a compiler to generate 'long' form instructions is a common option. This is of concern to the programmer for several reasons. If the program is to form part of a suite of programs it is essential to establish the conventions which will allow intermodule communication to occur. Within a module it might prove acceptable to let the assembler decide the appropriate format of the jump. Techniques exist to make the necessary adjustments to jump format if an extra word is introduced or removed, e.g. by changing from a short jump to a long jump, though by no means all assemblers have this facility. It is necessary to use the appropriate conventions when the low-level module has to be called from a high-level compiled program.

The temptation always to use long calls and jumps must be paid for in terms of larger and slower programs.

2.8.4 Relocatability and position independent code

Some order codes which support PC relative memory references allow a program to be written in such a manner that it will run correctly, without modification, wherever it is loaded. This is seldom entirely straightforward at the level of an individual module, which may well have to communicate with global data and call other procedures. For an entire self-contained program, with appropriate hardware facilities, relocatability may be achieved transparently. This has obvious advantages in the allocation of storage where programs may be called into memory on demand.

2.8.5 Code/data areas

The separation of code and data is supported by some architectures and is mandatory in others. Such separation allows the program to be protected by access control hardware from accidental overwriting. It also simplifies the production of re-entrant programs.

2.8.6 Re-entrancy

A re-entrant program is one that does not require initialisation and can be run 'simultaneously' as part of separate processes. It is invariant and does not modify itself. For a code section to be simultaneously invoked with different data, that data must be addressed using registers and avoiding any direct, fixed addresses for variables.

2.9 Physical addressing

Associated with every processor is a physical memory. The processor generates logical addresses, which are mapped to actual memory locations. The physical memory is usually a mixture of ROM and dynamic or static RAM.

2.9.1 Memory sizes

There are two dimensions to the memory size equation. The first is the size of the basic addressable unit. This is likely to be the byte, but may be the word. As most memory chips implement a 1 bit $\times 2n$ regime there are often multiples of nine chips, the ninth bit being used as a parity bit. In the case of more sophisticated error-correcting memory, the number of additional bits is greater.

As chip technology advances the value of n grows rapidly. Originally such a memory chip contained perhaps 1024 bits, (i.e. $n = 10$), but it may now contain a million bits. Thus it is economical to implement a million bytes in a single memory unit, e.g. circuit board, because the price of a chip is not proportional to the number of bits it is capable of storing, and the memory can be constructed on the same number of boards of essentially similar complexity irrespective of the chip capacity. The order codes and their associated address ability were not designed with all these advances in mind. However, the implication now is that physical memories are large and are no longer closely related to the logical address that the order code is capable of generating. Early designs were such that the logical address space and the physical address space were identical.

2.9.2 Bus widths

Memories are conventionally, but not universally, attached to the processor by a bus. This is an interface which permits the parallel transfer of data. The number of bits in parallel is known as the bus width. The bus width is not necessarily the same as the minimum logically addressable unit of storage. It follows that if one byte is requested, then two or more bytes may be transmitted to the processor. The wider the bus, the faster the processor may run, since it is delayed less often waiting for data.

2.9.3 Boundaries

One practical consequence of the bus width being greater than the minimum addressable unit is that wider entities may have to start on specific byte boundaries. Thus, in some machines, instructions and integers must be stored at even addresses, while real numbers occupying four bytes must start on addresses divisible exactly by four. The consequences of this arbitrary rule may be unexpected and may cause undetectable errors.

2.9.4 Paging

Analysis of the behaviour of executing programs shows that neither all the program nor all its data need to be available all the time the program is executing. Paging is a mechanism which allows a program to execute correctly even if not all of its code and its data are resident. The hardware detects when a reference is made to an address which is not available in physical memory, it suspends the executing program and then makes available that (portion of the) program or data from an external device, and the program execution may then continue.

This process makes certain demands on the hardware. It must be able to detect references to 'missing' addresses and to map logical addresses to physical addresses. It is also essential to be able to restart instructions which have been partially executed. This latter criterion has proved to be difficult to meet in the case of variable length instruction sets and in the case of auto-incrementing registers. It is not always easy to undo those steps which have been completed before the missing memory is detected.

Paging was originally used to fit a large program into a small physical memory. Subsequently it has been used to share a relatively large physical memory between several users, none of whom would have been able to address all the memory.

2.9.5 *Cache memory*

Because there are hierarchies of memory, where the fastest is the most expensive, the concept of caching has been developed to take advantage of the fast memory without excessive expense. The concept works for much the same reason that paging does. Practical experience shows that only a small part of a program or its associated data is active in any particular time slot. Cache memory is used to store recently accessed data and instructions to provide high-speed access. The memory access process looks to see if data is present in the cache before it accesses the main memory. Different manufacturers implement the process each in their own way; the only effect the user should see is improved performance. The process is built into the hardware and is not under programmer control.

2.9.6 *Read/write/execute protection*

Once the hardware implements the complex addressing mechanisms needed for paging or relocation, it is possible to add checks to each access. These checks are usually implemented on page-sized sections of the address space and can be used to prevent accidental overwriting (read-only access), or software theft, by allowing execute only access. It is also possible to mark pages which have been changed, which is significant in a paging environment as it is unnecessary to write out unchanged pages.

Some systems also provide an 'accessed' flag so the system can establish which code and data pages are currently in active use. Again these mechanisms are usually transparent to the low-level programmer.

2.10 Input/output

In nearly all computer systems it is essential to communicate with external devices. This is the process known as I/O. Common external devices are keyboard/screen devices, printers, disc drives and tapes. Nearly all external devices are slow in operation compared with the speed of the processor and memory. Understanding of I/O is very important as much low-level programming is concerned with peripheral interfacing either exclusively or as part of its task.

2.10.1 *Privileged instructions and protection*

It has become customary for the vast majority of programs to perform I/O using the facilities provided by an operating system. When privileged instructions are implemented they are used by the operating system to try to provide protection from erroneous I/O operations. Normally, the programmer will access these facilities by calling executive, or supervisor, facilities.

2.10.2   *Addressing devices*

External devices are assigned addresses. These may be either part of the logical address space or specific I/O port addresses. Such addresses are usually determined by external hardware and as such often assigned conventionally. Whichever method is chosen it is necessary to be able to send commands, read status and transfer data to and from a device. All processors implement mechanisms to achieve this.

2.10.3   *Interrupts and polling*

Because external devices are slow and unpredictable as to when they have data available, it is necessary to have a mechanism to know when they need attention. There are two principal methods:

(a) *Polling.*

In a polling regime, the controlling program periodically scans the devices which might have some action to report. The status of the device is interrogated and if action is needed, for example, to transfer in the latest keystroke such action is taken. It is important to ensure that the devices are polled often enough to prevent the loss of data and that the control program does not get into a loop and fail to poll at all.

(b) *Interrupts.*

In this method, when a device wants attention it raises a hardware flag which alerts the central processor. When the processor acknowledges that flag it interrupts what it is doing, and invokes an interrupt handling routine. The processor can only accept interrupts at certain points in its execution cycle; read/fetch next instruction time is usual. (Effectively interrupts are techniques for polling at the hardware level where it can be carried out more efficiently.) The processor must have the ability to inhibit further interrupts so that enough of the machine state can be saved so that the process interrupted can be restarted correctly. The detailed implementation of interrupts varies widely. Some processors have only one interrupt and the handler must identify the interrupting device, others have so-called vectored interrupts where each device invokes its own appropriate handler. Interrupts do not provide a totally secure mechanism to avoid data loss as the interrupt-handling system may be turned off when some crucial event occurs. It is usual for there to be special hardware to handle the knitters of two simultaneous events and to queue those which are pending. The design of interrupt handlers can be rather complex. It is important to ensure that the interrupt system is disabled for as short a period as possible to reduce the risk of data being lost. The handling code must preserve the environment so that it can restore it after handling the interrupt. Broadly, the choice is between completely servicing the interrupt in the handler, or queuing it so that it can be handled later. There is also a problem in loading the interrupt vector with the address of the handler. Some operating systems provide a mechanism to allow the user to provide his own handlers. In such cases there is usually a detailed set of rules to observe to ensure that the overall integrity of the design is maintained.

2.10.4 Direct memory access

When relatively large amounts of data are transferred in a block, e.g. a disc sector or a magnetic tape record, at a fairly high speed, then a device known as a direct memory access controller will often be used. The principle is straightforward; the DMA device is given the position of the data in memory, its length and the device concerned. It then takes bus cycles to transfer the data directly to memory without going through the central processor at all. An interrupt occurs when the transfer is complete or an error occurs. There are problems in specifying addresses as the cycle stealing process may well bypass any memory protection or relocation hardware. This is a particular problem in time-sharing systems. In such systems a user may have to wait for I/O completion, and another user gains control of the processor. It is very important that the memory concerned with the I/O process is not reallocated as the DMA is running autonomously.

Sophisticated device controllers may support gather-read and scatter-write. In this case a contiguous disc record is created by reading from different memory areas. The process is reversed on writing back to memory.

2.10.5 Traps

Traps are internal (software) interrupts. External interrupts are triggered by external events. Traps are caused by internal conditions created by hardware or software. Again traps affect the programmer primarily because he or she may have to handle traps caused by his (or other) programs. Typically traps are seen as interrupts by low-level programs.

(a) *Short-call mechanism.*

Some processors implement traps as a concise calling mechanism. This can save space if they are used to invoke frequently used services from the operating system. There is also the advantage that the invoking program does not need to know the addresses of the invoked service. This allows a new version of the operating system to be implemented without any change being needed to application programs.

(b) *Illegal instructions.*

Not all patterns of bits form 'legal' instructions, i.e. defined instructions. Some processors detect this condi-

tion and execute an illegal instruction trap. Illegal instruction traps can also be used to support missing
instructions so that, for example, software floating point
emulation code can be automatically entered.

(c) *Data errors*.

Data errors such as parity faults or division by zero can
cause traps.

(d) *Paging problems*.

A page trap is generated by a reference to a page non-
resident in memory. If the system supports demand
paging, i.e. it will read from disc the missing portion and
carry on, then the instruction so interrupted may be
partially complete. This causes considerable difficulties
in the design of processors and there are many examples
of errors in processor design in dealing with page faults.
(e) Power failure. For a short time after a power failure
in the external supply the processor can still execute. If
there is standby power for the memories or core memory
it is possible to shut the machine down in orderly fashion
so that it can restart properly.

(f) *Bootstrapping/IPL*.

Many processors can detect an external reset signal; this
causes a trap which in turn executes a power up initial
program load sequence. This start-up code must be held
in some permanent memory, e.g. ROM.

2.10.6 Pipe-lining/instruction caching

In the constant search for processor speed many machines
implement 'pipe-lining'. Using this technique the processor decodes several instructions at a time, the decoding of each being
started before the first has finished. Interrupts and jumps cause
problems but this overlap does give a speed increase. Another
technique is to hold instructions in a special instruction cache
memory. This enables short loops of code to be executed without
any instruction fetches from main memory, and thus produces
speed improvements.

In both cases the programmer needs to have intimate knowledge of the machine to use the mechanisms safely and efficiently.

2.11 Other architectures

The overwhelming majority of computers in use are based on
the above principles. There are other ways to design computers:

(a) *P-code machines*.

One example of such an approach is to build a machine
to do in hardware what is more often done by software.
The USCD Pascal system compiles into an intermediate

language known as p-code. This is usually interpreted by software, but processors have been built to execute it directly.

(b) *Parallel machines.*

Most parallel machines are groupings of independently executing von Neumann machines which cooperate on a single task. There are also machines, with array processors, which will perform the same operation simultaneously on all the elements of an array.

2.12 Assemblers and macro-assemblers

In practice most low-level programs are written either to interface to special-purpose hardware or to interface between programs written in high-level languages. Most low-level programs are written in macro-assembler, and the programmer must be aware of the properties of machines outlined above in order to produce efficient, reliable, modifiable code.

2.12.1 Basic assembler

Programs written using the mnemonic order code of a particular machine are said to be written in assembler or assembly language. Each processor has its own machine code and associated assembly language, even though some manufacturers try to conceal the fact and persuade users always to program in some higher level language. There are various important characteristics of assemblers:

(a) *One-for-one.*

An assembler allows (or forces!) the programmer to specify each machine instruction individually. This is known as one-for-one.

(b) *Syntax.*

Most assemblers allow one statement per line. The format is: LABEL OP-CODE OPERAND Comments The fields are conventionally separated by at least one blank character. Not all fields have to be present in each statement.

(c) *Labels.*

Labels are mnemonics which can be associated with instructions and with data. For most assemblers the syntax of labels is that they always start with an alphabetic character. The length of the name depends on the system. Sometimes the name can be long, but only the first few characters are significant. The number of characters allowed in external names, for inter module communication, is nearly always restricted to six or eight characters. Sometimes the '$' character and a few other punctuation marks are allowed in a name as well as alphabetic and numeric characters. Labels are always the first field on a line. There are two common conventions in use. The first is that a field starting in column 1 is a label; the other is that labels are terminated with a colon. This second convention permits multiple labels to be specified on a single statement.

(d) *Mnemonic op-codes.*

Associated with each instruction in the order code is a mnemonic 'op-code'. Conventions vary, but many systems provide mostly three-letter combinations for each operation. This is not a universal practice. It is the common intention that these letter groupings are meaningful, hence the term mnemonic.

(e) *Pseudo ops, comments, lay-out.*

In addition to the op-codes which correspond to machine instructions there are usually pseudo-ops. These allow the format of the print-out to be specified, storage locations to be allocated or labels to be assigned to constant values.

(f) *Operands.*

The third field is the operand field. What this contains is specific to the operation specified in the op-code. It is commonly an address or a constant (also known as a literal value or just literal). The operand can sometimes be modified; indirection or indexing may be specified. Sometimes there may be two fields if the instruction needs both a source and a destination address. It is customary to separate the sub-fields of the operand with commas. Some limited assembly-time arithmetic capability may be provided on the operand field.

(g) *Comments.*

The final field on a line is taken to be a comment. Comments are ignored and appear in the file and on listings simply as explanations. Some assemblers require the end of the instruction to be marked with a special character e.g. ; (semicolon). Where this is not the convention an * (asterisk) in column 1 is often used to indicate that the entire line is to be treated as a comment.

(h) *Constants.*

Facilities are provided for defining constants of all the data types supported, i.e. chars, bytes, integers and reals. In the case of bytes and integers, especially because they may be used as masks and flags rather than as numbers, it is usual to allow specification of constants in terms of single bits, or in octal, decimal and hexadecimal notations. Constants can be given a mnemonic name and can often be constructed using assembly time arithmetic and logical operations.

(i) *Storage allocation.*

Labels can be given to storage locations and blocks of storage. A frequent pseudo-op is block storage start (BSS). In this case the operand is the number of words to be allocated. Zero is permitted which gives a mechanism for multiple labels at a single location in those cases where it is impossible to specify multiple labels on a single line.

```
COMMENT |
********************************************************************************

File:           TEST12
History:        Started 9/8/92
Purpose:        Provides options to change the display to 40 or 80
                column mode
Format:         No calling conventions
*******************************************************************************|

            TITLE   test12              ;
            DOSSEG                      ;Conventional segment allocation
            .MODEL SMALL                ;
            .STACK 100h                 ; 256 byte stack

            .DATA
message     DB      "Select option: [4]0, [8]0, E[X]it ", '$'
newline     DB      13,10,'$'

            .CODE
start:      mov     ax,@DATA
            mov     ds ax
key_loop:   mov     dx OFFSET message   ; point to the message
            mov     ah,9                ; write code
            int     21h                 ; DOS write
            mov     ah,1                ; get a keyboard character
            i nt    21 h                ; DOS read
            push    ax                  ; save the character
            lea     dx,newline
            mov     ah,9
            int     21h
            pop     ax                  ; get character again
            cmp     al,'x'              ; was it exit?
            je      exit                ; yes - so go!
            cmp     al,'X'              ; was it exIt?
            je      exit
            cmp     al,'4'              ; 40 characters?
            je      set 40
            cmp     al,T8'              ; 80 characters?
            je      set 80
            jmp     key loop            ; Go for more

set_40:     mov     ah,0                ; service 0
            mov     al,0                ; 40x25 mode
            int     10h
            jmp     exit

set_80:     mov     ah,0                ; service 0
            mov     al,3                ; 80x25 mode
            int     10h
            jmp     exit

exit:       mov     al,0                ; error-level
            mov     ah,4Ch              ; DOS exit function
            int     21h                 ; call DOS
            END     start
```

Figure 2.1   A typical 80x86 assembly language listing showing conventional assembler syntax

(j)   *Code and data separation.*

It is generally desirable to separate code and data storage explicitly and some hardware provides facilities to achieve this. Assemblers supporting these hardware features allow a single program text to be divided into 'Psects' (program sections) and 'Dsects' (data sections). These are loaded separately and the allocation is handled by the loader.

2.12.2   Interfacing with high-level language modules

Assembly programs lend themselves to modular organisation. It is often the case that such programs have to interface with compiled code written in higher level languages. The output of all the different language processors must be expressed in a common relocatable binary language. The crucial point for communication is the concept of entry points and external references. A module can declare one or more of its labels as an entry point. Other modules can declare references to be external. There must be only one entry point declaration of a name but it can be used as an external reference by all the other modules in the system. In most assembly systems this produces a two-level naming structure. References are either global or local.

2.12.3   Assembly time arithmetic and logic for addresses and data

Constants can be constructed using assembly time arithmetic and logical operations. Not only does this give mnemonic significance to the value, but allows automatic recalculation of that value if one of the component values changes.

Address arithmetic is also possible but it must be noted that while two addresses can be subtracted to provide a constant difference, it is not possible to add two relocatable addresses.

2.12.4   Conditional assembly

An extremely powerful feature of an assembler is a conditional assembly option. By no means all assemblers support such a feature.

Basically, what is provided is a set of 'pseudo-ops' to give an 'if... then ... else ...' capability. Some value or relationship may be tested and depending on its logical truth or falsity one set of statements will be assembled rather than another.

The capability applies not only to code producing statements but may be used so that, for example, one constant value is used rather than another or one form of data structure is defined rather than another.

Some assemblers allow nesting of conditionals while others implement only a single level.

2.12.5 Macros

A macro in this context is a text body into which textual substitutions may be made at assembly time. Once defined it looks like any other op-code. Indeed, it may even be used to redefine an existing order. This contrasts with one-for-one assemblers as a macro instruction may translate to several real machine instructions.

Macros are sometimes provided to simplify the use of operating systems facilities invocation. They may be used to enforce conventions on the accessing of data fields, or in calling procedures and setting up parameter lists.

When invoked, the parameters, which are in the operand field, are substituted textually for the equivalent formal (or dummy) parameters of the definition. The connection between formal and actual parameters is positional.

Macros in some systems can be nested in their expansion so that a macro definition can contain other macros.

It is often the case that the macro expansion can itself be conditional on the number of parameters, so that procedure calls with variable parameter lists can be handled correctly.

2.13 Inter-module communication

A frequent task of the programmer is to write an 'interlude' code section to provide an interface between two modules compiled by different compilers, and probably written in different languages. The need for the interlude code is a result of each compiler designer choosing to use the addressing system in a different way and choosing to represent data in different ways.

What is common to all calling sequences is the need to be able to store a 'return address' so that, when the called module has completed its task, it can then return to the calling program at the correct point. Most modern processors achieve this by pushing the return address onto a stack.

It is in the form of an address stored on the stack that one difference between long and short calls manifests itself. This implies that there is a hardware-supported stack and that the user has allowed sufficient space for the stack to grow to save this return address. It is important to realise that the act of making the call has the side-effect of changing the stack pointer. Usually the stack is not used in the strict LIFO way, which allows access only to the top element, but to provide for dynamic local storage.

Most languages support the convention that local storage is allocated to a routine when it is called and that it is relinquished at module termination. This implies the existence of a stack frame, a template defining the conventional use of a section of memory. Each level of invoked program will have such a stack frame. There will therefore be conventions so that the local variable space of calling routines can be accessed (see Figure 3.2).

It is often the case that the stack pointer itself cannot be used for accessing stack frame elements, and another register, which will not be automatically altered by the calling hardware instruction, must be explicitly set to contain the value of the base of the stack frame.

This discussion has not included the passing of parameters. Although there are exceptions most languages allow the passing of parameters between modules in one of two ways. Parameters may be passed by value or by reference. Passing parameters by value does not present many theoretical problems. A solution is to place the values on the stack and allow the called routine to address them much as its own local variables. The only complication is passing by value items whose size is not known at compile time or which can be different at each call. Examples of this are strings and arrays. This problem is usually overcome by the use of descriptors which are fixed-size data items describing the size and layout of the variable-size data items. Passing parameters by reference is achieved by passing the address of the variable to the called routine.

The complications here are two-fold. First, in a segmented addressing scheme it may not be easy to pass the absolute address of a variable which is conventionally addressed as a register+displacement. The second problem may affect the re-entrancy of the code if the addresses are absolute and not register relative. It is unlikely that the typical low-level program will need to establish its own conventions. The programmer does need to understand the conventions adopted by others, especially compiler writers.

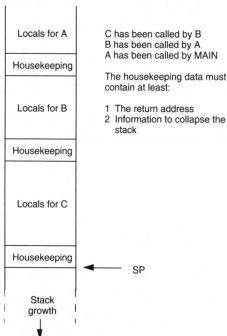

Figure 2.2   Use of stack frames

2.14   High-level languages

The development of programming languages has shown gradual trends away from machine dependence and towards greater orientation towards humans. The phrase 'high-level language' originally referred to the first of these, a language not specific to a particular machine architecture. Being more human-oriented came later. However, it is important to recognise that these two trends are distinct, and do not 8always pull in quite the same direction. It is also important to realise that, while this process has been going on for over 30 years, it is still some way from being completed, and looks set to continue for at least a decade or two more.

The steps taken in this process began with a move from pure machine code to symbolic assembly code, though still with a one-to-one relationship between assembler statements and machine instructions. Then came the addition of extra statements, not directly generating a machine-code instruction, but giving assembler directives, or simply adding comment for the benefit of human readers of the text. Comment remains to this day, which is one indication that the languages themselves are not as fully human-oriented as they might be. Directives also remain, not just in terms of 'pragmas' (assertions to aid program proving, and invocation of compiler options), but in the fabric of the language proper.

Type specification statements or declarations are descendants of assembler directives, though admittedly in some languages they do also generate code. For example in FORTRAN, type specification statements are 'non-executable' because they do not generate code directly, but in languages where declarations cause memory to be allocated dynamically when encountered during execution, they do generate code (e.g. to alter the value of a stack pointer) and so are 'executable' in FORTRAN terminology.

So from 'one statement to one machine instruction', languages moved to 'one-to-one or zero', and the next step was 'one-to-many'. The direct relation, in terms of textual sequence, between what one could now begin to call 'source code' and machine instructions still remained, but some source code statements expanded into several instructions.

One-to-one assembler instructions still lurk not far beneath the surface of many current high-level languages. The unconditional GOTO which many languages retain, despite two decades of vilification, is an obvious example. One-to-many mappings also exist, in forms such as simple conditional GOTOs, surviving curiosities like the FORTRAN statement function, and more sophisticated macro facilities. Use of single infixed operators was quickly followed by use of more general arithmetic expressions, with the development of algorithms to convert conventional-looking mathematical expressions with infixed operators to a form more suitable for translation into conventional, sequential, machine instructions. That form is often known as 'reverse Polish' for historical reasons, but is more usefully and descriptively termed 'post fixed'. The post-fixed form of $(a + b)$ is $(ab +)$ and that of $(a - b)/(a + b)$ is $(ab - ab + /)$.

It is interesting to note that direct use of postfixed form survives in the fringe areas of high-level languages on the borders with assembly language, most notably in the language Forth.

Although it can be seen that conversion of a post fixed expression into a sequence of machine instructions is fairly straightforward, already one has moved a long way beyond simple one-to-many assembler or auto code statements. The sequence of symbols operands and operations-changes greatly. Furthermore, one is not talking of one statement, but of an indefinite and potentially unlimited set of expressions of arbitrary complexity. In effect one has crossed the boundary between simple one-to-many conversion, into a more general form of translation in which any obvious relationship between the sequence of symbols in the source code and the corresponding machine code instructions has disappeared.

For simplicity we shall call this form of translation 'compilation', while recognising that variations such as 'interpretation' and use of intermediate code exists and that the strict definition of compilation is more specific. For this discussion, the differences between strict compilation and other forms of translation are unimportant. (It can be noted that post fixed expressions can be regarded as an embryonic form of intermediate code, albeit an abstract one.)

2.14.1 FORTRAN

Once the direct link between source code form and a sequence of machine instructions has been broken for arithmetic expressions, it is a short step to break that link for other computational processes. The first successful high-level language, for production rather than experimental purposes, was designed to bring to scientists and engineers the benefits of being able to write arithmetic expressions in programs in a fairly natural way, as its name FORTRAN (FORmula TRANslation) implies.

Thirty years later, FORTRAN remains one of the main programming languages of the world. It has developed, certainly, and FORTRAN 8X is a major development, but is still recognisably the same language. There are many reasons for the continued use of FORTRAN - some good, some debatable, some definitely bad. However, one reason must be the scale and nature of the benefits which FORTRAN delivered in usable form, compared with what had gone before, to its target users. Later languages offered further benefits, certainly, but for many those benefits are marginal, or seem so.

2.14.2 Machine independence

It is worth pausing here to reflect on the possibilities open at this stage. The technique of compilation (as opposed to conversion) had broken the connection between individual source code statements and corresponding machine code instructions. This, in principle, made possible the writing of programs which were machine-independent. That is, when a program was written the characteristics of the machine it would run on could be forgotten. Further, when it ran after compilation, it would work correctly on any machine, subject only to any limitations resulting from machine capabilities such as memory size or ranges of arithmetic. Since machine independence of programming languages would have been achieved, all programs could be written in the same language, and compiled to run on any (large enough) machine.

Because no dependence on machines would be left, the language for programming computers could be developed to be totally human-oriented. The compilers would convert programs into machine terms.

Three decades on, none of these possibilities has been realised. The twin aims of high-level languages, as indicated earlier, have not pulled in the same directions. All programs are not written in the same language. Programs often cannot be written without reference to machine characteristics. The languages, though human-oriented, are not wholly human-oriented despite claims to the contrary by devotees of particular ones. Perhaps the difference can best be expressed by saying that, while languages are not machine-specific, they remain machine-dependent. This is because, very often, one cannot be sure whether a program will run, or if it does run, what will happen, if it is transferred from one machine to another.

2.15 Abstract data types

In the case of data, high-level languages have steadily moved away from the storage associated models inevitable with assembly language, and the concepts of 'abstract data types' have gradually been developed. Nevertheless residues of machine dependence remain.

2.15.1 Arithmetic types

Assembly languages deal inevitably with storage units like machine words or bytes, and the hardware (or in more recent times, micro-coded) operations which are permitted on them. However, high-level languages have allowed programmers to refer to integers, reals and so on, and to mathematical operations on them. (Languages designed for real-time applications or for systems implementation of course have had to retain low-level features but they can be regarded as special cases.)

Mainstream languages, with their more usual arithmetic types, still show traces of machine dependence. Pascal does not have an exponentiation operator (an incompleteness which is the result of hardware limitations) while in contrast C has some extra operators because they map directly onto machine instructions of the PDP/11 on which the language was first developed. The ability to write $i + +$ instead of $i: = i + 1$ can be regarded as a useful abbreviation. Equally a way of making the compiler's job easier at the expense of making the programmer aware of how the operation works inside the machine. Note that Pascal and C are second-wave, not first-wave, high-level languages. There are many more examples of machine dependencies influencing recent high-level programming languages, so this is still a general limitation.

At least such machine-derived aspects of languages do not harm portability of programs, if they are written in ISO Pascal or C (when the standard is finalised). Much more serious is the fact that the ranges and in the case of real numbers precision of arithmetic values, are normally not specified in language definitions and standards. A program using only integer data may run correctly on one system but not on another, even though the system's basic power, in terms of speed and memory, is well capable of the job. The reason is just that this system's language compiler supports a narrower range of integers than the first. Worse, another system may run the program but produce incorrect results, because an arithmetic overflow is commonly regarded by language designers as a fault in the program rather than as a limitation of the processor. Hence it is not generally regarded as necessary for language standards to require compilers to signal overflow, or other undesirable events such as an attempt to divide by zero. Where there is no hardware overflow detector the result may be wrap round. With real number arithmetic one has not just the range problem. The precision of representation of values, and of the results of operations on values of a given precision, are left undefined, or implementation-dependent, or at best implementation-defined (which at least means that somewhere there should be a specification of what actually happens).

2.15.2   *Character data types*

Standards for character sets with 7-bit representation have been around for many years e.g. ISO 646. In the English speaking world this is normally referred to by the permitted USA national variant, ASCII language definitions and standards commonly define the set of characters needed to form programs, usually without reference to ISO 646, ASCII, or any permitted variant.

Additional characters supported by an implementation are normally left system-dependent, as are characters used in comments or character literal. Worst of all, collating sequences for characters are normally left system-dependent or at best only partially defined. This means that even if a program uses and handles only characters from the language's own basic character set (even if this is a subset of ISO 646/ASCII) it still cannot be guaranteed to produce consistent results when moved between systems.

After primitive beginnings, languages now tend to have reasonably complete facilities for handling both individual characters and character strings. Machine-dependence tends to show through, however, with the provision of built-in functions for mapping the available character set to or from a set of integers. These integers are normally identified with the internal machine representation which also of course provide the basis of variations in collating sequences). This provides some level of portability at the cost of the programmer needing to know about and program investigative and manipulative routines to work around the differences between internal representations. This makes extra work and prevents the programmer from thinking and working wholly in the right level of abstraction. This is all for the sake of ignoring the existence of well-established standards for character sets.

The excuse is, of course, that those not needing portability should not be required to sacrifice efficiency, but it is those who do want portability that tend to pay the price. At least FORTRAN 77 provided ASCII-based built-in functions as well as system-dependent facilities. The fault is as much that of the hardware designers as the language designers.

2.15.3   Boolean data types

Most languages contain, explicitly or implicitly, the concept of logical or Boolean truth values TRUE and FALSE, and logical operations upon them. Most languages have an explicit data type. Some languages only have Booleans implicitly, and generate Boolean values typically through the use of relational operations like >, < etc. on arithmetic or other values, for use in conditionals etc. These languages do not have the full panoply of a data type, so do not include literal values, variables, parameter passing, built-in functions etc.

Some languages have a bit data type, with values 0 and 1 and operations like logical multiplication, addition and negation to stand in place of the logical operations of Boolean types. There is often confusion between the two even though, at the abstract level, they are undoubtedly distinct despite the very obvious mapping which exists from one to the other. This is compounded by further confusion between the values and their representation. There is no reason, at the abstract level, to assume or need to know whether values like TRUE or 1 are stored as single bits, and certainly no need for language definitions or standards to specify that they must be, unless the language is explicitly designed for 'bit-twiddling' applications.

The distinction between logical and bit types is not very obvious at the single value level; the number of things you can do with a type with only two values is fairly limited. Further, it is easy to fall into the trap of assuming that TRUE and 1, AND Andy, are merely alternative syntactic representations of the same concept. The difference becomes clearer when aggregates are considered. Masking and shift operations make sense with bit strings but less sense with vectors of Booleans. However, logical values make more sense than bits when appearing in decision tables.

2.15.4   Derived and user-defined types

Early languages presented the user with some pre-defined types and that was all one had to work with. More modern languages allow programmers to define new types, either derived from built-in types or specified separately. Although derived and user-defined types are logically distinct in nature, they tend not to be so clearly distinct in practice because user-defined types are often derived from some base type that exists anonymously in the language. The only difference between this anonymous type and the built-in types is that the former is not available 'up front' but has to be invoked by a user definition.

Pascal, which pioneered user-defined types, at least in major languages, illustrates this well. One can define a new type:

type *colour: (red, blue, black, yellow)*

giving not just this set of values but the ordering

red < *blue* < *black* < *yellow*

whether this is meaningful or not. Also, if we need only four variables of this type we can write:

var *player1, player2, player3, player4: (red, blue, black, yellow)*

and this instantiation of the anonymous base type is itself also anonymous. The example above is a Pascal enumerated type (so called because one enumerates each specific value). In Pascal we also have again, whether relevant or not explicit type conversions between the values enumerated and a contiguous subset of integers from zero. In our case yellow, say, maps onto the integer 3. As well as showing that, in the case of Pascal, the term 'enumerated' can be taken in more than one sense, this demonstrates the 'abstraction' involved is really only a very thin veneer over an explicit hardware-related implementation model.

What makes Pascal enumerated types more than just the result of a sprinkling of syntactic sugar over type integer is that the arithmetic operations are hidden. If one does need them for an enumerated type, one has to use the type conversion functions and then of course one gets all of the operations, whether meaningful or not.

Derived types from actual (named and usable) types may be new types or subset types. In such cases we might write:

type *temperature* **is new** *integer*

or

type *year* **is** *range [1950 ... 1999]* **of** *integer*

Values of the derived type are the same as the values of (or the specified subset of values of) the parent type. A minimal provision of such a facility could simply use the name of the type as a documentation aid but have no other implications, e.g. declaring a variable:

temperature *bath*

would be the same as *writing*

integer *bath*

Further expressions like

bath + 5 or *bath + index*

(where *index* is an integer variable) would be admissible. However, this delivers only cosmetic benefit to the language user and the strong typing approach normally used requires **temperature** and **year** to be logically and syntactically distinct types from the parent **integer** (and of course each other). The implication is that explicit type conversions have to be provided when needed, e.g.

bath + **temperature***(index)*

The case of literal values is marginal but strict strong typing principles would require **bath + temperature**(5) as well.

To date, languages providing such a facility at all tend to take the soft option and assume that the derived type inherits all the properties of the parent type. However, multiplying one integer by another makes sense, but multiplying one year by another does not. In the example cited the safeguard is that the result of such an irrational operation would be outside the specified range of the subset type **year** but this is not true for **temperature**, where the same arguments apply. Adding one year to another or one temperature to another similarly makes no sense (although in other derived types, such as money in pence or weight in grams, the addition would make sense, since the zero of the counting scale is not arbitrary). However, subtracting two years or two temperatures does make sense, although the results are not of type **year** or **temperature** but are (pure?) integer numbers (of years or degrees).

This suffices to show that the primitive concept of type fostered by conventional languages is deceptively simple (actually it is over-simplified). Inheritance of properties (not just ranges of allowable values of derived types from their parents) is a complicated matter. To date languages which have addressed this issue at all have intended to use rather clumsy 'data-hiding' mechanisms. Here modules define derived types which are exported to the outside world. They also explicitly overload the operators intended to remain valid on inheritance, while hiding the actual parent type and the unwanted operations. This is workable but hardly elegant.

2.15.5 Pointer types

The value of an item of a pointer type is not one of a set of data values but a reference to some other item, which may be of any type (or none), including another pointer. At its crudest and most machine-oriented, the value is a machine address absolute, or relative to the base address of some allocated area of memory. In languages intended for systems implementation or other applications, like real-time, involving machine-level manipulation, pointers are types in their own right. Alternatively, they appear as an anonymous, basic type from which all others are derived. Languages like CORAL 66 underline this by allowing arithmetic operations on address values. Pointers are still effectively types in their own right if they are free pointers, able to reference any other object regardless of type. This occurs in weakly typed languages such as PL/1, or so-called (usually misleadingly) 'untyped' languages.

Pointers can be regarded as being of a derived type only if they are constrained to reference items of a specified type, which is the case in more modern languages with strong typing features. The language then has potentially as many 'simple' or direct pointer types as it has ordinary data types, including user-defined, derived and aggregate types. Of course it is possible to allow pointers to point to items of pointer type, to as many levels as needed, i.e. indirect pointers.

2.15.6 Union types

A union (or united) type consists of the union (in the set theoretic sense) of two or more existing types; that is, any value of any of the types forming the union is a value of the united type. Union types are uncommon if the term is used strictly enough to exclude 'casual' unions resulting from ad hoc type conversions in weakly typed languages. Of major languages, ALGOL 68 is the only one to address them seriously - in terms of providing explicit language features to support them.

Union types create numerous problems. One that is relatively easy to resolve concerns aiding. It could logically be argued that a union type is unordered, but it is probably more useful to regard it as partially ordered (using the ordering within the component types of the union). Further complete ordering is possible where, for example, components of the union are types all derived from the same ordered type. More difficult is the question of whether a permitted operation on values of the component types is valid on values of the united type. However, if, for example, the union is of **character** and **integer**, this applies equally to x + y if + means integer addition or character concatenation, or x*y if y if * is a replication operator which might be used in, say:

'GO!'*3 -> 'GO! GO! GO!'

That, however, can be dealt with alongside the operation inheritance problem of derived types. Most difficult is the problem of ambiguity of values, e.g. the status of the value red in the union type created from the two user-defined types

type *billiards = (red, white, spot)*

type *croquet = (red, yellow, blue, black)*

and the resolution of ambiguity in uniting values of pointers at one level with those at another.

ALGOL 68 avoided the first by not having subset or enumerated types and resolved the second by banning 'incestuous' types where the components of a union were too closely related. Other languages avoid union types or tend to brush them into well-policed corners like input/output. Effectively they present a problem in language design not yet totally resolved.

2.15.7　Aggregate types

In some discussions, aggregate types (also known as constructed or compound types) are also described as 'derived types'. Since the concept of aggregation already contains the idea of building a new type from components of existing types, it is more helpful to reserve the term 'derived' explicitly for simple types which are monolithic or atomic in structure.

To clarify this point and dispose of a common confusion, a set which contains only one element is distinct, structurally and logically, from the element itself. Similarly, string of length 1 is distinct from the single items it contains, as is an array with one element from the element, or a record with one field from the field.

2.15.8　Set types

The value of a set type is, strictly, an unordered collection of values drawn from one or more base types, or one type if unions are included. The usual set theoretic operations and concepts can be provided for such types. In most languages set types have to be simulated by the programmer, using other aggregate types such as arrays or lists, and the only major languages supporting them directly are Pascal and its derivative Modula 2. However, in Pascal, as with various other features, the way it is provided is based on a particular machine-oriented model which results in restrictions both on allowed base types and the sizes of sets. Indeed, a notorious shortcoming of many Pascal implementations is the failure to support even a natural requirement like a set of all the available characters. It is to be hoped that Modula 2, once standardised, will be free of such shortcomings.

2.15.9　Lists

A list is a sequence of elements, which may or may not be homogeneous and may include sub-lists. Here the natural concepts and operations are of (total) ordering, and additions or deletion of elements, including list concatenation. Other features can be added, such as indexing the elements. In most conventional languages lists have to be simulated, e.g. using records linked by pointers, or, if even those are not available, arrays. This is clumsy at best, and often inefficient. However, lists are provided in so-called 'list processing' languages, of which by far the best known is LISP, and rule-based languages like Prolog. In LISP the list is so fundamental that all data and control structures are represented in that form. Hence while lists come naturally, many other things come in a clumsy and unnatural way, or in some versions through 'alien' imports.

2.15.10　Strings

A string is a homogeneous list of simple elements, usually indexed, and often confined to character, or characters and bits. With characters normally represented by a single byte (or two or three in the case of large character sets like Kanji), the machine orientation is clear, although some languages put a thicker veneer over it than others, such as identifying a string with a vector of characters, with a special notation. In such cases, the string *'lemon'* is regarded as an abbreviation for the vector $['l', 'e', 'm', 'o', 'n']$. In C the distinction is made even clearer, using different delimiters for character and string values, so that "*x*" denotes a character string of length one containing the character *'x'*. This avoids type ambiguities of one-element literal that can occur in other languages.

The machine orientation is also revealed by the limited range of operations available. These are usually confined to concatenation and extraction of single elements, or perhaps sub strings, which are easy and efficient to implement.

Character strings are provided in most languages, with various fixes of greater or lesser clumsiness to cope with non-printing characters, especially **<CR>** (carriage return), **<LF>** (line feed) and **<HT>** (horizontal tab). Bit strings are much less common, and even then can come with machine-oriented restrictions such as fixed (byte or word) length. PL/1 is the only major language to provide a full range of facilities. However, it does not have a Boolean type (or in PL/1 rather a Boolean attribute), bit strings of length one doing duty for the truth values. Other languages identify Boolean with bit types, despite the distinctions mentioned earlier, in the sense of providing bit-string operations on arrays of logical. Pascal provides very explicitly machine-oriented, and machine-dependent, operations for packing and unpacking arrays, where the intent is to provide efficient storage. This is a point that the programmer must be conscious of and deal with, rather than take for granted as high-level abstraction would demand. Some degree of explicit machine orientation is probably inevitable with bit strings, given the applications that are likely to need them.

2.15.11 Arrays

The array is the oldest and most fundamental data structure. It is an interesting case since, although very little removed from an explicit machine model of storage, it also meets very important application needs. Especially in science and engineering, these arise from mathematical concepts like subscripted variables, vectors and matrices. We thus have the happy, and of course not wholly accidental, situation where machine orientation and application orientation are working together and not in conflict.

An array is a homogeneous structure of elements which are accessed individually, or collectively as sub-arrays or slices (cf. sub-strings) by indices. The dimensionality of an array is indicated by the number of subscripts needed to specify an individual element.

A one-dimensional array needs only one index and is often called a vector. This does not, however, imply that such a data structure has the properties of, nor can accept the operations of, vector algebra in mathematics. An array needing N indices (or subscripts) to reference a single element is N-dimensional.

Some discussions treat the case $N = 0$ (no subscripts required), implying a non-aggregated value, as equivalent to the base type of the array. This, however, goes against the way that languages treat arrays, which is based on a more or less explicit implementation model. This consists in general of a storage map containing information about the dimensionality (N) and range(s) of subscripts, followed by a contiguous block of storage containing the elements. Some implementation models are much more explicit than this, especially in older languages. For a scalar (base) value to be regarded as an array of dimension zero, which makes sense at the most abstract or mathematical level, the stub of the storage map, with $N = 0$, would still remain in this case. Also, with scalars as arrays of zero dimension one would expect all types to be 'array able', which is not the case in most languages. The only major language which contains explicitly the concept of dimensionality zero is APL, which anyway started its life as a mathematical notation. ALGOL 68 comes closest of the rest, with its 'rowing' coercion (automatic type conversion) converting a Scala into a vector of length one, though the motivation there seemed mainly to cope with distinguishing characters from strings of length one.

Incidentally, some languages, such as Pascal, and some textbook treatments use the term 'scalar' more restrictively, so that, say, a single record, being an aggregate, could not be so regarded even if the language allows arrays of records. (Pascal does not.) Others, whether or not containing the concept scalar, regard arrays as possible base types for other arrays so that a two-dimensional array is regarded as a vector of vectors, a three-dimensional array as a vector of two-dimensional arrays, etc. With this treatment, $A[i,j]$ is regarded as equivalent to $A[i][j]$, though this does not necessarily imply that the second form is syntactically acceptable. This could be regarded as merely notational convenience were it not that the implied storage model is that the elements of a 2×2 square array A would be stored in the order $A[1,1]$, $A[2,1]$, $A[1,2]$, $A[2,2]$ - something which could be of importance in some circumstances.

The implication of a storage map followed by a contiguous block of homogeneous elements is, of course, that the memory address of a specific element can be simply and quickly calculated from the values of the subscripts. In modern systems the addressing is likely to be logical or virtual, rather than physical, with the actual accesses left to the hardware andor operating system, but the principle is still clear. In the first FORTRAN standard (1966) this consideration was taken even further; an expression representing an actual subscript could be no more complicated than a linear function of a single simple (integer) variable, on grounds of efficient calculation in hardware registers.

Virtually all languages support arrays of elements of simple base types using integers or subscripts. Strictly, the type of an integer subscript is the derived sub-range type between the lower and upper bounds specified but that implies strict index bound checking, which even now not all languages require. Some languages have a default subscript lower bound (usually 1, occasionally 0) but the practice in older languages of a fixed lower bound has largely been abandoned, as has limiting dimensionality to a small number like $N = 2$ or 3.

However, it is still the case that the facility for addressing cross-sections or slices is not widely available. This is true also for operations on complete arrays, apart from input and output. Where such operations are defined in the language they tend to be element-by-element. (A common mistake of mathematically trained beginners, unless warned, is to assume that $A \times B$, where A and B are both square $M \times M$ arrays, is the matrix product instead of the element by element product) This reflects the single sequential processor provenance of most major languages, and will doubtless gradually change as vector processors, and data flow and other non-von Neumann architectures become more prominent. Thanks to its foundation in mathematics, APL still has the widest array-based facilities of the major languages.

Most languages still adhere to the basic concept that the index type is integer, and for many of the major applications this reflects the need. However, of the well-known languages Pascal introduced the idea of using other types as index types, provided that these were discrete, and exact. Given the mapping to integers which Pascal built in such types, this was cheap to provide but at the same time gave an improvement in language expressiveness and a liberation from implicit assumptions. Nevertheless, the basic picture of an array is that of a block of contiguous elements of one or more dimensions.

2.15.12 *Tables*

In this discussion a table is like an array, in that its elements are all of the same type, but indexing is not by a necessarily sequential subscript but by a reference value indicating content. The distinction is perhaps best brought out by an example. Suppose the non-integer index type of an array were a ai- lment, user-defined enumerated type representing the months of the year, and a vector were produced of the months in which the birthdays of eight people fell. The vector might look like:

Index	Jan	Feb	Mar	Apr	May	Jun	Jul	Aug	Sep	Oct	Nov	Dec
Birthdays	0	0	1	0	2	1	0	1	0	2	0	1

where the index values Jan Dec are clearly mapped onto the integers 1 - 12. A table of the same data might look like:

Index	Mar	May	Jun	Aug	Oct	Dec
Birthdays	1	2	1	1	2	1

Although this display has been ordered by the natural ordering of the indices, in contrast to arrays, there is no assumption of contiguity. The indexing in a table is indirect whereas that in an array is direct. Of course, an implement or may choose to map a table of the kind in this example directly onto an array, since this may well be more efficient. However, tables have the capability of handling a potentially unlimited number of different index values which it may be hard to specify in advance. An example is counting the number of occurrences of words used in an arbitrary text written in a given character set.

In almost all languages this kind of aggregate has to be simulated by the programmer, with all the indirect addressing provided explicitly, though Snobol (designed specifically for text handling and analysis) does have some facilities of this kind.

2.15.13 *Record types*

A record is an aggregate consisting of one or more fields that are in general in homogeneous. Individual fields are referenced by identifiers. known as field selectors or tags. Indexing is inappropriate because of the inhomogeneity. In principle the fields are unordered, although there are clear implementation advantages to keeping them in a fixed order internally so that tags can be identified with fixed address offsets from the start of the record. This concerns the programmer only in that it is possible to exploit it by allowing a list-like notation for a complete record, e.g. ["*John*", *23*, *male*] to represent the value of a record of a (user-defined) type *person* with fields name (string), *age* (subtype of integer) and *sex* (user-defined, two-valued, unordered). Such a record would normally have its own identifier, e.g. *trainee*, and a notation provided to select fields, using the tag identifiers. Most languages use a dot or period notation, so that *trainee.age* (or *age.trainee*, depending on the language) would be of type integer (the specified sub-type) and have the value *23*.

Usually fields are allowed to be of any type, including arrays, other records (permitting nested or hierarchical record structures) or pointers (normally to other records). Use of pointers to other records of the same type allows the construction of linked lists, trees, and other general data structures.

Languages vary considerably in the facilities they provide for manipulating records. Some allow record-to-record assignments. In strongly-typed languages the types would have to match. PL/1, being weakly typed, allows assignments between any records of the same size and shape (including nested sub-records) provided any needed type conversions can be performed. PL/1 also provides a very useful 'by name' assignment between records totally different in size and shape. where assignments are carried out field by field if the field identifiers are the same (and any needed type conversions can be done).

Assignments and other manipulations can always be done at the individual field level, at least if they themselves are not aggregates, but this can get tedious where many fields are involved, even with tic help of program text editors. Though not having record-to-record assignment, Pascal has a WITH statement to ease the burden. Within its scope, field identifiers can be used on their own and automatically associated with the specified record. In PL/1 a field identifier can be used unqualified, as a variable name in its own right. However, this is often less useful than might appear at first sight. To exploit it, field names may need to be specified unnaturally to keep them distinct. However, PL/1 does not allow user-defined type names, so multiple records of the same kind have to be specified by declaring one and then creating 'clones' by declaring others to be LIKE that one. So when LIKE is used, the field names are automatically duplicated, entailing some form of qualification when using field names.

Finally, while procedures, and possibly modules, may be used to aid manipulation of records in user-defined ways, many languages place restrictions on what can be done, e.g. returning a record as a function value.

Records first appeared in a major language in COBOL because of the obvious need for them in commercial data processing, but their value is now recognised much more widely. Exceptions among major languages include FORTRAN 77 (but FORTRAN 8X will have them) and APL, although APL arrays are so versatile that the need is less acute. One further development needs to be mentioned that of the variant record. In this case not all records of a given type have the same structure. There is a common part, which all share, and a variant part, which can differ from record to record according to some selection criterion (the equivalent for data of the case constructs in control flow). This concept was introduced in Pascal but has not yet found its way into languages generally. Despite its obvious utility for some applications (e.g. for personnel records where the variant part can contain different fields relevant to different categories of staff) there seems to be no generally agreed feeling within the programming language community that this is a successful feature. Clearly it does increase complexity in handling the records, both for implementors and for programmers, although it could be argued that for programmers using the feature, the complexity is there in the application anyway.

2.16 Control constructs

Conventional languages (sometimes called *procedural* languages) are essentially flow-of-control driven, based upon vow Neumann architecture or elaborations thereof. Control structures in conventional languages reflect this flow-of-control approach to computing and hence to language design. Machine and assembly languages are ordered sequences of commands. The statements, more accurately termed 'commands', of most high-level languages show that evolving relationships between machine instructions and language statements have in most cases still not gone so far as to break with this underlying assumption of sequentiality.

Given the conventional flow-of-control approach, five general kinds of control flow structure can be distinguished: sequential, parallel, branching, looping, and procedural. There is little to be said about sequential flow, since almost all languages based upon the flow-of-control approach take for granted the rule that program statements will be executed in textual order unless another control flow mechanism is explicitly involved. This discussion will therefore concentrate on the other four mechanisms.

2.16.1 *Parallel flow*

This kind of flow is the most recent to appear in high-level languages because of the previous assumption of single sequential processors. Hence it is here out of chronological sequence but is more logically and conveniently dealt with first.

Few current major languages have any explicit parallel processing constructs, although some have had them added as later developments (e.g. concurrent Pascal). Simula 67, as a simulation language, contains features to support the simulation of parallelism. It was nevertheless designed for conventional single processors, as was ALGOL 60, the algorithmic language on which it was firmly based. ALGOL 60's successor (ALGOL 68) did have some primitive constructs to support parallelism.

Early real-time languages such as CORAL 66 tended, like Simula, to assume a single processor and mimicked parallelism through interrupts. Often these were not specified in the language but provided instead by dropping down into machine code or assembler. It was not until the late 1970s that major, as opposed to experimental, languages began to emerge which contained genuine parallelism.

The most prominent example is Ada, designed to US Department of Defense (DoD) specifications, with particular emphasis on use in embedded, real-time systems. In Ada, parallel tasks can be programmed as separate modules but can be synchronised through the use of a rendezvous mechanism. The Inmos language Occam, which can be regarded equally as an assembler for the Inmos Transputer as a high-level language, takes a different approach. The programmer explicitly specifies whether a given block of instructions is to be executed SEQuentially or in PARallel. Viewed side by side, Ada and Occam illustrate the wide range of styles and approaches encompassed by the term 'high-level language', as do in a different way - COBOL and APL. Ada is a complex, feature-rich language, whereas Occam is spartan to the point of asceticism.

Parallelism in languages is still in its infancy, studied by numerous researchers but not yet subjected to fierce pressure from the needs of industry. It is the most obvious (to the current observer) growth point in the language design because the present means of expressing parallelism have barely been used so far. Language is a means of formulating thought as well as expressing it and there is little doubt that people will think 'parallells', or at least think non-sequentially, when languages capable of expressing such thoughts are better developed and more widely available.

2.16.2 Branching

Making a decision between one possible course of action and another is a central feature of automatic computation. From the earliest days machine codes had to have 'jump' instructions, both unconditional and conditional. Hence branching is the earliest and most basic form of flow of control in high-level languages.

In the crudest form of branching, various points in the program are labelled in some way, e.g., by numbering or naming statements, so that they can be branched to from elsewhere. An unconditional branch is then achieved by a statement of the form GOTO label and a conditional branch by IF condition THEN GOTO label. All early languages contained such facili- ties and most still retain them. Their assembler level derivation is obvious, a label being a thinly-disguised machine address of an instruction and the term 'high-level' is a dubious epithet. FORTRAN had (and still has) a variation, the 'arithmetic IF' where a jump occurs to one of three labels (numbered statements), depending on whether the value of a given arithmetic expression is negative, zero or positive.

One step away from direct machine language association can be achieved by allowing the IF to control statements other than a GOTO. However, a much bigger step is to have the IF control in a group of statements rather than just one. The move from machine orientation is virtually complete by adding an ELSE part also controlling a group of statements as an alternative to be used when the IF condition fails. This can readily be mimicked using IFs and GOTOs indeed, it can be achieved directly in machine code or assembler - but then it is up to the programmer to build the constructs and maintain their integrity. This means that good program design principles must be adhered to so that casual jumping to labelled statements within the groups (so-called 'spaghetti programming') is avoided. Machine code and IF/GOTO constructs will not help in this respect, whereas high level IF ... THEN ... ELSE constructs do.

ALGOL 60 provided the ELSE part of the branch. It also first introduced (in a major language) the concepts of 'statement bracketing', where a sequence of statements is turned into a compound statement by use of the statement brackets BEGIN and END, and of 'blocks' (see below). Hence both the IF/THEN and the ELSE of a logical branch statement could be made to control compound statements. This concept rapidly spread to most other major procedural languages, although it was not until 1977 that it entered standard FORTRAN.

For true integrity of such a construct, entry to a compound statement should only be through the BEGIN (i.e. a jump to a labelled statement within the statement brackets is not allowed from outside). This is to say that the scope of a label is confined to within the BEGIN ... END brackets immediately surrounding the statement which it labels. This was not fully recognised in ALGOL 60, even though the concept of scope of identifiers was central to the design of the language. For integrity of IF ... THEN ... ELSE, the controlled compound statements should themselves not be labelled, or at least the scopes of any such labels should be confined to that construct. That again was not fully recognised at the time.

By analogy with arithmetic brackets, statement brackets can be nested, allowing arbitrarily large and complex constructs to be formed. ALGOL 60 was the first major example of what became a huge family of so-called 'block structured' languages which exploited this idea to varying extents. ALGOL 60 was (and remains) the single most influential high-level language ever designed, through its exploitation of nested blocks as a means of controlling scopes of identifiers, and hence access to the entities they named. It was two decades before the limitations of this approach seriously began to concern many people in the mainstream of the languages community.

2.16.3 *Loop constructs*

Loop constructs can be regarded as even more fundamental to computing than branch constructs, if only because of the relative cost benefit ratios between getting a computer to perform a simple task iteratively and getting it to take a complex sequence of decisions. The importance of iterative processes will be reduced by parallel processing, especially when the ready availability of parallelism leads to the development of new parallel algorithms. There is an analogy with the availability of sequential machines which led to the development of iterative algorithms in preference to the 'one-shot' algorithms more suited to hand computation.

Nevertheless, even when this and the growth of non-algorithmic languages are both taken into account, iterative constructs in conventional procedural languages are likely to remain of importance for a good time yet.

At the machine code level, loops can readily be constructed by the use of conditional andor unconditional jumps. Where the jump to continue the loop is backwards in the sequence of instructions and to the exit is forwards, beyond the range of the loop. This is easy to simulate in simple high level languages with Its and Duties, albeit with the same weaknesses and insecurities as are present at the machine level.

Oddly, the commonality of approach to mainstream aspects of computing, such as branching, found in most conventional high-level languages does not extend to loop constructs. Many variations exist at a more fundamental level than sync tactic expression and skirmishes still break out from time to time between supporters of different styles. Part of this can be attributed to the past need for sequential iteration to fill the gap left by the absence of parallelism, but once this is allowed for, unresolved differences remain. The discussion that follows applies when the cyclic nature of the computation in a loop is inherent, rather than merely the consequence of having to do the same thing a number of times using a sequential rather than a parallel machine.

In this case it is worth taking a more general, top-down approach to the question of loop constructs than has applied hitherto. Ignoring for the moment the possibility of nested or multiple loops, the most general form of loop consists of a cycle with multiple entries and multiple exits, rather like a traffic roundabout met by a number of one-way streets. The smallest number of both entrances and exits is theoretically zero. A loop with no entrances is not very interesting (and not a problem, however specified), so it does no harm to assume at least one entrance. Most loops need some initialisation anyway. However, loops with no exits definitely exist, especially for real-time control applications where, once set up, the loop should continue to operate indefinitely, until the process is interrupted by some external agency: operator action, the power failing, the machine wearing out, etc. Some languages contain such facilities explicitly, e.g. Ada and ALGOL 68, whereas others leave it to the programmer to use a simple backward GOTO (which at the machine-language level is all it amounts to).

Multi-entrance loops can be created by GOTOs but within major high-level languages a single entrance, via a keyword (such as DO, FOR, REPEAT etc), is virtually universal. APL is different, as usual, but almost everything one might wish to do with loops can be done in APL by using operators 'functions' as APL prefers to term them. This does, admittedly, sometimes require a certain amount of ingenuity.

This common practice of a single entrance is a consequence of the conventional sequentiality of written text as much as it is of the sequentiality of processors. Of course, in the outer program surrounding the loop, one can always use some construct or another to reach the entrance from several different points in the program. However, as far as the loop is concerned, all processes start at the one entrance.

Given that there is a single entrance, what of the number of exits? The received wisdom of structured programming is that 'single-entrance single-exit' loops are best since this facilitates the testing of the loop as a single entity. However, it is important to be clear about what 'single exit' means. Maverick jumps to any accessible label in the surrounding program are clearly excluded (though most languages permit them). What should be made of EXIT statements which transfer control from anywhere in the text of the loop to where the 'actual' exit is? This is equivalent, in the traffic roundabout analogy, of cutting across the central reservation. Viewed from the outside, there is still a single exit, at the textual end of the loop construct, so that the loop can still be regarded as a single entity as far as testing is concerned. However, some purists, or ascetics, argue that a mid-cycle EXIT is analogously dangerous to cutting across a traffic roundabout and should be outlawed accordingly.

Not surprisingly, given these differences of view, different languages resolve these issues in different ways. It often comes down to how the language designers resolve the tradeoffs between safety and convenience.

The earliest loop mechanisms were conceived in terms of performing the same operation repetitively on each of the elements of an array. Almost inevitably this led to the concept of a 'control variable' to determine progress through a loop, with this variable being closely associated, if not identified, with the index of the relevant array. However, it became rapidly apparent that the concept of repetition whether or not to ape parallel processes on sequential machines was far more fundamental to automatic computation than the mere manipulation of array elements.

This was indeed clear even before high-level languages started coming in. Nevertheless, it has been taking a long time for realisation of this to be reflected in languages. The fact that an array is a data structure of major application importance, despite its primitive nature, is presumably a factor in this.

For array handling applications where it is necessary for an index to step through a sequence of values, practice varies between languages from having a loop construct with an explicit control variable, to a more general form where a control variable can be specified if required, with the explicit form being more common. Even here practice varies. In some cases the control variable is confined to that role; in others it is an ordinary variable. The latter is useful if, say, one wishes to carry out of the loop the index value of an element with a particular property that the loop has searched for. The former is more secure but can lead to some clumsiness if an index value is to be preserved. Although an index is 'naturally' an integer, some languages permit control variables of type real. This has the danger of cumulative errors as the number of increments increases. Pascal allows any discrete type, as it does for array indices, but confines the size of the increment to the value of one (upwards or downwards) or the equivalent in non-integer types (immediate successor or predecessor). It is probably this use of enumerated and other types to control loops that caused in Pascal the restriction for integers to a step length of 1, since anything else would be likely to lead to some rather messy syntax.

Another matter concerns whether the language permits the increment and final value of the control van able to be altered by the code in the body of the loop. For very good and obvious reasons of security, languages have increasingly tended to prohibit this, by various syntactic and semantic means.

One immediate variation of the control variable incremental loop is to make the variable itself implicit rather than explicit if it is not specifically needed in the loop for indexing or other purposes. Examples are COBOL's DO N TIMES, which covers the majority of cases very simply, and ALGOL 68's rather more flexible but perhaps less graphically expressed method. Here the starting value, finishing value and increment of the control variable can all be specified but the variable itself remains anonymous.

Most control variable loops are of the type where the termination condition 'has the control variable reached or gone beyond its limit value?' is tested on initial entry. This means that the actual loop body may on occasion not be executed at all, e.g. in FOR $i :=$ 1 TO n DO in Pascal when $n < 1$. This seems to make sense but there was certainly a school of thought in the early days, persisting until quite recent times in some areas, that it was wrong to require the computer to go to the trouble of setting up a loop if it was not to be executed at all, i.e. the 'zero trip loop' should banned. However, zero trip in such cases is undoubtedly the norm.

This can be regarded as a special case of the single-entrance, single-exit loop where the one exit is immediately after the one entrance. The more general form of this kind of loop is usually known as the DO ... WHILE loop, i.e. 'Do what follows WHILE the following condition holds', the implication being that if the condition fails at the outset the loop is not executed at all. Many procedural languages have this in some form or another.

Pascal provides not just the incremental loop and the DO ... WHILE loop but a REPEAT ... UNTIL loop, i.e. 'REPEAT what follows UNTIL this condition is satisfied'. The roundabout model would show this as the single exit appearing immediately before the single entrance, i.e. the loop will always be executed once before the condition is tested. Issues that do still remain, however, are the number of exits allowed (in the sense of jumps to the one-textual-exit from places textually or logically remote from the end of the loop body), and whether a single exit can be anywhere other than immediately before or after the single entrance. ALGOL 68 bravely tried to unify all possibilities, particularly to allow the second possibility, though in a way which was never syntactically convincing. A cruder, less structured, but perhaps more effective way is to have an indefinite loop (unconditional DO ... END DO or the like) with one or more EXITs (or, rather, EXIT IFs) placed in the loop body wherever required. That does exist in one form or another in some languages.

Nested loops do not cause a great problem apart from the question of exits. Should an EXIT other than a 'normal' one (i.e. normal exhaustion of index values or whatever) exit only from the loop in which it occurs (i.e. control is transferred to the next level up) or be free to terminate several levels at once?

The argument for the former is that the same result as normal exit is more logical and often what is needed anyway. The argument for the latter is that an 'emergency' in an inner loop probably means that one wants to stop the whole process. A counter-argument is that one cannot always assume that, and what does one do if one wants to continue the outer loop? A third suggestion is that people should be given the choice, but then we are talking about labels and the syntax becomes messy!

2.16.4 Blocks

In itself a block is not a control flow structure at all, since any change in flow is determined externally to it, but it is worth considering in its various forms because it represents an important stage in the transition from individual statements. The simplest block does no more than parcel together some statements, enabling them to be treated as a single, but compound, entity. Conventionally such a block consists just of a sequence of statements, but letting them be parallel, or a mixture of sequential and parallel, makes no material difference. Most languages display this concept in one form or another even if they do not have the explicit BEGIN ... END statement brackets of ALGOL 60, or their equivalent. The parcelling has the conceptual if not logical effect of separating off a section of program and giving it, in however tenuous a form, an individual identity.

The next step in separating a block from its environment is to add the concept which might be called (albeit grandiosely) 'access integrity', restricting access to the block to a single entrance the BEGIN or its equivalent as already described above. However, this means making GOTO destinations (labels) local to the block, which is merely a special case of making user-defined entities local to the block. If entities are to be referenced, internally or externally, they need identifiers of some kind, so effectively this means limiting the scope of identifiers to the particular block in which they appear. This can be done either implicitly or explicitly. The implicit approach may, for example, be appropriate for GOTO destination labels, since it hardly makes sense to have duplicate labels in the same block and the repetition is easy to detect. The explicit approaches is to have declarations local to the block. This was the line taken in the pioneering and influential language ALGOL 60, in which the term 'compound statement' was used for parcelling statements and the term 'block' reserved for the case where there were internal declarations whose scope was confined to the block. Many other languages, with variations, have since followed this pattern.

The next issue, perhaps of no great importance on its own but certainly so in conjunction with others, concerns whether a block is open or closed. An open block can include references not only to entities which are within its own scope but to those within the scope of any surrounding block, subject only to name clashes. This is the classical block-structured pattern adopted by ALGOL 60 and its many derivatives. However, this assumes a nested block structure. In some languages blocks can be disjoint, in which case the question arises as to whether access to data is global, or local, or can be either. In COBOL the structure of the procedure division is a sequence of paragraphs, which are blocks of a kind, but the data defined in the separate data division is shared globally. In FORTRAN 77, which is not block-structured either, the separate program units are disjoint and symbolic names (i.e. identifiers) and labels are local. Hence by default access to data is local, and data can only be shared by parameter passing in a procedure calling mechanism, or by specifying that data is to be held in COMMON. This FORTRAN concept of COMMON storage, a shared data area, is very machine-oriented and there is no data typing association. Indeed, another of the ideas behind COMMON was that, as well as allowing data sharing, it could be used to allow the same area of storage (then scarce and expensive) to be reused for different purposes. This is something a simple dynamic stack implementation method for a block-structured language takes care of automatically.

Getting the FORTRAN COMMON storage associations right is entirely the programmer's responsibility, which has led to untold numbers of faults in FORTRAN programs. About the only aid a programmer has is a special BLOCK DATA program unit, the sole purpose of which is to permit areas of COMMON to be named. These names, like the names of the procedure (function and subroutine) program units, are available globally and used at link-edit time to make the requested associations.

Of course even with a disjoint block structure, the individual blocks can themselves be block-structured on ALGOL 60 lines. This is the case with PL/1, the classic 'pantechnicon' language which contains almost everything. In FORTRAN 77 program units IF blocks and DO loops can be nested but this has no access implications apart from jumps. In COBOL even that does not arise since a jump is possible only to the start of a paragraph.

The advantages of block structuring are its flexibility and the control over flow of execution and access to data that it affords, without too much need to be aware of machine-level considerations. The advantages of a disjoint structure are that it permits separate compilation and hence the building of libraries of pre-compiled, reusable routines which can be accessed without the programmer needing to worry about or even be aware of their internal workings. The marriage of these two concepts together with that of procedure calling eventually led to the modern idea of a 'module'.

2.16.5 Procedures

The basic idea of procedure-calling goes back to the early 1950s, though the germ of the idea can be found even in Ada Lovelace's description of Babbage's Analytical Engine. At its simplest, it consists of a jump which carries with it the memory of where the jump was made from. Thus, when the (appropriately marked) end of the relevant section of code is reached a jump can be made back to immediately after the point of the program from which the jump came. The section of code 'called' in this manner is referred to as a routine. The term 'procedure' is typically reserved for a routine which transfers parameters and a result.

The routine-calling mechanism is easily implemented in machine code by writing the return (jump) address in a special location in the routine. This enables the routine to be called from many different places in the program, and the return to be made to the appropriate place each time. Very early on in computer design machine code instructions, and even special registers, were provided to facilitate routine calling.

In some high-level languages the procedure-calling mechanism is very little removed from this primitive idea. Although some versions of BASIC have more sophisticated procedure calling with parameters the simpler versions of the language e.g. the Minimal BASIC standard have a simple GOSUB <label> statement. This is just a GOTO with a 'come from' link added. After the jump processing continues just as normal until a RE-

TURN statement is reached when the link is invoked and a jump is made back to the statement following GOSUB. Note that if another GOSUB is encountered before RETURN the original link is lost and hence nested procedure calls are not possible though a good BASIC implementation will at least warn if this occurs.

In COBOL each paragraph is named by an identifier, like a heading, and this can be used either as a label for the destination of a GOTO, or to invoke a procedure call. Hence from within a paragraph PARA2 one might either GOTO PARA5, with no return, or PERFORM PARA5 which means that at the end of PARA5 the return is made to the sentence (statement) in PARA2 following the PERFORM command. Note that even this primitive structuring of COBOL is enough to permit nested calls.

COBOL also allows a succession of paragraphs (in textual order) to be called, by naming both the first and the last, e.g. PERFORM PARA5 THRU PARA8. Hence any group of one or more paragraphs in text sequence is potentially callable as a procedure. These very simple mechanisms work in BASIC and COBOL because in those languages data is shared globally and so parameter passing is unnecessary. However, COBOL does also have a facility, CALL USING, for another complete program to be called. For languages with local data, whether block-structured or not, then parameter passing becomes a virtual necessity. If parameter passing is not available, information has to be passed by global data. It is easy to show that, whether a procedure is confined to just one program or it is to be part of a library, it is preferable for it to have no global references at all and to communicate with the outside world solely through parameters. This sounds rather rigid, and in fact the module concept allows more flexible and powerful means of communication, as we shall see later.

There are many different ways of passing parameters. It is a topic which sometimes gives rise to confusion, usually caused by one of three factors:

- (a) taking for granted that what one is used to in one language applies to others;

- (b) taking a model (e.g. a mathematical model) which is inappropriate or inadequate for a computational process

or

- (c) taking too machine code-oriented a model.

Approaches to parameter passing are strongly inter linked to approaches to data typing. The modern approach is best exemplified by Ada, where parameters are specified as IN, OUT, or INOUT. As the terms imply, IN parameters supply information to the procedure, OUT parameters return results and other information to the outside world at the conclusion of the call, and INOUT parameters do both. Pragmatically, Inputs are best regarded as the means whereby procedures can be used to update the entities which they name.

2.16.6 Functions and subroutines

In the preceding discussion of procedures, one thing has been left on one side - how the procedure is actually called, which is tied up with what the procedure is supposed to do. The term 'procedure' has been used here for any block of code which can be invoked from elsewhere in a program and can return control there once it has completed its business. ALGOL 60 and many of its derivations use the term in this generic sense, but others do not use it at all, e.g. FORTRAN 77 distinguishes between Functions, which return a value through the function name, and Subroutines, which do not, and are invoked differently. Pascal, confusingly, uses the term FUNCTION in the FORTRAN sense but uses PROCEDURE for the other cases, that do not return a value. In ALGOL 68 the distinction is of little significance because of that language's integration of statements and expressions.

At the cost of some redundancy it saves confusion to refer to 'function procedures' and 'subroutine procedures'. The call of a subroutine procedure is then, in conventional languages, a standalone statement in its own right. Calls can take place among assignment statements, I/O statements (which in many languages are in the form of calls of in built procedures) and the rest. In all cases the name of the procedure and the actual parameters to be used in the call have to be supplied.

There are two main variations. Some languages have specific keywords or commands introducing the call, e.g. CALL in FORTRAN or PERFORM in COBOL, whereas in other languages the call is implicit, the name of the procedure being enough. A more modern variation, yet to find its way into the majority of major languages, is to have default settings of parameters specified in the procedure definition, so that in the call only variations from the defaults need to be specified. As with operating system commands, from which this idea is derived, this can be done either position ally, or by using the names of the formal parameters as keyword. An example, not taken from any particular language, might be:

PROCEDURE SEARCH (AREA = ALL, KEY = NAME)

where the formal parameters are AREA and KEY with ALL and NAME as the defaults.

Here one might write a call as

CALL SEARCH(,AGE)

CALL SEARCH(KEY = AGE)

This is certainly a more user-oriented style of call, especially for procedure libraries, and one that is likely to spread. Since function procedures return a value, a call is placed where the value is needed, appropriate to the type of the value returned, typically within expressions. Most languages restrict the values returnable in this way to basic simple types like INTEGER, REAL, CHARACTER etc. that are supported by the language, though for full generality this ought to extend to user-defined types, aggregates, pointers, or indeed even procedures, as 'first class values' in the sense of polymorphism.

2.16.7 Modules

If the secret of successful engineering of large, complex artifacts is the availability of tested, reliable components with standard interfaces and properties, then the module is an attempt to provide a mechanism for turning software building from a craft into a genuine engineering discipline.

The modern concept of modules brings together a number of strands from the past, some of them quite old: the separation of procedure heading from procedure body, 'the inheritance by derived types', the inheritance of properties and procedures of parent classes in the class concept of Simula. Even the humble and mundane block data facility of FORTRAN can be seen as having a germ within it of the idea of a module.

Since modules are a comparatively new concept, their form of provision has not yet settled on a commonality of style as with procedures (such as IF ... THEN ... ELSE, etc).

Of the major languages only Ada and Modula 2 fully provide a module facility, though at the time of writing such a facility is planned for inclusion in FORTRAN 8X - a sign of the times. However, in general the main distinguishing features of a module facility are the following:

(a) Separation of module specification and module definition.

(b) Modules package together type definitions, procedures, operators etc.

(c) Modules explicitly export 'public' facilities available to other modules, and import facilities from other modules that they need.

(d) Implementation details, which may include further 'private' types, procedures etc., are hidden from the outside world.

(e) A 'client' module does not necessarily import all of the facilities of a 'server' module, only those that it needs.

2.17 References and bibliography

Barnes, J. G. P. (1982) *Programming in Ada*, Addison-Wesley

Barnetson, P. (ed.) (1985) *Research and Academic User's Guide to the IBM PC*, IBM United Kingdom Ltd

Birwhistle, G. M., Dahl, O-J., Myrhaug, B. and Nygaard, K. (1973) *SIMULA Begin*, Petrocelli/Charter

Booch G. (1988) *Software Components with Ada*, Benjamin Cummings

Burns, A. and Wellings, A. (1989) *Real-time Systems and thei Programming Languages*, Addison-Wesley

Cardelli, L. et al (1988) *Modula 3 report*, DEC Systems Researc Centre Report 31

Cardelli, L. and Wegner, P. (1985) *On understanding types, dat abstraction and polymorphism*. Computing Surveys, 17, 471-52

Danforth, S. and Tomlinson, C. (1988) *Type theories and object oriented programming*. Computing Surveys, 20, 29 72

Davis, S. (1993) *C++ Programmers Companion*, Addison Wesle

Department of Defense (1983) *Reference Manual for Ada Pro gramming*, ANSI/MIL-STD 1815A

Ghezzi, C. and Jazayeri, M. (1987) *Programming Languag Concepts*, 2nd edn, Wiley

Griswold, R. E. and Griswold, M. T. (1973) *A SNOBOL 4 Primer* Prentice-Hall

Higman, B. (1977) *A Comparative Study of Programming Lan guages*, 2nd edn, Macdonald

Hill, I. D. and Meek, B. L., (eds) (1980) *Programming Languag Standardisation*, Ellis Horwood

IBM (1970) *PL/1 language specification*, document numbe GY33-6003-2

Iverson, K. (1962) *A Programming Language*, Wiley

Jensen, K. and Wirth, N. (I985) *Pascal User Manual and Repor* 3rd edn, Springer-Verlag.

Kemeny, J. G. and Kurtz, T. (1985) *Back to BASIC*, Addison Wesley

Kernighan, B. W. and Ritchie, D. M. (1978) *The C Programmin Language*, Prentice-Hall

McCarthy, J., Abrahams, P. W., Edwards, D. J., Hart, T. P. an Levin, M. I. (1965) *LISP 1.5 Programmers Manual*, 2nd edn, MI Press

Meek, B. L. (1978) *Fortran, PL/1 and the Algols*, Macmillan

Meek, B. L., Heath, P. M., and Rushby, N. J. (eds) (1983) *Guide to Good Programming Practice*, 2nd edn, Ellis Horwood

Meissner, L. and Organick, E. (1984) *FORTRAN 77 teachin structured programming*, Addison-Wesley

Pagan, F. P. (1976) *A Practical Guide to Algol 68*, Wiley

Purdum, J. (1985) *C Programming Guide*, 2nd ed, Que

Sammet, J. E. (1969) *Programming Languages: History an Fundamentals*, Prentice-Hall

Steele, Jr., G. L. (1984) *Common LISP: the Language*, Digita Press

Stroustrup, B. (1985) *The C++ Programming Language*, Addison-Wesley

Tucker, A. B. (1995) *Programming Languages*, 2nd edn, McGraw-Hill

Wexelblat, R. (ed.) (1981) *History of Programming Languages*, Academic Press

van Wijngaarden, A. et al. (1976) *Revised Report on the Algorithmic Language Algol 68*, Springer-Verlag

Wirth, N. (1977) *Modula: a language for modular multiprogramming*. Software - Practice and Experience, 7, 3-36

Wirth, N. (1982) *Modula 2*, 3rd edn, Springer-Verlag

Wirth, N. (1983) *Programming in Modula 2*, Springer-Verlag

Wyatt, A. (1992) *Using Assembly Language*, Que

Chapter 3
Operating Systems

3.1 Introduction

Operating systems have existed for nearly 30 years. During that time they have moved from rather simple notions of managing the hardware on behalf of a single user or several users using a machine serially to provision of increasingly complex functions to, first, a number of users sharing a large machine and latterly, to a number of semi-independent users geographically distributed who nevertheless wish to share resources such as data, processes and processing power.

This chapter addresses two objectives: explaining what an operating system is, how an operating system works (in fairly general terms), and the significance of different operating system 'styles', explaining how to use an operating system from the point of view of the software engineer and programmer.

Three major classes of operating system are considered in turn. First are the simple, single-user operating systems of the sort popular with personal computers, comparing Digital Research's CP/M, Microsoft's MS-DOS, IBM's PC-DOS and occasionally the UCSD p-System to see how different operating system designs resulted from a common hardware base. In each case the major parts of an operating system, e.g. memory management and disc and file organization and management, are described.

Next, multiprogramming operating systems are looked at, which of necessity are more complex than simple systems, and again the major parts (memory management, storage and file organization and management, process management), three well-known multiprogramming operating systems are reviewed. Unix, VMS, and MVS, are compared.

Finally, multiprocessing and distributed systems are reviewed with examples drawn from MVS (which can also be a multiprocessing system) and a multiprocessing adaptation of Unix. Lastly the ways the programmer can access operating system services are discussed.

3.2 Basic concepts of operating systems

An operating system is the software which intervenes, at the lowest level, between the hardware of the machine itself, its peripherals, any applications software, possibly sensors and actuators in the 'real' world and, of course, the 'user'. The 'user' means primarily the software engineer, the programmer, system programmer or systems manager, but not the end user, who often perceives only the 'system' presented by an application. The operating system acts as an intermediary between the require ments of the hardware and the needs of the programmer. It removes from the programmer the need to be concerned with the low-level details of data transfer from main memory to a secondary storage device and it coordinates the disparate elements of the machine's operating environment, acting as a scheduler of work, an arbiter (on multi-user systems) between the conflicting demands and needs of users and a protector, ensuring that one process cannot corrupt another.

In addition, the operating system presents most users with some kind of interface (unless a more indirect interface is provided for an end user solely by an application program, as is in the case, for example, in form-filling programs for data entry purposes) usually called the command interface, in the form of a set of commands or menu-choices. The command interface in turn arbitrates between the user and a series of general-purpose utility programs (which provide simple, basic services such as a file maintenance, printing services and so on) and those applications programs which can be invoked by the command interface. The command interface which the operating system presents the user gives that user a virtual model of the machine he or she is using. For this reason, dissimilar machines with similar or the same operating system present the user with nearly identical virtual machines. Figure 3.1 outlines the basic structure of an operating system.

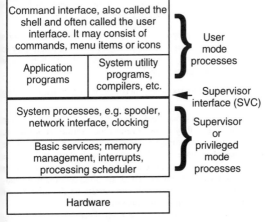

| **Figure 3.1** | *A diagrammatic representation of an operating system's architecture showing the relationship of the command interface, system utility programs, system services and basic services. Application programs are not part of the operating system, but can be invoked by commands in the command interface (or invoked directly when the end user logs on to the system).* |

Of course, hardware is a significant influence on an operating system. For example, if the hardware supports paging structures (see below) then an operating system can use paging to provide a virtual memory (where the size of an application is limited by the structure of the address rather than by the real size of a machine's main memory) for an application or other process. However, if the hardware on which a system will run does not support paging, then the operating system must use some other form of main memory management and cannot provide a virtual memory. Unix 4.3 BSD and System V provide an example of this: the operating system provides paging where the hardware has the necessary supporting structures.

Direct memory access (DMA) is a hardware facility allowing two or more processors access to the same memory and allows the use of, for example, channels (input/output processors) in conjunction with a main processor. The operating system exploits this in the way it carries out input and output operations. Buffers combined with asynchronous input/output (I/O) where I/O is carried out by a channel processor and the main processor can be switched to other tasks while the I/O operation is carried out independently require the use of DMA hardware structures. If these are not present, I/O must be synchronous, that is, the processor must wait for I/O to complete before continuing.

At present, there are three major categories of general purpose operating system. They are:

(a) the simple, single-user operating system, such as is available on micro and personal computers;

(b) the multiprogramming operating system which supports several users simultaneously or allows a single user to run several processes simultaneously, or both, on a single processor; and

(c) the multiprocessing, network or distributed operating system.

All of the last group are distinct types, but all have features in common in that they allow several processors to cooperate to some degree in providing the user with a service. In addition, there exist special-purpose operating systems particularly designed for critical or high-performance applications such as real-time or transaction processing work. These are often referred to as real-time executives. This text will concentrate on the three major categories of general-purpose operating system.

All operating systems are the result of compromises made by the operating system designer between:

(a) the capabilities of the underlying hardware, the needs and demands of the users, where not all classes of user may be in agreement as to what is needed.

(b) mutually exclusive choices among methods and techniques, for example, choosing a particular scheduling technique may make it impossible to do real-time processing.

(c) stringencies of resources time and money.

(d) marketing considerations such as eventual cost or complexity of the product.

For example, choosing to use a round-robin scheduler, where each process is given a discrete time interval in turn in which to use the processor, is suitable for a time-sharing system but cannot be used for a system which must support real-time applications. As a result, no one operating system is suitable for every possible application and one of the choices to be made in designing an application system may be the choice of an operating system.

Broad categories of application include: real-time, transaction processing, interactive systems and batch systems. These range from those which are driven by external events (real-time, including networking, and transaction processing) through those which must give precedence to fairness of treatment for all users (interactive multi-user systems) to those which require little or no human intervention but are characterized by a very high volume of repetitive processing work (such as occurs in the preparation of periodic accountancy reports). The requirements of the particular classes of application which dominate may thus dictate the choice of operating system. Many operating systems can accommodate more than one type of application, but the application with the most stringent requirements must be given precedence. For example, the Digital Equipment operating system IAS is designed around the provision of real-time services, but time not used for providing such services is available on a lower priority to interactive (or on the lowest priority, to batch) processing applications. On the other hand, Unix is designed for interactive computing use and is wholly unsuitable for real-time applications without considerable modification.

3.3 Simple, single-user operating systems

Originally, all operating systems were single-user and simple. Computers were 'shared' serially by means of booking a unit of time such as an hour and having exclusive use of the machine for that hour. This type of system has returned to prominence with the advent of the micro- and personal computer, although many of these systems have been extended somewhat to allow some degree of multiprogramming (explained below). Popular single user systems today are CP/M, MS-DOS and PC-DOS. CP/M is primarily known as an eight-bit architecture operating system, though it has a 16-bit counterpart, CP/M-86. MS-DOS and PCDOS are very similar systems designed for use on IBM PCs (in the case of PC-DOS) and compatibles (MS-DOS).

Such systems resemble each other in that they all are based on the same fundamental assumptions:

(a) that the user 'owns' (or at least has the major share of use of the machine).

(b) that shared data is a matter for private arrangements between users.

(c) that since only one user at a time will be using the machine, there is no question of having to provide elaborate scheduling facilities or to ensure fairness.

There is also no question of providing real-time services, which is not to say that small machines of this type have not been put to use in real-time applications. There is an increasing need to provide some degree of multiprogramming, for example, to allow the user to run one application while printing the output from another. Services provided by the operating system for the user are very basic: the operating system manages main memory, provides input and output services to limited numbers and classes of devices such as printer, disc and modem; it manages space on secondary storage media such as discs and provides simple file-handling capabilities (renaming, copying, deleting); it provides for the loading and the start of execution for applications.

This last named service can be organized such that an application is invoked automatically at the end of the system's start-up procedures. For example, a PC used by a secretary can automatically be put into a word processing application at the end of system start-up. The operating system usually also provides some form of spooling program so that printing can be carried out without locking the user out of the system.

All other services are generally left to specific applications which the user can purchase or design and develop him or herself. As a result, most such operating systems are fundamentally similar. All of those mentioned provide a command-based interface to the user: the user types in a short command on the keyboard in order to initiate a response. A few other systems have different interfaces: the UCSD p-System proves a hierarchically arranged menu system where commands are invoked by typing a single letter as shown in a menu; the Apple Macintosh, Atari ST, Commodore Amiga and PCs using Windows provide a WIMPS interface (windows, icons, mouse, pointer or pull-down menu systems) in which the user is presented with a window a virtual screen on a visual display unit which contains icons — pictorial representations of commands and objects such as discs and files to which the user points by using a mouse.

3.3.1 Memory management in simple systems

One of the primary concerns of an operating system is the management of main memory, which is a limited resource even in single-user simple systems. There are two basic problems to be solved in the management of memory. A primary concern is the protection of different parts of a process (a running program) from each other, the protection of the fundamental parts of the operating system itself (lest the machine be disabled) and the protection of the data in main memory in some measure from inadvertent destruction. (The system generally cannot protect data from a user's stupidity, but it can protect, for example, the program code from being overwritten by data and vice versa.) A secondary

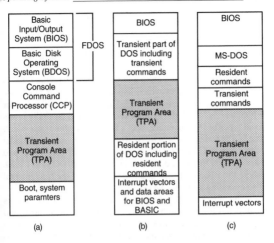

Figure 3.2   **Memory maps of small single-user operating systems:**

(a) CP/M; (b) PC-DOS; (c) MS-DOS.

These vary in reality according to hardware factors such as main memory size. The low addresses are shown at the bottom Applications program (transient) areas are shaded. No scale is implied.

concern is the loading of program code and data for execution. Given that such systems are very simple, memory management is correspondingly simple.

The operating system of most such systems generally consists of two parts: the essential part which must be resident in order for the system to continue to function, and a 'transient' part which resides in memory only when the operating system is first loaded or when one of the transient functions is invoked by the user.

In Figure 3.2, certain parts of the command interface and the system processes and basic services must be resident and protected, while less commonly invoked commands, application and utility programs and some of the less frequently used system functions can be transient, and invoked as required and overwritten when necessary. At any time, any space in memory occupied by a transient function can be overwritten, that is, used by something else such as a user's data file or an application program. In the case of CP/M, the operating system must be partially reloaded when its transient area has been overwritten. Other systems leave such transient functions to be reinvoked explicitly by the user when he or she issues a transient command or invokes an application program or utility.

The most fundamental parts of the essential portion of these small operating systems are the bootstrap, which is usually in hardware or in firmware in read-only memory (ROM), though parts of a bootstrap program may be software; basic system routines such as memory management; the input/output (I/O) subsystem; and the command interpreter.

The input/output subsystem is normally divided into two parts: one is concerned with character input and output such as keyboard input, screen output and print output, and the other is concerned with devices which handle data in larger blocks — usually discs. The first may be called the basic I/O (sub)system or BIOS, as it is in CP/M. (In other systems, BIOS normally refers to all types of I/O.) In either case, a BIOS is machine dependent; that is, the code must be written afresh for each make and model of machine and is not portable to a dissimilar machine. The second part is called the basic disc operating system (BDOS) in CP/M, where the BIOS and BDOS together are called the fundamental disc operating system (FDOS).

The function of the character-based slow-device BIOS or its analogue is to carry out basic input and output operations to and from slow devices such as keyboards, the character-based screen (although bit-mapped screens are different), and printers or devices made to appear to the system as printers. This is accomplished by the use of printer, serial transmission line, keyboard and screen primitives, special character handling routines, and a small type-ahead buffer or queue on which individual input characters are assembled until they form a meaningful unit (e.g. a command terminated by a carriage return). The function of the disc management portions of the operating system is to map logical units of data to the cylinder, track and record units of the disc using disc primitives.

The command interface, which is called the console command processor in CP/M, is also an essential part of a small operating system. Without it the system is disabled as it cannot interpret commands and carry out the appropriate actions.

Some commands themselves may also be essential. Generally these are the simple and basic commands which allow the user to access data in files or load application programs or transient commands. Commands which are essential are often called built-in (CP/M) or internal (MS-DOS and PC-DOS). Commands which are not essential, and therefore need not be resident permanently in memory, are called transient or external and are treated differently by memory management routines. Although the 'map' of memory for systems may differ, the philosophy of protecting the essential parts of the operating system from inadvertent overwriting means that these are typically stored in such a way that they are either below (at lower addresses) than the more volatile transient area where applications appear, or they are separated from the transient area by less essential parts of the operating system. Figure 3.2 shows memory use by three such systems.

From the programmer or software engineer's point of view, it is possible to use all of the transient program area (TPA) for an application, though an application can 'steal' space from the console command processor (CCP) in CP/M or from the transient parts of DOS or the transient commands in either of the two DOS systems before a crisis is reached which will cause a system error.

When loading the operating system, most systems, including small systems, begin with a firmware bootstrap which loads a small portion of software which in turn loads further software until all the operating system or all essential parts of it are resident. This process usually begins at the lowest address, loading 'upwards', then moves to the highest possible address and loads downwards', leaving the portion in between free for applications. When the user invokes an application, the operating system then loads this from the lowest available address above the lower essential parts of the operating system and loads 'upwards' until the application is loaded. Any data files then invoked will be copied in portions into the remaining parts of the transient area above the application program.

Data in such buffers may be copied to disc as necessary when more room is needed for further data in main memory. Such buffer copying is done, not to the original file, but to a temporary work area on disc. It is only when the user signals that the file is to be written, usually by means of a save or quit (with save) command, that the file on disc is written (or overwritten, as the case may be). Thus, space on disc acts as a temporary extension where necessary of main memory. Note that this should not be confused with paging; see below.

3.3.2 Disc and file organization and management

The second major function of a small operating system is to manage disc space and file organization on behalf of the user. Small systems make the assumption that the system user is the owner of the discs and files and has control over who accesses them. Thus, disc and file management is not concerned with identifying ownership nor with protecting data from unauthorized access. This makes such systems very simple, but vulnerable to accident, unauthorized access and malicious mischief.

Disc management is concerned with two things: the identification of free space and the identification of user and system files. At a lower level, this means that space on a disc must be mapped in some way, and the map must be able to identify free space and to indicate where to find the data in named files.

Files are identified by means of a form of record called a file control block (FCB). This will contain, at the minimum, the name of the file and a pointer to the location of the file on disc. File control blocks are concentrated together at a known location on the disc called a file directory. In most systems the disc's primary file directory resides on, say, tracks 1 and 2 of each disc. An entry in this directory may point to a file which is itself a directory, thus achieving an hierarchical arrangement of directories and data files.

The FCB entry may, in addition, contain other data useful for the control of files; it may contain the date the file was last accessed or changed, the size of the file and the type of the file. A command to show the contents of a directory will generally display this data, with variations which the user can invoke by means of parameters to the command.

Disc and file management within CP/M

CP/M's techniques of disc and file management allow dat for a single file to be scattered throughout the area of a disc in se sized sectors. As sectors arc assigned to a file, their location i noted in a part of the FCB called the disc allocation map. If a fil contains more sectors than can be noted in a single file contro block's disc allocation map, the file is allocated more than on FCB. Each disc, in addition, contains an allocation bit map, whic records, for each group of eight contiguous sectors (called cluster) whether that cluster is used or is free space. It does this b having one bit for each cluster; a 1 indicates that the space is use and a 0 indicates that the cluster is free.

When a disc is accessed for the first time in a session, it allocation bit map is copied to main memory. When a file i accessed by means of an 'open', an FCB in main memory i allocated, with the name specified by the user in the comman compared with the names in the FCBs in the directory. If a matc occurs, the information in the disc's FCB is also copied to mai memory. For a new file, the FCB is initialized in the disc' directory. A 'close' operation causes the new information in th main memory FCB to be copied to the disc's corresponding FCB

When space is allocated or freed, the corresponding bit in th bit allocation map is set and both the main memory and disc copie are kept in step, since the user may remove a disc at any time When a file needs new space, BDOS searches the bit allocatio map to find a free cluster, which is then allocated to the file, wit corresponding changes to the bit allocation maps and the mai memory copy of the FCB made at the time.

Disc and file management within MS-DOS and PC-DOS

MS-DOS and PC-DOS use a different technique. Disc spac is divided into sectors, and four contiguous sectors are groupe into an allocation unit (AU), as it is called by MS-DOS, or cluster, as it is called by PC-DOS. Space on the disc is recorde in a file allocation table (FAT). Each FAT entry contains 12 bits If all bits are set to zero, the AU/cluster is free space. Otherwise the bits represent either a pointer to another AU/ cluster in the list or, if all bits are set to ones, this indicates that this AU/cluster i the last one in a file. Files are named in FCBs in a directory. Thi entry contains the file name, an attribute indicator (system o user), the time and date of last update, the number of the first AU cluster in that file, and the size of the file. To access a file, the FCF is read, the pointer to the first AU/cluster of the file is used to poin to the correct entry in the FAT, and that entry in turn points to th next AU/cluster allocated to that file, and so on to the last one Notice that the FAT does not contain data, merely the address o the next AU/cluster of data. There is a further step required, whic is to map the AU/cluster number in the FAT to a real AU/cluste on the disc itself. This technique is known as block-oriented fil mapping and is shown in Figure 3.3.

Note that direct access to data on any AU/cluster at random requires that the data's position relative to the beginning of the fil be known, that the ordinal AU/cluster within the file can b

File allocation table

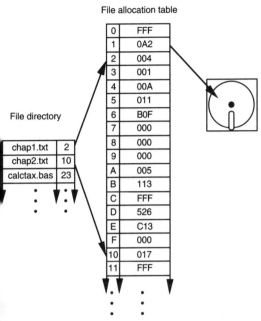

0	FFF
1	0A2
2	004
3	001
4	00A
5	011
6	B0F
7	000
8	000
9	000
A	005
B	113
C	FFF
D	526
E	C13
F	000
10	017
11	FFF

File directory

chap1.txt	2
chap2.txt	10
calctax.bas	23

Figure 3.3   **Block oriented file mapping in MS-DOS and PC-DOS. Note that the file 'chap1.txt' shown in the file directory begins at AU/cluster 2, that the FAT entry at 2 points to the next portion of the file (004) and the file continues from there to 00A, then 005 and ends at 011.**

determined and that chain of pointers in the file allocation table be followed to find the correct AU/cluster. Only then can the mapping between the AU/cluster number and the actual AU/cluster on disc be made and the data accessed.

Disc and file management within the p-System

The p-System uses a third strategy, whereby files are stored in contiguous sectors. To find sufficient space for a file, the system looks for the largest available empty space and uses it (the worst fit algorithm). The space for a file is allocated at once when the file is saved, rather than as the file grows. As old files are deleted, areas of free space result into which new and probably smaller files will be put and subsequently deleted; the process may eventually clutter the disc with such small free areas that no usable free space remains. It is then incumbent on the user to compact space on the disc. This process groups all files together and all free space together, leaving one large chunk of empty space. Then the process of filling the newly consolidated space with new or growing files begins anew. Thus, when an existing file is changed and grows as a result, it must be allocated new space and the old space it occupied before it 'grew' becomes one of the fragments of free space.

The special advantages of contiguous allocation are the speed with which the file can be accessed, and the ease with which any data can be located directly if its position relative to the beginning of the file is known. The disadvantages are fragmentation resulting from deletions and re-allocations and the consequent need for user intervention to maintain an ample pool of contiguous free space.

3.4 Multiprogramming operating systems

For most people who have used any shared computer environment, the multiprogramming operating system will be the most familiar of the three classifications given here. Such systems are available on everything from quite small machines (such as the larger PCs), through the popular and widely available minicomputers to the very large mainframe. The philosophies on which such systems are based, however, vary widely and the various examples show greater diversity than is true of small, single-user operating systems. Three will be considered in some detail: Unix, Digital Equipment's VMS, and IBM's MVS. Multiprogramming systems make the following assumptions:

(a) More than one process will be resident in memory at one time.

(b) Each resident process will require some attention from the processor (i.e. the processor itself becomes a resource which the operating system must manage).

(c) Simultaneously resident processes will appear to execute concurrently.

This means that the operating system must mediate between active processes in the matter of allocating main memory and allocating processor time, and that the latter must be done in a way which guarantees that all processes resident and capable of running share the processor temporally in a reasonably fair way. In addition, most multiprogramming systems are also designed for use by multiple users simultaneously, so that:

(a) A process is associated with an owner.

(b) Data (in files) has designated owners or authorized users and those owners or users must be able to control access by other users to that data.

(c) Users simultaneously 'logged on' must receive service in a way which suggests to each that he or she has control of his or her own virtual machine.

In practice, most systems of this type today are time-sharing or interactive systems, which additionally means that fairness among simultaneous users must also be guaranteed. Additionally, the job of preventing one process from interfering with another becomes much more complex.

3.4.1 Memory management in multiprogramming systems

The problem of protecting the operating system and applications programs also exists in multiprogramming systems, although it becomes more important to guarantee the integrity of the system, because error by one user cannot be allowed to deny service to others. Conceptually, portions of the operating system are usually loaded beginning at the lowest possible address and loaded 'upwards'; these usually constitute the most essential parts of an operating system. The more 'public' services and areas within a multiprogrammed operating system are then usually loaded from the highest address 'downwards'. Examples of such public services are some I/O routines and shared buffers. The area between then becomes available for loading applications and user time-sharing session areas.

In practice, a scarce resource has always been space in main memory. While the scarcity can be relieved partly by adding more memory, as is often the case in microcomputers, there is a ceiling which is imposed by the addressing structure of the hardware size of the address registers or sometimes the physical construction of the machine on how much can easily be added. Most present-day multiprogramming operating systems relieve the scarcity by means of using a high-speed medium such as a drum or fixed-head disc as an extension of main memory. Systems using such approaches are often referred to as paging or virtual memory systems.

It has long been a practice to disassociate the addresses of an executable (object) program from real addresses by making a program relocatable. This is done by making all address references within a program relative to the start of the program (i.e. the 125th byte or word of a program has a displacement from the start of the program byte or word zero of 124), assigning a real address to the start of the program when the program is loaded for execution, and calculating all address references within the process as the starting address plus the displacement. The concept of virtual storage further disassociates addresses from the contraints of real addresses by interposing an additional layer or two of indirection in address translation, as described below.

Observations have shown that programs exhibit a property called locality, that is, frequent reference to the same or closely adjacent instructions such as sequential code execution, the place-

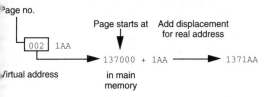

Figure 3.4   A simple address translation.

ment of related variables near one another and traversal of array (spatial locality) or within a short period of time such as occurs in loops, subroutines, stacks and certain types of variables which are near one another (temporal locality). From these observation developed the theory of a working set of pages, which says tha any program can be divided into sub-units and some number of sub-units will be referenced repeatedly in such a way that only tha group of subunits will be active and, without seriously affecting efficiency, other sub-units need not be resident in main memory

The subunits are generally called pages and are small (e.g 4K), but units of other sizes can be used. It is even possible to use two (or more) different sizes of unit simultaneously, as will be shown. Figure 3.4 shows a simple scheme for using one level of indirection (pages) in addressing to allow disassociation of on part of a program from another without disturbing the apparent o virtual sequence of addresses.

The practical effect of locality means that only the working sets of active processes need be in memory simultaneously, and memory can be managed as simple, small units allocated to and recovered from active processes as required. In an example of a common memory management scheme, a program is divided into fixed-size sub-units of 4K each, called pages and that these page are numbered sequentially from zero. It does not matter that page be in nor that they be adjacent in main memory, so this scheme i called virtual addressing. Any address within a program is thus a virtual address that must be translated to a real address either on disc or in main memory as described below by some translation process which maps virtual addresses to real addresses. Further physical (real) memory itself is also divided into 4K units called page frames, and that an auxiliary medium such as a high-speed fixed-head disc has its space divided into 4K units called page slots. When a program is loaded, all of it is loaded into page frame in memory, and those pages not referenced are gradually marked as 'not needed'. As the operating system requires more space i copies marked pages out to page slots on the disc. When any page not currently in main memory is referenced, a page fault occurs and the operating system then searches for the true location of the page, fetches it from its slot and finds a frame for it. The mapping of page to frame to slot is accomplished by containing the information in tables.

Figure 3.5 shows one example. To find virtual address 0021AA which consists of page number 002 and a displacement into the page of 1AA bytes, use the page table origin register to find the page table. The virtual address page number (002) gives the displacement into the table, and the pointer at that entry give the start of the page in main memory or its location (if not in the main memory) on auxiliary storage. If a page is in main memory simply add the lower-order part of the address, the displacement 1AA, to the starting address of the real page to obtain the real address. If the page is not in main memory, interrupt execution of the current instruction, locate the page on auxiliary storage using the page table, write the page to main memory and re-execute the interrupted instruction.

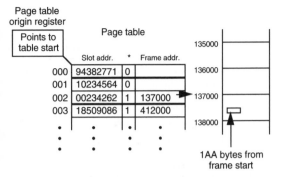

Figure 3.5   *A mapping arrangement for paged memory management Note that the page number of the page is a number relative to the beginning of the program (or segment,). There needs to be one page table origin register for each active process. A three-digit (hexadecimal) page number with 4K-sized pages allows an exceedingly large program. The column marked '*' identifies a bit indicating whether or not a virtual page is in main memory; that is, it indicates whether or not the frame address is valid for this page.*

A variation on paging is the use of segments, which may be of fixed or variable size and are generally larger than pages. The mechanism for mapping segment numbers to actual addresses in main memory (or on auxiliary storage) is very similar, but the segment table contains additional information, on segment size and often on access control information.

A third variant, used by the operating system MVS, combines pages and segments. In MVS, 64K segments contain 16 4K pages, and a program can contain up to 4096 segments (more if run on the newer extended architecture mainframes). A segment table origin register points to the segment table for the program; entries in the segment table point to the appropriate page table, which in turn points to the location of the page. Assistance from hardware structures in the form of additional registers and associative memory make the process efficient.

A system-wide table is used to keep track of each of the running processes, whether they are resident, partly resident or not resident at all. A process likely to have a long wait, for example for some slow peripheral device, is swapped out (removed to auxiliary storage in its entirety) in order to free memory for other processes.

Processes (or in some cases pages) which are read-only (variously termed pure or re-entrant code) can be treated differently from processes which contain internal variables which are modified in the course of execution. Since read-only code is never modified internally, it can be executed apparently simultaneously by several users or parent processes. A frequently used editor or a compiler is one example of this type of code. The advantages of being able to treat such code differently are that only one copy need be resident regardless of how many people are using it (thereby saving main memory space), and since that copy tends to be heavily used, it becomes a working set which remains resident and thereby provides better service. In terms of memory management, systems like Unix handle such code explicitly by maintaining a special table for read-only processes.

Memory management within VMS

As with most modern multiprogramming systems, VMS is paged. Each process in VMS is assigned a limit to the number of pages which can reside in main memory simultaneously the resident set limit. This limit is adjusted dynamically up to a maximum based on the fault rate. Thus a new process, which will have a high fault rate as frequent references are made to pages not yet resident, will exhibit a rapidly increasing resident set limit.

A reference to a non-resident page results in the pager gaining control of the system and using the virtual address referenced to find the page table entry for the faulted page, as described above. The page is found on the auxiliary storage device and read in, and control is passed back to the instruction which caused the page fault. When the number of pages resident reaches the limit, a page frame is 'stolen' from the process's own set, on a first-in, first-out (FIFO) basis. Pages yielded by a process are put on either a free page list (if they have not been modified) or a modified page list. If a page on either list is referenced, it is simply 'reclaimed', thereby avoiding excessive paging I/O. Pages on the modified list must, of course, be written to auxiliary storage in order for the space they occupy to be moved to the free list and re-allocated. But modified pages are not written out until the list achieves a certain size. This also avoids excessive paging I/O, as pages can be written out in clusters. Further efficiency is achieved when clusters of modified pages belonging to the same process can be written out contiguously.

VMS also uses swapping. When VMS swaps a process in or out, it swaps the entire resident set. (Some systems swap out the entire set but page in pages one-by-one upon reference rather than swap in.) Any newly swapped-in process is guaranteed at least one time-slice before it is eligible to be swapped out again. In order to find the space to swap a process in, VMS looks to the free space list, or may write the modified page list to auxiliary storage in order to free those pages, or it may choose to swap out another process of lower or equal priority.

Memory management within Unix

Unix was not originally a paged system; it used swapping instead. The Unix version BSD 4.0 was the first version to use demand paging. Now versions 4.0 BSD and above, and System V, support paging when installed on machines with memory architecture based on pages and which are capable of re-executing instructions that must be terminated because they reference a page not in main memory. Paging is thus 'grafted onto' an older memory management system based on space occupied by a whole process or space occupied by objects associated with a process.

To understand the way in which Unix manages space in main memory, it is necessary to look at the construction of a process. A program, when compiled or assembled, results in an executable file which consists of headers, program text, a machine representation of any data that has initial values plus an indicator of how much space should be allocated for uninitialized data, and other items like the symbol table. When loaded, the process consists of at least three regions: one for program text, a data region and a stack region.

Each process is described to the operating system in a structure called the per process data structure. This in turn points to a region table. The page table for the region is in the region itself. Each page table entry is associated with a disc block descriptor, which points to and describes a 'slot' on auxiliary storage. The page table entry describes a virtual page, points to a page in main memory and to that page's corresponding entry in the page frame table. When a page is paged out, the disc block descriptor associated with the page table entry contains the necessary information for locating the page on auxiliary storage. The structures in the operating system which support paging are shown in Figure 3.6.

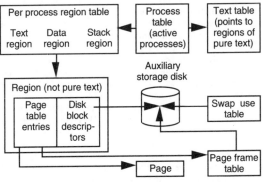

Figure 3.6   *Structures for memory management in Unix.*

Memory management within MVS

MVS maintains the concept of a unitary process, and in fact, of a unitary image of user process and system. Each process, which may be the session of one interactive user, has its own virtual address space which is the maximum 'width' of the addressing structure and thus is 16Mb (older IBM mainframe architectures) or 2Gb (extended architectures) in size. The virtual image is one which conceptually contains a complete copy of the operating system and the process, its dependent tasks, buffers and so on. In fact, because the operating system is largely made up of re-entrant code, there is actually only one copy which is shared among all active processes. However, the virtual process image continues to include an apparent private copy. This fiction allows applications to occupy up to 16Mb or 2Gb of space including whatever is occupied by the operating system itself.

With the aid of associative memory for efficiency MVS divides the address space (process image, including the virtual private copy of the operating system) into 64 K segments which are further subdivided into 4 K pages. An address space control block (ASCB) describes, at the highest level, the address space occupied by a process, and acts as the entry in the dispatching queue (see below). The ASCB points to the real address of the process's segment table and indicates its length. The segment table in turn points to one page table for each segment, and the page tables point to locations in main memory or auxiliary storage as described above.

Note that MVS maintains information in control blocks which are entities in linked lists rather than use tables, as is done in Unix.

3.4.2 Storage and file organization and management

Because multiprogramming, multi-user systems are shared simultaneously by many people or processes, the problem of identifying files clearly and of assigning ownership and granting the owner rights which he or she can extend to co-workers, and of managing complex arrangements of space on secondary storage devices, needs to be addressed.

The differences between systems are probably their most noticeable to users in this area in particular. Generally, however, systems maintain a two-level structure: one level is directed at devices (such as discs), and the other at files of data.

Structures for devices are analogous to the BIOS portions of small, single-user operating systems. They contain tables of available devices which record device type and status information and point to the appropriate device driver. Each class of device must have a low-level device driver, which is a unit of software or hardware that performs interface functions such as the passing of addresses and interrupts, the buffering of data and the detection of errors; thus it communicates between a peripheral device and the operating system. In Unix, devices are divided into two major classes: character-oriented devices and block-oriented devices and are listed in two tables, the 'cdevsw' and the 'bdevsw'. MVS simply keeps a table of all available devices in order of device number, which dictates paths to a device via channels and relative priority; this contains the necessary descriptive information within each entry in the table. MVS's scheme allows access to a device via more than one channel, thus reducing 'channel busy' wait states.

Structures for keeping track of files may either assign files to definite owners (such as is true of both Unix and VMS) or ignore the question of personal ownership and assume that the organization which controls the system is 'owner' of the files, the strategy adopted by MVS. This has important implications for the sharing of files and for the protection of files against unauthorized access. Where a file has an individual owner, the owner has 'rights' over the file which he or she may then grant, in full or in part, to other users. Both Unix and VMS have a conceptual hierarchy such as that shown in Figure 3.7.

In most circumstances, an owner wants to restrict the more powerful permissions; for example by restricting 'delete' and perhaps 'write' to him or herself, while granting the less powerful permissions of, say, 'read' to his or her working group while allowing the 'world' to have 'execute' permission for files which are executable. In many systems, the more powerful permission implies that the person granted it also had all the permissions below it in the hierarchy, that is, that 'delete' permission implies the ability to write to the file, read and execute it, but the 'write' permission includes only the further right to read a file if that is possible. 'Read' implies character format, while an executable file is unreadable, so these two are mutually exclusive categories.

Other systems, such as MVS, were designed around the notion of an organization being responsible for and therefore 'owning' data in files. MVS does allow an individual to protect his or her files by associating passwords with them. Otherwise, it is assumed that all files are shared by anyone who can name them unless an application provides file control at a different level. Password and other optional security systems (authorized program facility, cryptography), however, are complex and can be used in combination, separately or at different levels. Authorized program facility (APF) identifies 'trustworthy' and 'untrustworthy' programs, for example, and limits the access of the latter to certain parts of the system.

Files are named in a file directory, but the construction of the directory structure again varies from system to system. Both VMS and Unix make possible, and use for their system files, a hierarchical directory structure. Thus the user can organize his or her files under a series of directories, as shown in Figure 3.8.

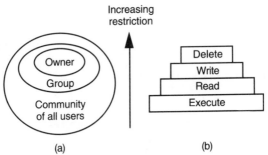

Figure 3.7   *Concepts of individual ownership, hierarchy of access and hierarchy of permissions (a) a concept of 'who shares' (b) a concept of how a file can be shared.*

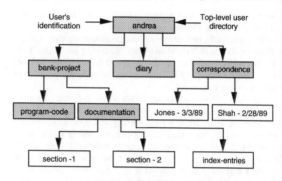

Figure 3.8 *A hierarchical directory structure. Shaded boxes are directories, clear boxes are data files.*

In this case, Andrea, upon logging on, would be 'pointed at' her highest level directory, which is actually a sub-directory of a system master directory. To access her correspondence with Shah from the end of February, she would have to specify a path by noting that the file Shah-2/28/89 is to be found by traversing the directory called correspondence. Or, she could change her default directory to correspondence and access the letter shah-2/28/89 directly. If, while accessing this, she wished to refer to something in section-1 of the bank project's documentation, she could specify the full path: up one level to andrea and then traverse, in order, bank-project and documentation to the file section-1.

MVS uses quite a different organization. It has a 'master' directory called the system catalog, which may have subsidiary catalogues. This is a hierarchical arrangement but is invisible to the user, who simply specifies a file name. The catalogue entry

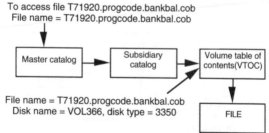

Figure 3.9 *MVS's arrangement of catalogues and VTOCs, and file access. The user sees this not as a means for organizing personal files, but for accessing any file. Some semblance of a hierarchical structure can be made to appear through the use of name levels, but there are no special directories implied at each level, and no 'path' through these to a particular file.*

contains a pointer to additional information about the file held on the volume table of contents (VTOC) of the disc on which the file actually resides. It is the combination of the entries contained in the catalogue and the VTOC which gives sufficient information to access a file successfully. If a user knows the specific location of a file, i.e. the name of the disc, he or she can access the file directly, circumventing the catalogue. In fact, it is possible to keep files without registering them in any of the catalogues; this can provide a small measure of security. See Figure 3.9.

3.4.3   Sharing processor time

To multiprogram efficiently, a system must have:

(a) one or more processes ready to run which are resident or can be made resident in main memory,

(b) a means of deciding among them which shall run next,

(c) a means of pre-empting one running process in favour of another.

The first point implies that the system must maintain the status or state of a process. A process can be:

(a) ready to run and resident;

(b) ready to run but not resident, in which case it must be swapped or paged in, see 'Memory management' above;

(c) not ready (also called blocked);

(d) actually running.

Systems choose which process to run next by choosing from among either the ready and resident, or the ready but not resident. Blocked processes normally are blocked because they are awaiting some event which they have triggered, such as the completion of I/O, or because they have put themselves in a wait state to await some external event, such as the arrival of a message from a network connection.

In addition, systems normally assign a priority to processes and may vary the priority dynamically within limits. Some systems, such as MVS, will also allow the user to request a particular priority in some circumstances, such as in the submission of a batch job, and will allow the system operator to vary priorities manually. A job, in this sense, is defined by the user, who can group one or more programs together for execution, to be executed serially, defining the job with a job statement or card. An end-of-job marker statement defines the end of a job, or if that is missing, the next job statement defines the end of the previous job. The programs within a job so delineated need not be related, but usually are. The job is the unit dealt with by the high-level scheduler; see below. Choice among processes which are of equal status, i.e. there are several processes which are ready and resident, may then be made on the basis of their relative priorities or, if priorities are also equal, on the basis of their position in a queue of ready processes. Priority can also be made the basis by which one process can pre-empt another (see the description of VMS below).

There are a number of commonly used scheduling algorithms. Briefly described, they are:

(a) FIFO. This implies a queue and the selection of processes in order in the queue.

(b) Round-robin. Each ready process is given a quantum of time in turn.

(c) Shortest-job-first (or next). This requires an estimate of the required time to do a job and favours jobs which promise to be quick. A 'guillotine' usually takes care of cheats.

(d) Shortest-remaining-time. Also requires an estimate of the required time to do a job; the algorithm must also record the time used and in selecting processes favours those which are nearest to finishing.

(e) Highest-resource-ratio-next. Seeks to correct some of the biases of shortest-job-first and does so by calculating a dynamic priority as a function of the estimated service time (i.e. how much time is required to do the job) and the amount of time the process has already had to wait, such that longer waits will cause the priority to increase.

A system may have scheduling on more than one level and may use more than one of these algorithms. The first 'scheduling barrier' is whether the user or program will be allowed access to the system at all; this is higher job-level scheduling. Once admitted to the system, the second 'barrier' is whether the program or session will become a process; this is intermediate level scheduling.

Once a process has been formed the final 'barrier' remains, for its lifetime, whether at any opportunity to run it will be granted access to the processor itself; this is low level scheduling. Different algorithms may apply at each of these levels, and a hierarchical arrangement of several algorithms may apply at any one level. For example, ready processes may be selected by, say, shortest-remaining-time, but if several have equal estimates of remaining time they may then be chosen by either a round-robin arrangement or by the time spent on the queue (FIFO).

Multiprogramming within VMS

VMS divides processes into three major classes which it uses to establish a broad group of priorities. It recognizes time-critical processes (real-time), time-shared (interactive), and background (batch or computation-bound) processes and assigns these, broadly, high, medium and low priorities respectively. On a scale of 32 priorities, the system manager can subdivide time-critical applications into high-priority and low-priority realtime and can control the actual priorities assigned to these groups and to the swapper, which is a system process that frees space in memory by removing inactive processes to secondary memory, or brings such inactive processes back into main memory when they are again ready to run.

An algorithm controls the priorities of time-shared and background processes, subdividing these into I/O bound (requiring higher priority), less I/O bound, and computation bound (the lowest priority). It then seeks always to provide realtime services for real-time tasks, and then to balance interactive and background work to maximize throughput while providing a good service to highly interactive use (I/O bound). The algorithm varies priorities dynamically within these broader ranges. The scheduler always chooses the process with the highest priority in the ready-and-resident group. Events, such as the completion of I/O, move processes into this group. Each process receives a quantum of time, but real-time processes are exempt from the expiry of their quanta. Processes can be preempted before their quanta expire, but until the quantum does expire, a process remains in the set of ready-and-resident processes, with occasional exceptions (such as when swapped out because service is required by a higher priority non-resident process or when entering a wait state).

Multiprogramming within Unix

Unix is a time-sharing system, geared to program development and interactive use. As such, its scheduler is a round-robin scheduler, guaranteeing 'fairness' to each member of a community of interactive users. Background tasks can be started, but have a low priority and run in what is virtually a 'soak up' mode, using time not otherwise devoted to serving interactive users. Processes can voluntarily 'sleep' (enter a wait state) or will be blocked upon issuing an I/O instruction. Then they will be woken up by the occurrence of an event, such as arrival of the type of message they process or the completion of the I/O, and returned to the ready state, from which they will have access to the processor for a quantum, in round-robin fashion. If several processes are asleep awaiting a common event, such as the availability of space in memory, the occurrence of the event wakens all of them and the scheduler then chooses one on the basis of priority, which varies dynamically according to the character of the process. Because Unix's scheduler does not allow a process to be awoken and returned to execution immediately the event it awaited occurs, Unix is unsuitable for real-time applications, as no guarantee can be made how soon a process will be scheduled after its waking event occurs.

MVS is a complex and very large operating system, and its scheduling is correspondingly complex. It uses the three levels of scheduler, as described above. Additionally, it divides work which is ready to run into units termed either service requests or tasks. Service requests arc small units of work designed to reduce overheads and increase parallelism on multiprocessors where these exist. Service requests have a higher priority than tasks and can be dispatched (selected by the scheduler) to any address space. Tasks, on the other hand, belong to a particular address space, are larger and have a lower dispatching priority.

Work can also be thought of as belonging to a domain, which is similar to the main categories used by VMS (see above); each domain has assigned to it a relative priority. The lowest priority might be batch jobs. the next lowest might be high-priority batch work, then non-trivial interactive use, with the highest priority given to trivial interactive use. (Trivial refers to the resources required, not the perceived importance of the work.) Each unit of activity equivalent to an address space is called a transaction, which for batch jobs is the job as defined by the user's job control language and for interactive use is the time from when a user's address space becomes ready until a terminal-generated wait state occurs, as for example happens when a response is returned to the user. The installation defines the transaction types to which each transaction will belong and associates a type with a performance group which is then assigned a performance objective. Each MVS system has an installation performance specification (IPS) which sets installation requirements for each performance objective.

The terminology is somewhat confusing, but a domain is a category of work (e.g. interactive, batch), a unit of work (for example a user executing an interactive command) is a service request or a transaction, and a performance group defines a set of performance objectives for a particular domain may give rise to many tasks of various types with each type in turn are associated with a performance group. The complexity, or sophistication, of the scheduling allows for very fine tuning of the system.

A part of the system, called the system resources manager (SRM), uses the IPS to determine which task of all the active tasks should be given access to the system's resources. In addition to attempting to meet the specification set in the IPS, the SRM tries to optimize resource use. The SRM is, however, not a low-level scheduler but an intermediate-level one, as it controls a number of other functions which in turn control resources.

The SRM controls the:

(a) *Resource manager* (RM), which monitors system-wide resource use and determines which resources are under or over-used.

(b) *Storage manager* (SM), which controls main and auxiliary storage and acts as paging supervisor and swapper.

(c) *I/O manager*, which manages the assignment of devices to a process, builds the control blocks necessary to control I/O and attempts error recovery.

(d) *Workload manager*, which measures resource use and maps the service rate to the service specification in the IPS.

(e) *CPU manager*, which monitors the processor and seeks to reduce delay.

The service rate is a linear combination of the amounts of three basic resources: processor time, an I/O request count, and page-seconds over the lifetime of the transaction. A computer-dependent adjusting factor is included. Each performance objective sets a minimum amount of service that any of its transactions must receive during any processing interval. The resource manager, CPU manager and the workload manager can vote on swap decisions; the SRM controls swapping and vote counting.

The low-level scheduler is the interactive use manager for MVS systems. Choice of a process is based on queues of ready processes; the ASCB (address space control block) which describes the address space also contains pointers to the preceding and following ASCBs in a queue, forming a two-way linked list which comprises a low-level scheduling queue. ASCBs for address spaces which become ready are inserted in the queue according to a priority which changes dynamically, but the queue is serviced by the low-level scheduler in FIFO order.

The high-level scheduler for batch work is software called the job entry subsystem (JES) which exists outside MVS 'proper'. It supports multicomputer systems and some degree of distribution (see below), queues incoming requests, translates and parses job control language, and at the other end controls printing and the punching of cards. Thus it controls entry into and exit from the MVS system 'proper'.

3.4.4 Serialization, concurrency and the prevention of deadlock

A problem which arises when several processes execute simultaneously is the possibility of two or more processes seeking to gain access to some unsharable resource at the same time. This is clearly unsatisfiable and access to such a resource must be serialized in some fashion. A greater danger is the possibility of deadlock occurring. A deadlock occurs when one process obtains use of an unsharable resource and needs a second unsharable resource, while a second process has been allocated the second resource but needs the first to continue, see Figure 3.10. Neither process can proceed until the other relinquishes the contested resource. Deadlock detection. in this case, is simple but in general the detection of deadlock and the determination as to which process should 'back off' is difficult. Hence avoidance or prevention is a better solution although some systems do support mechanisms for deadlock detection and recovery.

There are some resources where concurrent use by different processes do not matter. For example, two or more concurrent processes reading an entry in a database simultaneously is no problem. Since all are reading and none is changing the entry, one can be assured that the information each reads is current and identical to that seen by all other processes. However, should one process want to update an entry, it is wise to ensure that only that process has access to the entry for the duration of the update. Otherwise, reading processes may obtain inconsistent information, or nearly simultaneous updates may corrupt the entry en-

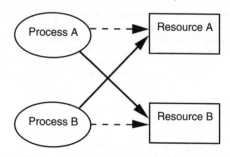

Figure 3.10   A schematic representation of deadlock

tirely. In this case it is important for the application or the operating system to ensure that the resource is serializable, that is, that concurrency is controlled in each instance where this is necessary.

Another way in which the update of an item of data can become corrupted is when the update is partial or incomplete. For example, a transaction shifting money between one account and another must subtract the amount to be shifted from one account and add it to the other account. Failure part-way through means that one account will lose money but the other will not gain it. Another example is failure part-way through updating the pointers on items in a two-way linked list when inserting or deleting an item from the list. This can cause problems in operating systems which depend on queues and linked lists.

To prevent partial update, it is necessary to define atomic actions. These are actions which will either complete with certainty or will return all objects on which they operate to their state before the action started. Thus, failed atomic actions are always restartable, since upon failure of the action to complete all objects return to the state they had before the action began. The system will always be in a known, consistent state.

Machine code instructions are atomic. They will always complete or the system will return to the state it was in before the instruction started. Ensuring atomicity means that one must be able to synchronize a given set of events, to make certain that they occur in a particular order. This means being able to serialize sub-actions such as access to any resource (which may be a data item).

To serialize a resource in a shared environment, mutual exclusion can be instituted. This means that whatever process gets hold of a resource which must be serialized, it does so in a way which will exclude access by any other process. To prevent excessive degradation of service, the duration of any period of mutual exclusion should be as short as possible, which means in practice identifying the minimum sub-set of any resource which needs mutual exclusion.

Mutual exclusion can be implemented by use of semaphores, which are primitive signals that indicate either that a resource is held under mutual exclusion (in which case processes which need that resource in effect form a queue) or it is not held under mutual exclusion (in which case a process, for example one of a waiting queue, can seek to obtain the resource itself). While a process has a resource under mutual exclusion it should be made uninterruptible. If it is interrupted, the resource it holds becomes unavailable and remains unavailable until such time as the process again becomes active and completes the portion of work which requires mutual exclusion.

Deadlock is often caused by allocating resources to processes in a piecemeal fashion in systems which use mutual exclusion. Thus, one method of preventing the possibility of deadlock is to allocate resources to a process in a single act, or if piecemeal allocation seems preferable, to disallow mutual exclusion. A third necessary condition to deadlock is the use of non-preemptive scheduling algorithms. Any process allocated a resource under mutual exclusion will be able to hold that resource indefinitely if it is not pre-emptable. However, the apparently obvious solution of designing an operating system without piecemeal allocation, with pre-emptive scheduling and without mutual exclusion is not acceptable in most cases. Pre-emptive scheduling, for example, has a relatively high overhead; mutual exclusion may be a necessity. A number of allocation and deadlock detection and recovery algorithms exist which address the problem of piecemeal allocation. It is the difficulty of avoiding deadlock while satisfying other objectives which forces the use of deadlock detection and recovery mechanisms.

3.4.5 *Interprocess communication*

It is often desirable to allow processes which share a system to communicate in some way. Among the many possible ways of communicating there are:

(a) Message-passing, where one process can send a message to another.

(b) Use of common storage or buffers.

(c) Use of shared files.

(d) The use of signals (software interrupts) and flags

(e) Passed parameters, which can be passed by value or via the medium of a pointer to the location of the parameter.

Of these, the first two allow greatest flexibility and the last is the most static. The inter-process communication facilities of Unix are primitive, limited to parameter passing and signals. Files can be shared, but concurrency control is a matter for voluntary mutual agreement among the users rather than something enforced by the operating system.

VMS allows the use of event flags (a bit which describes status) which processes can use to synchronize themselves, a mailbox facility (message-passing) and shared storage. VMS users can also share files provided all sharers are reading (not writing). Writing on indexed and relative files can be done concurrently, with protection against concurrent access for writing occurring at the record level.

In MVS, tasks can communicate via shared storage the common system area (CSA) which is used for communication between tasks which do not share the same address space. Message-passing between sub-tasks and shared buffers are a matter for the application. All three systems make use of parameter passing, but, for example, Unix's 'default' mode is passing by value, while MVS always passes by reference.

3.5 Multiprocessing and distributed systems

Multiprocessing systems are those which include two or more processors working together to accomplish work. MVS, described earlier, is a multiprocessing system as well as a multi-programming system. Network operating systems are those in which each host computer has its own operating system but also has communications processes which carry out network control functions. Distributed systems can be defined as those where hardware, control or data are distributed geographically.

The distinction between these classes of system is often the subject of debate. Generally, network systems can be considered as those where the presence of the network is made visible to users and users must take overt actions to invoke network functions. In distributed systems, and indeed in multiprocessing systems, the fact that there are a number of different processors communicating and cooperating tends to be invisible to the user. Hence the user is very likely to be unaware of which processor is carrying out his or her work.

There is also considerable debate about where the border between multiprocessing and distributed systems lie. A rule of thumb is to consider whether message-passing is the only possible mechanism for cooperating. Message-passing can, of course, be used even in single processor systems as a means of inter-process communication. But as distance increases, the time between sending and receiving communication also increases and at some point this reaches a stage where message-passing becomes the only viable means of communication. For example, two systems closely adjacent can share files by means of a physical switch or direct wiring, but beyond a certain distance, the sharing is more economically and simply accomplished by sending data from a file to a remote processor in the form of a message, however long.

Multiprocessing systems can best be classified according to their relationships, or the closeness of the coupling between them. One possible relationship is that of master and slave, such as that demonstrated by IBM's mainframe attached processor (AP) systems running MVS. Both processors share a single main memory, the master processor provides all the I/O, scheduling and resource management services and the other processor (the attached processor) is devoted to processing work under the direction of the master. Any interrupt occurring in a process in the AP causes a second interrupt in the master processor. Some master-slave arrangements are not so rigid as that of IBM's AP systems; the master may only be the director or dictator, but not have exclusive control of all resources.

Another form of multiprocessing system is called separate executives, whereby each processing element has its own operating system, controls its own I/O devices and files and processes only its own interrupts. I/O devices may be switched between processors through intervention by an operator or a master processor, which may also control access to global data.

Coupling, on the other hand, may range from the very tight (where all processors are semi-independent and have both local memory and shared global memory), to very loosely coupled arrangements where processors have only local memory and share a communications channel.

In symmetrical systems the single operating system floats between identical processors such that only one processor is host to the operating system but any processor is capable of being the host.

MVS, running under the JES3 job entry subsystem, is an example of a separate executives arrangement. (Processors need not be proximate in JES3 systems, but as the master schedules work for all the other processors, where processors are distant, the 'jobs' are sent in the form of messages.)

There are several possible models of distributed system, including:

(a) A local-area network used as a form of 'bus' to connect multiple processors in a multiprocessing-type system.

(b) Local processors with local memory sharing discs and files on a network (the 'workstation' model).

(c) Personal computers interacting with larger hosts such that smaller applications with a high degree of interaction run on the PCs and larger applications and files reside on a larger host.

(d) A community of democratic equal hosts interacting, using an extension to the operating system to provide address extension.

Multiprocessing systems have much in common with multiprogramming systems. In addition, they have added problems of more complex deadlock prevention and concurrency control and load balancing. They are more expensive, but in return offer increased reliability and improved performance, although two processors in a multiprocessing system do not perform at twice the rate of a single processor! The degree of coupling and especially of data sharing dictates to a large extent the degree of performance improvement; unshared data gives the best performance improvement, while global data gives the least.

One of the major objectives of distribution is to render the fact that a system is distributed as transparent as possible. This can be achieved in several ways. For example, Sun Computer's Network

File Server attempts to mimic the hierarchical directory and file system of Unix so that the whole distributed file store appears as though it were on a single system. A common mechanism is the remote procedure call (RPC), which attempts to mimic, from the programmer's point of view, an ordinary procedure call statement. However, the procedure call must be 'bundled' into a message along with any parameters to be passed, must be reliably sent to the remote host and reliably invoke the remote procedure, which must then execute and return control and any parameters to the invoking procedure on another machine.

Time is of crucial importance in any consideration of distributed systems. Synchronism over considerable distance is difficult, since in a distributed system working over a network using message-passing as an information exchange mechanism there is no common clock. Delays in message transmission do happen, as do failures of hosts and failures in the network. Thus, applications must take into account the possibilities of these occurrences. If distances are very great or the likelihood of delay is great, it may be necessary for the 'working' process to send reassurances to the invoking process as commonly the invoking process must wait a 'reasonable' time before making the assumption that the remote host is unreachable or has failed to complete the transaction. In distributed file systems, a part of the file store may become suddenly unavailable, although this may be compared to a similar problem occurring in a single, centralized file store due to failure of a device or group of devices. A further consideration for many is the security of a distributed system; encryption of messages and other protective measures may be necessary and add to the overhead burden of such a system.

Thus, while distributed systems provide fault tolerance, increased power, and power closer to the user, developers must be aware that the state of the system is not easily determined from any one node and different nodes may simultaneously have different views of the system state. The time taken to pass messages is not insignificant and may add to delay perceived by the user. The working address space available to a user may be smaller than would be the case on a large single system or in a multiprocessing system.

MVS and IBM's VM (Virtual Machine) operating systems support multiprocessor systems, however a job, once assigned to a particular processor or close-coupled processor complex, remains there until completed. Calls to services on other processors outside a close-coupled complex are not supported and hence these do not constitute true distributed systems. Sun Computer's Network File Server, a service added to Unix 4.2 BSD, provides a distributed system of form (b) above. Grapevine was developed at Xerox and is an interesting case study of a distributed system, its advantages and its problems. A large number of rather ad hoc systems of type (c) exist and are rapidly becoming more common. IBM's SNA and SAA network architectures and DECnet support developments of this type. These are ad hoc in the sense that organizations are assembling them from a variety of equipment often using or developing a wide variety of applications software designed for distributed use. Thus, each is unique to its organization. As yet, no manufacturer provides a complete system, including applications, which can be purchased entire. Research examples exist of most types.

3.6   Accessing system services

In most systems, requests for system services are provided for applications by code inserted at compilation time by the compiler of high-level language programs. For example, read and write statements call on system I/O services and these calls are inserted into the object program by the compiler when it compiles high-level language statements that are of the read or write type.

In CP/M, MS-DOS and PC-DOS, as well as service requests made by the compiler (or interpreter) from a high-level language on behalf of the programmer, a more direct form of access to system functions is accomplished at the Assembler level by executing an instruction to call the system function, with the required function number in a register designated for the purpose. In MS-DOS the instruction is:

INT 21H

and the function number must be in the AH register.

For example, placing 03H in the AH register and executing INT 21 H will cause the system to wait for a character from the defined auxiliary port to arrive; when a character does arrive it will be returned to the AL register. Another method used by some programmers is to access directly the system jump table, but this causes problems of portability between versions of MS-DOS and PC-DOS, which have the jump table at different addresses.

In MVS, system services are numerous. Access to such services is normally provided by the compilers for high-level language applications, but more direct access is available at the Assembler level by executing the SVC (supervisor call) instruction, where the operand is the number of the service wanted. For example, SVC 13 opens a file whose identifiers are already established by earlier code. (It is worth noting that most system error codes above 00F in MVS are related to the SVC which detected the error, S013 and S213 errors, for example, are errors which occurred during attempts to open a file and were detected by the SVC13 routine, while S214 occurs when a file cannot be closed properly for example, because there is insufficient room to write the end of file marker and is detected by SVC14, the file close routine.) Some utility programs, for example the SORT utility, contain numbered 'hooks', often called 'exits', which can be invoked from either high-level or assembler language programs. SORT, for example, contains 'exits' E15 and E35 which allow the programmer control over the input to and output from the sorting process, respectively.

In Unix, which is largely written in a high-level language (C), calls to system services can be made more directly in C or Pascal programs. In this case system services are provided by pre-written modules which can be invoked by calls. For example, in C a 'fork' (which creates a new child process) is simply invoked by:

```
main()
    { int ppid;
      signal (SIGINT, signal monitor);
      if (fork( ) = = 0)
         {
         /* body of fork code run in child process */
         }
    }
```

In this fragment of code two system services have been invoked. Fork has already been mentioned and is invoked in the 'if' statement. The other system service invoked is signal, invoked in the line above. All such system services are documented in the Unix manual which is provided on-line in Unix systems.

VMS provides system services as functions which can be invoked from high-level languages such as FORTRAN and Modula-2 more directly than is the case with any of the systems above except Unix. The programmer using VAX/VMS utilities must adhere to the VAX Procedure Calling and Condition Handling Standard in order to avoid problems. Utilities are grouped. For example, there is a utility set for: the access control list (ACL), the command language (CLI), conversion (CONV) and data compression and expansion (DCX), and invocation uses these abbreviations in the form:

ACLEDIT$EDIT *item-list*

> where ACL is the set, EDIT is the function, and 'item-list' is the parameter.

3.7   References and bibliography

Bach, M. J. (1986) *The Design of the Unix Operating System*, Prentice-Hall

Brinch-Hansen, P. (1971) *Short-term scheduling in multiprogramming systems. In Third ACM Symposium on Operating Systems Principles*, pp, 103-5

Coulouris, G. F. and Dollimore, J. (1988) *Distributed Systems: Concepts and Designs*, Addison-Wesley

Deitel, H. M. (1984) *An Introduction to Operating Systems*, Addison-Wesley

Denning, P. J. (1968) *The working set model for program behavior. Communications of the ACM, 11*, 323-33

Draper, S. (1985) *The nature of expertise in UNIX. In Human-Computer Interaction - Interact '84*, Shakel, B. (ed.), North-Holland

Hoare, C. A. R. (1985) *Communicating Sequential Processes*, Prentice-Hall

Keller, L. S. (1988) *Operating Systems: Communicating With and Controlling the Computer*, Prentice-Hall

Kernighan, B. W. and Ritchie, D. M. (1978) *The C Programming Language*, Prentice-Hall

LeLann, G. (1981) *Motivations, objectives and characterization ot distributed systems. In Distributed Systems: Architecture and Implementation. An advanced Course.* (ed. B. W. Lampson et al.) Springer- Verlag

Lucy, S. (1984) *MS-DOS User Book*, Sigma Press

Maekawa, M., Oldehoeft, A. and Oldehoeft, R. (1987) *Operating Systems: Advanced Concepts*, Benjamin/Cummings

Microsoft Press (1993) *MS-DOS Programmers Reference* (Version 6), Microsoft Corporation

Solomon, D. W., Halliday C. M., Busch D. D., Stanley T. S., (1989) *MS-DOS User's Guide*, Que

Thomas, R., Rogers, L. R. and Yates, J. L. (1986) *Advanced Programmers Guide to UNIX System V*, Osborne McGraw-Hill

Chapter 4
Discrete mathematics

4.1　Introduction

This chapter gives a summary of the discrete mathematics which underlies the process of software engineering. Topics covered are those that a software engineer needs to know in order to produce formal specifications, either algebraic (e.g. OBJ or CLEAR), model-oriented (e.g. VDM or Z), or using a process algebra or calculus (e.g. CSP, CCS or LOTOS).

Sections of this chapter are devoted to logic, set theory, functions, relations, and algebras. The account is kept at an elementary level. A more advanced and specialist treatment would probably embark on domain theory, universal algebra, category theory, and topology, which are used to explain the semantics of specification languages such as those mentioned above, and also of some aspects of programming languages. The chapter concludes with a brief introduction to the specification languages, Z and VDM.

4.2　Logic

4.2.1　Propositions and predicates

Logic — the calculus of propositions and the calculus of predicates is an essential part of discrete mathematics for software engineering. A logic of propositions is needed to make assertions about properties of objects in the application domain which the software is to model. Propositional and predicate calculus are needed to make statements about programs, in particular to assert that they meet specifications, and that parts of programs have certain effects, such as establishing a relationship between the values of particular variables.

A proposition is a statement which is either true or false. A predicate is a formula such that when its variables are assigned values (of an appropriate type) it becomes a proposition. Examples of propositions are:

Proposition	Value
$7 > 3$	True
$4 = 5$	False
$\{3,4\} \subseteq \{4,3,6\}$	True
The sun is shining	?

Examples of predicates are:

$$x > 3$$
$$y = z - 7$$
$$S1 \subseteq S2$$

4.2.2   *Logical connectives*

Propositions can be formed from other propositions by means of logical operators or connectives. The logical connectives are:

¬   not
∧   and
∨   or
⇒   implies
⇔   equivalence

The logical connectives in general capture the intuitive linguistic ideas of 'not', 'and', 'or', 'implies' or 'if ... then ...', and 'if and only if'. Their meanings can be defined by truth tables. If P, Q, R are propositions, then so are:

¬ P
P ∧ Q
P ∨ Q
P ⇒ Q
P ⇔ Q

Hence compound propositions can be constructed:

P ∧ Q ∧ R
P ∧ (Q ⇒ R)
etc.

The precedence conventions are in the order given above, so that: ¬ P1 ∧ P2 ∨ P3 ⇒ P4 ⇔ P5 is taken as:

$$((((\neg P1) \wedge P2) \vee P3) \Rightarrow P4) \Leftrightarrow P5$$

However, it is good practice to insert brackets even where it is unnecessary, if this improves readability. The meanings of the connectives are defined by the following tables:

P				¬*P*	
true				false	
false				true	

P	*Q*	*P* ∧ *Q*	*P* ∨ *Q*	*P* ⇒ *Q*	*P* ⇔ *Q*
true	true	true	true	true	true
true	false	false	true	false	false
false	true	false	true	true	false
false	false	false	false	true	true

The meaning given to implication sometimes causes difficulty when the operand on the left is false. It may help to consider such colloquialisms as 'If it rains today I'll eat my hat', where both component propositions are false, but the compound proposition is considered true. Likewise if one is given a request 'If you're driving to Birmingham today will you take this package with you?', then one is complying with the request by not driving to

Birmingham and not taking the package. Likewise, one is also complying by travelling to Birmingham by train and taking the package anyway.

The variable letters such as P, P1, Q etc. may also stand as propositions. In that case the proposition has a truth value only when its constituent variables are 'interpreted' by being assigned a truth value themselves. However, a proposition may have the same value for all interpretations of its constituent propositional variables. If a proposition is true for all interpretations, it is called a tautology. If a proposition is false for all interpretations, it is called a contradiction.

The following are examples of tautologies:

$P \vee \neg P$
$P \Rightarrow P$

The following are examples of contradictions:

$P \wedge \neg P$
$true \Rightarrow false$

The truth values of compound propositions can conveniently be calculated by means of truth tables. The technique is to construct a table containing a number of lines, the number being 2n where *n* is the number of propositional variables in the proposition; this is the number of possible combinations of the truth values of the propositional variables. A column is drawn for each propositional sub expression, ending with a column for the total proposition. The truth values for each column are then filled in, using the truth tables for the primitive operators.

For example, suppose we wish to establish that:

$(\neg P \vee Q) \Leftrightarrow (P \Rightarrow Q)$

is a tautology. We proceed as follows:

P	Q	$\neg P$	$\neg P \vee Q$	$P \Rightarrow Q$	$(P \vee Q) \Leftrightarrow (P \Rightarrow Q)$
true	true	false	true	true	true
true	false	false	false	false	true
false	true	true	true	true	true
false	false	true	true	true	true

The final column containing 'true' for all combinations of truth values for P and Q shows that it is a tautology.

Truth tables can be used to verify a number of well-known laws. These state that each member of a pair of propositions have the same truth value. The most well known of these are as follows:

$P, \neg \neg P$	
$P, P \wedge P$	
$P, P \vee P$	
$\neg P \vee Q, P \Rightarrow Q$	
$P \wedge Q, \neg(\neg P \vee \neg Q)$	De Morgan's Law
$P \vee Q, \neg(\neg P \wedge \neg Q)$	De Morgan's Law
$R \wedge (P \vee Q), (R \wedge P) \vee (R \wedge Q)$	Distributive Law
$R \vee (P \wedge Q), (R \vee P) \wedge (R \vee Q)$	Distributive Law

$P \wedge Q, Q \wedge P$	Commutative Law
$P \vee Q, Q \vee P$	Commutative Law
$P \Leftrightarrow Q, Q \Leftrightarrow P$	Commutative Law
$P \wedge (Q \wedge R), (P \wedge Q) \wedge R$	Associative Law
$P \vee (Q \wedge R), (P \vee Q) \vee R$	Associative Law
$P \vee \neg P, true$	
$P \wedge \neg P, false$	

All these laws can be proved from the truth tables. The meanings of the operators can alternatively be given by means of axioms, in which case the above laws can be proved from the axioms by natural deduction.

A sentence in predicate calculus is a proposition which may contain variables, constants, functions, and predicate symbols which stand for truth-valued functions. In addition to the logical operators of propositional logic, in predicate calculus one may also construct sentences using universal and existential quantifiers.

A sentence in predicate calculus consists of any of the following:

1. the truth values true or false

2. a predicate $p(t_1,...,t_n)$ where p is a predicate symbol and $t_1,...,t_n$ are terms

    $\neg P$ where P is a sentence

    $P \wedge Q$ where P,Q are sentences

    $P \vee Q$ where P,Q are sentences

    $P \Rightarrow Q$ where P,Q are sentences

    $P \Leftrightarrow Q$ where P,Q are sentences

    $\forall x.P$ where x is a variable and P is a sentence

    $\exists x.Q$ where x is a variable and Q is a sentence

    $\exists! x.Q$ where x is a variable and Q is a sentence

The last three forms are called 'quantified expressions'. $\forall x, P$ means that P is true for all values of x, and $\exists x, P$ means that P is true for some value of x and $\exists! x, Q$ means that there is a unique x such that Q is true. $\forall$ is called the universal quantifier, and $\exists$ and $\exists!$ are called existential quantifiers.

Terms may be built from variables, constants, functions and predicates; a term is any of the following:

1. A constant.

2. A variable.

3. A function application $f(t_1,...,t_n)$ where f is a symbol of arity n and $t_n,...,t_n$ are terms.

Generalising, predicates may be regarded as special cases of functions and the truth values as particular constants. Function, and predicate symbols may be infix (in which case $\wedge$, $\vee$ etc. are predicate and hence function symbols) and a term may also be a sentence. Predicate calculus is usually typed, in which case variables are designated as being of a particular type, and arguments of functions have to match the types expected. Then the quantified expressions are of form:

$$\forall x{:}T,P$$
$$\exists x{:}T.P$$

where T is a type.

A sentence in predicate calculus has a truth value when all free variables are assigned values conforming to their type. This is analogous to the proposition symbols in propositional logic being assigned truth values, resulting in the proposition which contains them having a value. Examples of predicates are:

$$x > 3$$
$$y = z - 7$$
$$S1 \subseteq S2$$
$$\forall x{:}\mathbb{Z}.x*x \geq 0$$
$$\exists y{:}\mathbb{R}.y*y = 2$$

where $\mathbb{Z}$ and $\mathbb{R}$ are the sets of integer and real numbers respectively.

In the above, x, y, z would have numeric types and S1, S2 would have types whose members were sets. The symbols $>$ and $\subseteq$ are examples of predicate symbols.

Predicates are used to express conditions in many contexts in computer science: in assertions about the values of variables in a program, in pre- and post-conditions in VDM and other techniques based on Dijkstra's weakest pre-conditions, in loop invariants, and elsewhere. So, for example, in a relational database, if a relation R is transitive, i.e. is such that whenever, for entities in E, e_1Re_2 and e_2Re_3 we have e_1Re_3, this can be expressed in predicate calculus:

$$\forall e_1,e_2,e_3{:}E.(e_1Re_2 \wedge e_2Re_3) \Rightarrow e_1Re_3$$

4.3 Set theory

Set theory is relevant to software engineering for many reasons. It is one of the principal foundations of mathematics. It provides a useful model of various styles of type theory which, in turn, are the basis of abstract data types and data types in programming languages.

Sets can be defined axiomatically, and this is the best formal treatment of the subject. It is also intuitively helpful to think of sets as collections of objects, and this is the approach we shall take in this brief account. In fact the mathematically defined theory of sets can stand as a theory of collections of objects, just as the mathematically defined theory of numbers can stand as a theory of measurable quantities such as mass and length.

A set may be thought of as a collection of any objects of any kind.

The collection is unordered, and no distinguishable object can occur in it more than once, i.e. all objects in a set can be distinguished one from another.

There is thus a relation 'belongs to', written as an infix symbol we write:

$x \in S$

to indicate that x is a member, or belongs to, the set S. x may or may not be a set. The operator $\in$ is thus a predicate symbol, since an expression of the form $x \in S$ is either true or false.

Throughout this account, the words 'element' and 'member' are used interchangeably. One also denotes the negation of set membership by $\notin$. Thus:

$x \notin S$

means the same as:

$\neg(x \in S)$

A set is identified by its members. This means that two sets Sl and S2 are equal, i.e. the same set, if and only if they have the same members.

A set with a finite number of members $x_1, x_2, ..., x_n$ can be denoted:

$\{x_1, ..., x_n\}$

Since the members of a set are in no particular order, the order of the $x_1, ..., x_n$ is irrelevant. Also, since there is no concept of repetition of the elements, repetitions of any of the values x are irrelevant. Thus the following all denote the same set:

$\{1, 2, 3\}$
$\{3, 1, 2\}$
$\{3, 1, 3, 2, 2\}$

and the set they denote has three members. (Note that the last form may not be legal in some specification or programming languages.) It follows that the empty set, that set which has no members, is denoted:

$\{\}$

Other forms are also written, for example O. Since a set is identified by its members, it follows that there is just one empty set, the identity of which is independent of the way in which it is defined. Thus, for example, the set of numbers greater than two and less than one is the same set as the set of planets in the solar system which are larger than Jupiter. Sets may also be defined implicitly, by means of the properties of their members. If $P(x)$ is a predicate in which the variable x occurs free (see next section), then:

$$\{x | P(x)\}$$

denotes the set of all values x such that $P(x)$ is true.

4.3.1 Free and bound

The value of an expression like $x \wedge y$ depends on the values of the variables x and y. In such a case x and y are said to occur 'free' in the expression. On the other hand, in an expression like $\{x | P(x)\}$, x is said to occur 'bound'; the value of the expression does not depend on any value which x might have in its surrounding context. The variable x plays much the same role as it does in the (more familiar) expression:

$$\sum_{n=1}^{n} A_x$$

A more rigorous definition follows:

A variable x is said to occur free or bound in an expression e under the following circumstances:

1. x occurs free in the expression x, i.e. the expression which consists solely of the variable x.

2. If x occurs free in the expression e, then it occurs free in the expression (e).

3. If x occurs free in the expression e, then it occurs free in the expression $f(e_1, e_2, ..., e_n)$ where one of $e_1, ..., e_n$ is e, and f is a function or predicate symbol. This is also true for infix forms of the function or predicate symbol.

4. If x occurs free in the expression p, and x and y are different variable symbols, then x occurs free in each of:

   (a) $\forall y.p$

   (b) $\exists y.p$

   (c) $\{y | p\}$.

5. If x occurs free in e, then x occurs free in $\{e_1, ..., e_n\}$ where $e = e_i$ for some i, $1 \leq i \leq n$.

6. x occurs bound in each of:

   (a) $\forall x.p$

   (b) $\exists x.p$

   (c) $\{x | p\}$.

7. If x occurs bound in e, then x occurs bound in (e).

8. If x occurs bound in the expression e, then it occurs bound in the expression $f(e_1, e_2, ..., e_n)$ where one of $e_1, ..., e_n$ is e, and f is a function or predicate symbol. This is also true for infix forms of the function or predicate symbol.

9. If x occurs bound in the expression p, and x and y are different variable symbols, then x occurs bound in each of:

    (a) $\forall y.p$

    (b) $\exists y.p$

    (c) $\{y \mid p\}$.

10. If x occurs bound in e, then x occurs bound in $\{e_1, ..., e_n\}$ where $e = e_i$ for some i, $1 \leq i \leq n$.

    If the variable y does not occur free in p, then the following pairs of expressions are equal and interchangeable:

$$\forall x.p \qquad\qquad \forall y.p_{(x \to y)}$$

$$\exists x.p \qquad\qquad \exists y.p_{(x \to y)}$$

$$\{x \mid p\} \qquad\qquad \{y \mid p_{(x \to y)}\}$$

Where $p[x \to y]$ denotes the expression p with all free occurrences of x replaced by y.

Example:

Logic and set theory are useful for formally expressing assertions about, for example, the desired effect of a program:

$$\forall i,j \in \{x \mid x \in \mathbb{N} \land x \leq \text{len file}\}.i \leq j \Rightarrow \text{KEY}(\text{file}(i)) \leq \text{KEY}(\text{file}(j))$$

All the items in the file are ordered by their KEY fields.

$$\forall p = \text{Personnel}.\text{Job\_title}(p) = \text{"supervisor"} \Rightarrow \text{Grade}(p) \geq 6$$

Everyone in the personnel database whose job-title is 'supervisor' has a grade of at least 6.

4.3.2   *Set operators*

Operators on sets allow new sets to be defined in terms of existing sets. Again, the meaning of the set operators can be defined axiomatically. Here we shall define set operations constructively, in terms of their membership relations, since this matches more easily the intuitive view of sets as collections of objects which is already taken.

1. *Set union*. $S \cup T$ where S and T are sets, is the set satisfying: $x \in (S \cup T)$ if and only if $x \in S$ or $x \in T$

2. *Set intersection.* S∈T where S and T are sets, is the set
   satisfying: $x \in (S \cap T)$ if and only if $x \in S$ and $x \in T$

3. *Set difference.* S – T where S and T are sets, is the set
   satisfying: $x \in (S - T)$ if and only if $x \in S$ and $x \notin T$

The effect of these set operators can be depicted by so-called 'Venn diagrams'. These are shown in Figures 4.1 to 4.3.

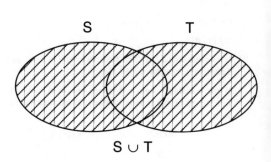

$$S \cup T$$

Figure 4.1   *Union*

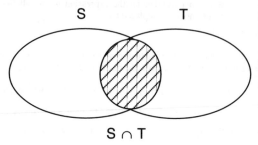

$$S \cap T$$

Figure 4.2   *Intersection*

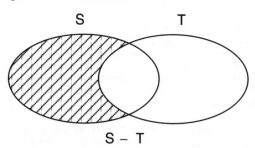

$$S - T$$

Figure 4.3   *Set substraction*

Certain facts are easily proved from the definitions:

$S \cup T = T \cup S$	Commutativity
$S \cap T = T \cap S$	Commutativity
$(S \cup T) \cup R = S \cup (T \cup R)$	Associativity
$(S \cap T) \cap R = S \cap (T \cap R)$	Associativity
$S \cap (T \cup R) = (S \cap T) \cup (S \cap R)$	Distributivity
$S \cup (T \cap R) = (S \cup T) \cap (S \cup R)$	Distributivity
$(S \cup T) - R = (S - R) \cup (T - R)$	
$(S \cap T) - R = (S - R) \cap (T - R)$	

$$\{x_1,...,x_n\} \cup \{y_1,...,y_m\} = \{x_1,...,x_n,y_1,...,y_m\}$$
$$\{x/p\} \cup \{x/q\} = \{x/p \vee q\}$$
$$\{x/p\} \cap \{x/q\} = \{x/p \wedge q\}$$
$$\{x/p\} - \{x/q\} = \{x/p \wedge \neg q\}$$

Since the set operators $\cup$ and $\cap$ are associative and commutative, distributed forms of these are often used. Given an index range $1 ... n$, one may write:

$$\bigcup_{i=1}^{n} S_i \qquad\qquad \bigcap_{i=1}^{n} S_i$$

Likewise, given an index set I, one may write:

$$\bigcup_{i \in 1} S_i \qquad\qquad \bigcap_{i \notin 1} S_i$$

The meaning is, for each respective case:

$\{x \mid \exists\, i \in \text{I}.x \in S_i\}$	for distributed union
$\{x \mid \forall\, i \in \text{I}.x \in S_i\}$	for distributed intersection

For the $1 ... n$ forms, the index set I can be taken as

$$\{i \mid i \in \mathbb{Z} \wedge 1 \leq i \leq n\}.$$

Distributed and $\wedge$, and distributed or $\vee$ can be defined in an analogous way.

4.3.3   Set relations

Three set relation operators are in common use. These are $\subseteq$ (subset), $\subset$ (proper subset), $=$ (equality). If S1, S2 are sets, then the expressions:

$$S1 \subseteq S2$$
$$S1 \subset S2$$
$$S1 = S2$$

Each have the value *true* or *false*.

The subset relation is defined as follows:

$S1 \subseteq S2$ if and only if all members of $S1$ are also members of $S2$.

The proper subset relation is defined:

$S1 \subset S2$ if and only if $S1 \subseteq S2$ and there is at least one member of $S2$ which is not a member of $S1$.

Equality of sets has already been defined:

$S1 = S2$ if all members of $S1$ are members of $S2$ and all members of $S2$ are members of $S1$.

The subset relation can be illustrated by the Venn diagram, shown in Figure 4.4.

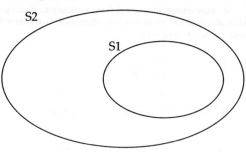

$$S1 \subseteq S2$$

Figure 4.4   Subset

The following facts follow immediately from the definitions:
$$S1 \subset S2 \Leftrightarrow S1 \subseteq S2 \wedge \neg(S2 \subseteq S1)$$
$$\Leftrightarrow S1 \subseteq S2 \wedge S1 \neq S2$$
$$S1 = S2 \Leftrightarrow S1 \subseteq S2 \wedge S2 \subseteq S1$$
$$S1 \subseteq S2 \Leftrightarrow \forall x.x \in S1 \Rightarrow x \in S2$$
$$S1 = S2 \Leftrightarrow \forall x.x \in S1 \Leftrightarrow x \in S2$$

If $S1 \subseteq S2$ then $S1 \cup S3 \in S2 \cup S3$
If $S1 \subseteq S2$ then $S1 \cap S3 \in S2 \cap S3$

4.3.4   Cardinality

For finite sets, the cardinality of the set is equal to the number of its members. A unary (or monadic) operator is used for this:

card S   is the number of distinct members of S, when S is finite.

'card' is not defined for infinite sets. Various symbols are in common use for this operator, in particular:

|S| and   #S

The following facts can easily be shown:

card { } = 0
card S1 + card S2 = card (S1∪S2) + card (S1 ∩ S2)

4.3.5 Powersets

The powerset operator applied to a set S gives the set of all its subsets. We write:

$$\mathscr{P}S$$

which is defined:

$$\mathscr{P}S = \{x | x \in S\}$$

Since, for any set S, S ⊆ S and { } ⊆ S, it follows that:

{ } ∈ $\mathscr{P}S$
S ∈ $\mathscr{P}S$

In computer science (and software engineering) it is often useful to consider the set of all finite subsets of a set S. This is easy to define, and is sometimes written:

$$\mathscr{F}S$$

The definition will be given when we have dealt with functions. Of course if S is itself finite, then its powerset will also be finite, and so $\mathscr{P}S$ and $\mathscr{F}S$ will be the same. For a finite set S, the cardinality of its powerset bears the following relationship to the cardinality of the set itself:

card $\mathscr{P}S$ = $2^{\text{card } S}$

4.3.6 Cartesian product

If S and T are sets, a further set can be constructed which is the set of ordered pairs of members of S and T. We write:

$$S \times T$$

to denote the set of pairs (x, y) such that $x \in S$ and $y \in T$.

Since 'pairs' have not yet been defined, this definition is strictly not meaningful. An intuitive concept of ordered pair is that the order of the elements of the pair is significant and that repetition may perhaps be allowed. To give this idea more formal substance, we need to define operators on the set which is denoted $S \times T$.

First a constructor of pairs of any two sets S, T (and indeed, S and T may be the same set) can be defined, 'make$_{S,T}$' takes a member of the set S and a member of the set T, and yields a member of the set $S \times T$.

The second operator, 'first$_{S,T}$', takes a member of the set $S \times T$ (i.e. a 'pair') and yields a member of S:

first$_{S,T}$(make$_{S,T}(x, y)$) = x

Likewise, a third operator, 'second$_{S,T}$', takes a member of the set $S \times T$ and yields a member of T:

$$\text{second}_{S,T}(\text{make}_{S,T}(x,y)) = y$$

When the context is clear, and this is more usual, the subscripts S, T are omitted. Also the 'make' operator is not normally named, and the mix-fix notation:

$$(\_,\_)$$

is used to construct pairs. The underline symbols indicate the positions of the arguments when the operator is applied to specific values. Thus the above may be rewritten in a more abbreviated way:

$$\text{second}((x,y)) = y$$

Occasionally for pair-construction, other brackets are used, for . [_,_] or <_,_>.

Example

The complex numbers may be regarded as the Cartesian product

$\mathbb{R} \times \mathbb{R}$ of pairs of real numbers.

We can generalise the foregoing concept by constructing multiple Cartesian products. If $S_1, S_2, ..., S_n$ are sets, then the Cartesian product of *n*-tuples is written:

$$S_1 \times S_2 \times ... S_n$$

or

$$\underset{i=1}{\overset{n}{\times}} S_i$$

A corresponding 'make' operator is defined:

$$\text{make}_T(x_1,...,x_n)$$

where $x_i \in S_i$, $1 \leq i \leq n$, and:

Selection operators are likewise defined:

$$\text{select}_{T,i}(x_1,...,x_n) = x_i$$

for $1 \leq i \leq n$. If k is a tuple which is a member of T, instead of writing:

$$\text{select}_{T,i}k$$

more often one writes $k(i)$ or $k[i]$. The selection operators are often known as 'projections'.

The cardinality of a Cartesian product is related to the cardinality of its components:

card (S x T) = card S * card T

In general:

$$\text{card} \; \overset{n}{\underset{i=1}{\times}} \; S_i \; = \; \overset{n}{\underset{i=1}{\prod}} \; \text{card} \; S_i$$

Examples

There are numerous examples of Cartesian products, and tuples which are members of them, in software engineering. Arrays in programming languages are one. An array of n integers is a representation of a member of the Cartesian product:

$$\times_{i=1}^{n} \mathbb{Z}$$

where $\mathbb{Z}$ is the set of integers.

4.3.7 Labelled Cartesian products

An elaboration of multiple Cartesian products, whose members are n-tuples or tuples, is the concept of 'labelled' or 'tagged' Cartesian product. This concept is used mainly in computer science contexts rather than in mathematical ones, since it provides a convenient mathematical model of files, tuples in databases, Pascal-style records, etc.

Let L be an arbitrary set of labels or tags. It is convenient for L not to be of finite cardinality, so as to provide an unlimited source of labels. Then a labelled or tagged Cartesian product can be constructed from a number of constituent sets $S_1,...,S_n$ and the same number of distinct labels $L_1,...,L_n$ where $L1 \in L$, $1 \le i \le n$, and defined by the following notation:

$$T \quad = L_1{:}S_1 \times L_2{:}S_2 \times ... \times L_n{:}S_n$$

When T is defined as above, it denotes a set with operators 'make-T' and 'select-T'; 'make-T' takes members of the sets $S_1,...,S_n$ as arguments and yields a result which is a member of T:

make-T($s_1,s_2,...,s_n$)

where

$s_i \in S_i$, $1 \le i \le n$

The select-T operator takes a member of T as its first argument and a member of L as its second argument. To be well defined, the member of L must be one of the $L_1,...,L_n$ occurring in the definition of T. The select-T operator yields as a result a member of the set S_i which corresponds to the label which stands as its second parameter; this will be the selected component of the tuple which is a member of T.

The definition of the operators and the set T is captured by the following rule. If $t \in$ T is such that:

$t = \text{make} - \text{T}(s_1, s_2, \ldots, s_n)$

where $\text{T} = L_1{:}S_1 \times \ldots \times L_n{:}S_n$ then:

$\text{select} - \text{T}(t, L_i) = s_i$

for each $1 \leq i \leq n$.

4.3.8 Notation

In the definition of a tagged Cartesian product the product symbols 'x' are frequently omitted. The `select-T` operator is often simply written as $\_.\_$ or $\_(\_)$, so that in the above definition one would write:

$t.L_i = s_i$

or:

$L_i(t) = s_i$

The set T is determined from context, by the term t.

Example:

Pers =   NAME:Text
            AGE: N
            OCC: Text
            SALARY: N

Let:

fred = make-Pers("Fred", 40, "Hacker", 9500)

then:

fred.NAME="Fred"
fred.AGE = 40

4.4 Functions

Given two sets, S, T there is a set of functions from S to T, denoted S→T. If f is such a function, then f belongs to this set, i.e.:

$f \in$ S→T

So S→T is the set of all functions of this type.

Given a function f as above, and a member x of S, then f may be applied to x to yield a member t of T. t is often said to be the 'image' of x under f. Function application is an operator whose usual syntax is $\_(\_)$, e.g.:

$f(x) = t$

(In texts following an older tradition, function application is sometimes written: xf.)

Functions are usually considered as 'total', which means that for every $x \in$ S, the application $f(x)$ of f to x is defined. Functions which are not total are said to be 'partial'. Familiar examples of partial functions are 'square-root' applied to real numbers, which is not defined for negative numbers, and division, which is not defined for a second argument of zero.

The notation S→T is usually taken to mean the set of total functions from S to T. Another often used notation is T^S. The set of partial and total functions is sometimes written:

$$S \leftrightarrow T$$

although S→T is often used with this meaning.

The collection of values in S for which f yields a value in T is called the 'domain' off Thus:

$$\text{dom} f = \{x \mid x \in S \land \exists y \in T f(x) = y\}$$

Likewise the collection of members of T to which f maps some member of S is called the 'range' off Thus:

$$\text{ran} f = \{y \mid y \in T \land \exists x \in S. f(x) = y\}$$

For $f \in$ S→T, T is called the 'codomain' of f. There is no accepted term for S, although if f is total, then S = dom$f$. For partial f, the term 'source' has been suggested for S. Unfortunately, there is little general agreement about many of these terms; for example, 'range' is often used to mean 'codomain' as defined above.

Associated with any function $f \in$ S→T, there is a set of pairs called the 'graph' off, defined:

$$\text{graph} f = \{(x,y) \mid (x,y) \in S \times T \land f(x) = y\}$$

Because any function f applied to a member x of its domain yields a unique value, the set of pairs which constitute the graph of f has the following uniqueness property:

$$\forall x \in \text{dom} f, y_1, y_2 \in \text{ran} f. (x, y_1) \in \text{graph} f \land (x, y_2)$$
$$\in \text{graph} f \Rightarrow y_1 = y_2$$

Conversely, any subset of $S \times T$ which conforms to this condition is associated with a unique function. Because there is very close association between a function and its graph, they are sometimes considered identical. In the Z notation, for example, functions are defined as being their graphs.

For $f \in$ S→T and $S1 \subseteq$ S, a function restriction operator can be defined, which restricts the domain of f to $S1 \cap \text{dom} f$. The function $f \mid S1$ is defined such that:

$$\text{dom}(f \mid S1) = S1 \cap \text{dom} f$$

$$(f \mid S1)(x) = f(x) \text{ for } x \in S1 \cap \text{dom} f$$

$(f \mid S1)(x)$ is not defined for $x \in S - (S1 \cap \mathrm{dom}\, f)$

An extended function can be defined, given $f{:}\mathrm{S}{\rightarrow}\mathrm{T}$. The extended function, usually also denoted by f (by 'abuse of notation'), is of type $\mathscr{P}\mathrm{S} \rightarrow \mathscr{P}\mathrm{T}$, and is defined such that, for $S1 \subseteq S$:

$$f(S1) = \{y \mid \exists x \in S1.y = f(x)\}$$

If $T1 = f(S1)$, $T1$ is sometimes called the 'image' of $S1$ under f. In some computer science contexts, it can be useful to consider the 'finite functions' from S to T, that is, partial functions whose domains are finite. For example, such finite functions can be an abstraction of arrays. An n-dimensional array whose elements are of type T and whose indices range from l to m is a representation of a finite function which is a member of $N{\rightarrow}T$ (or, synonymously, TN). There is no accepted notation for distinguishing finite partial functions from general partial functions. In the $\mathbb{Z}$ notation the symbol $\twoheadrightarrow$ is used, but this is not widely recognised.

Thus, given sets S, T, we can construct new sets $S{\rightarrow}T$, $S{\rightarrow}T$, being the set of total and partial functions respectively from S to T. These can again stand as abstractions of data types in computing, as well as abstractions of computations, i.e. algorithms, and programs whose executions calculate the results of applying the abstract functions. This gives rise to questions as to whether we need to distinguish finite functions as abstractions of finitary data types, i.e. types whose values contain finite information, or even whether we should distinguish computable functions at the abstract level.

These are debatable questions. Provided a function is finitely representable, for example, by an algorithm with a finite description, there is no reason why it should not be an abstraction of a value of some data type. Indeed, in several high-level languages, procedures are treated as first-class data objects, for which nonfinite functions would be required as abstractions.

It is certainly not possible to represent non-computable functions in a computer program, and so one might think that restricting the class of functions in a specification to computable functions would make it more difficult to specify unimplementable requirements. However, this is not usually done. To enable general proofs that any given function definition defines a computable function would require excessive restrictions on the expressibility of the logical calculus used for the definitions, to the point of negating their usefulness.

4.4.1 *Function composition*

Given functions $f \in R{\rightarrow}S$ and $g \in S{\rightarrow}T$, a 'function composition' operator o is defined:

$$g \circ f \in R{\rightarrow}T$$
$$\forall x \in \mathrm{dom}\, f.(g \circ f)(x) = g(f(x))$$

Function composition is associative, i.e. given $f \in R{\rightarrow}S$, $g \in S{\rightarrow}T$, $h \in S{\rightarrow}T$, then:

$h \mathrm{o} \, (g \mathrm{o} f) = (\, h \mathrm{o} g \,) \mathrm{o} f$

since, for any $x \in \operatorname{dom} f$:

$(h \mathrm{o} \, (g \mathrm{o} f)) \, (x) = ((\, h \mathrm{o} g \,) \mathrm{o} f)(x) = h(\, g \, (f \, (x \,)))$

A statement in a programming language can be regarded as a function which transforms values of the variables in whose scope the statement lies. Given two such statements S1 and S2, their sequence:

S1;S2

has the effect of $f2 \mathrm{o} f1$ where S1 has the effect of the function $f1$ and S2 has the effect of $f2$. For this reason, in some contexts, the statement combinator ';' has been adopted as a mathematical notation, so that:

$f1; f2$

means the same as:

$f2 \mathrm{o} f1$

4.4.2 Functions of more than one argument

Functions can in general have more than one argument. A function f with two arguments, each of which belongs to a set S,T respectively, is characterized:

$f{:}S,T{\rightarrow}R$

where R is the codomain of f. f is then applied to two (or more) arguments, by writing:

$f(x, y)$

where $x \in$ S, $y \in$ T.

This notation is traditional and familiar from school mathematics. It can be explained in terms of functions of one argument in two separate ways. The first is to treat the arguments as a tuple belonging to a Cartesian product, thus:

$f{:}S \times T{\rightarrow}R$

Then the function application uses the tuple construction (x,y). The second way of explaining a function of more than one argument is by 'Currying'. A Curried function takes the arguments one at a time and produces a new function, until the last argument is taken. Thus:

Curry $f: S \rightarrow (T \rightarrow R)$

When Curry f is applied to an element of S it yields a function which, when applied to an element of T, yields an element of R. This technique can be extended to any number of arguments. Currying functions enables them to be treated in terms of λ-expressions, and also gives rise to a more succinct explanation of partial functions.

4.4.3   Properties of functions

For the set of functions $S \rightarrow S$ mapping a set S to itself, there is a special function called the 'identity' mapping or function, id, which maps each member of S to itself. Thus:

$$id(x) = x \text{ for all } x \in S$$

It follows that for all functions f $\in S \rightarrow S$:

$$id \circ f = f = f \circ id$$

If $f,g \in S \rightarrow S$ are such that $f \circ g = id$, then g is called the 'inverse' of f. It follows that f is also the inverse of g because:

$$g \circ (f \circ g) = g \circ id = g$$
$$g \circ (f \circ g) = (g \circ f) \circ g$$

so:

$$g \circ f = id$$

The inverse of a function f is written f^{-1}.

A function $f \in S \rightarrow T$ is called 'one one' or an 'injection' if, for each $y \in ran f$, there is at most one $x \in dom f$ such that $y = f(x)$. This is expressible as:

$$\forall x_1, x_2 \in dom f.f(x_1) = f(x_2) \Rightarrow x_1 = x_2$$

It follows that, for an injection f, if f is finite:

$$card \, dom f = card \, ran f$$

A function f $\in S \rightarrow T$ which is such that ran $f = T$ is called a 'surjection' and is said to map S onto T. A total function which is an injection and a surjection is called a 'bijection' or a 'one one correspondence'. A bijection has the property that its domain and range are of equal cardinality. This fact can be used as a definition of cardinality: a set S is of cardinality n if there is a bijection from S to the range of natural numbers $\{1:n\}$. We can then extend the idea of cardinality to define cardinality of infinite sets: two sets S and T have the same cardinality if there is a bijection from S to T. A set S is said to be countable if either S is finite or if there is a bijection from S to N. A set is said to be uncountable if it is not countable. The following standard results are easily proved:

$\mathbb{Z}$ is countable
$\mathscr{P}\,\mathbb{N}$ is uncountable
$\mathbb{N}\rightarrow\mathbb{N}$ is uncountable
$\mathbb{N}\rightarrow\mathbf{B}$ is uncountable
$\mathbb{R}$ is uncountable
$\mathscr{F}\mathbb{N}$ is countable

Where:

1. $\mathbb{Z}$ is the set of integers
2. $\mathbb{N}$ is the set of natural numbers
3. $\mathbf{B}$ is the set of truth values, true and false
4. $\mathbb{R}$ is the set of real numbers
5. $\mathscr{P}$ stands for powerset
6. $\mathscr{F}$ stands for finite powerset

Any Cartesian product of countable sets is countable.

Since, in general, computer programs transform input values to output values in a predictable, definable, and deterministic way, functions are abstractions of computer programs and of many of the constructs which occur in computer programs. In general any construct in a program is an implementation of a function which transforms values of inputs and variables in whose scope the construct lies, to new values of those variables, and possibly output values. Examples of such constructs include statements, 'functions' (e.g. Pascal functions), procedures, expressions.

4.4.4   Disjoint union

A further way of constructing a set from existing sets is by means of the 'disjoint union', 'discriminated union', or, simply, 'sum' operator (all of these being synonymous).

Given two sets, S, T, a new set can be constructed which is usually denoted:

S ⊕ T

or simply:

S + T

(Note the symbol ⊕ is used for other purposes in the Z language.) This set is intuitively like set union, except that if S and T share members, then these are represented in S ⊕ T by distinct copies of themselves. Thus S ⊕ T can be modelled by the union of disjoint copies of S and T. However, the definition of S ⊕ T is given by axioms relating the operators which can be applied to it. These operators are:

```
inj1:S→S⊕T
inj2:T→S⊕T
proj1:S⊕T→S
proj2:S⊕T→T
```

The operators above are related by the rules:

For $x \in S, y \in T$:
proj1(inj1(x)) = x
proj2(inj2(y)) = y

Frequently, when the context permits no risk of ambiguity, the injection and projection function applications are omitted.

Disjoint union can be modelled by constructing the union of isomorphic copies of S and T, by, for example, labelling the copies of the members of S with the label '1', and the copies of the members of T with the label '2'. Thus if $x \in S \cap T$, then $1{:}x$ and $2{:}x$ will separately be members of $S \oplus T$. These can be modelled in a computer program by records which have an appropriate label field.

Clearly:

$$\text{card } (S \oplus T) = \text{card } S + \text{card } T$$

It also makes sense to talk about $S \oplus S$, and $\text{card}(S \oplus S) = 2*\text{card } S$. Like (Cartesian) products, disjoint unions, or sums, can be extended to a multiplicity:

$$\bigoplus_{i=1}^{n} S_i$$

denotes the disjoint union of *n* sets, and:

$$\bigoplus_{i \in I} S_i$$

denotes the disjoint union of an I-indexed family of sets. The corresponding injection and projection functions are, in both cases:

$$\text{inj}_I\colon S_i \to \oplus S_i$$
$$\text{proj}_i\colon \oplus S_i \to S_i$$

with the set of rules:

$$\text{proj}_i(\text{inj}_i(x)) = x \text{ for } x \in S_i$$

It is, of course, perfectly possible, and straightforward, to define a concept of labelled or tagged disjoint union, with the injection and projection functions being distinguished from each other by the tag which labels the component set S_i, in an analogous way to tagged Cartesian products. This is slightly less common, however, and we shall not pursue the details here.

4.4.5   Sequences

The multiple Cartesian product:

$$\bigtimes_{i=1}^{n} S_i$$

can be further extended to a general sequence, in the case where all the Si are the same set S. The following abbreviation is used:

$$S^n = \overset{n}{\underset{i=1}{\times}} S_i$$

A sequence S* of elements over S is defined:

$$S^* = \underset{n \geq 0}{\cup} S^n$$

Thus S* contains as elements all tuples of the form:

$\text{make}_S{}^n(x_1,...,x_n)$

where $x_1,..., x_n \in$ S. These elements of S* are more often abbreviated: $[x_1,...,x_n]$

The context usually determines to what set S_n the sequence belongs. S0 is taken to be that set containing just one member, the empty sequence. So:

S0 = {[]}

Other brackets for delimiting sequences are in common use: < > and ( ).

The empty sequence, abbreviated [], is strictly:

$\text{make}_S()$

for some S. However, it is usual practice to consider all such empty sequences identical, i.e.:

$\text{make}_S() = \text{make}_T()$

even when S≠T. However, the semantic situations in which the distinction arises are infrequent in practice, and it is possible to define the semantics of the empty sequences either as being distinguished by their type or not.

The same selection operator is defined on sequences as is defined on multiple tuples. If $[x_1,...,x_n] \in$ S*, then select$_S$:S*, N→S is defined:

$\text{select}_S ([x_1,...,x_n],i) = x_i$
for $1 \leq i \leq n$.

This operator is usually abbreviated;
if $t = [x_1,...,x_n]$:

$t(i) = x_i$

or:

$t_i = x_i$

Other operators are defined on sequences. Assuming $t = [x_1,...,x_n]$, $hd:S^* \to S$ and $tl:S^* \to S^*$ are defined:

$$hd\ t = x_1$$
$$tl\ t = [x_2,...,x_n]$$

The above are not defined when applied to empty sequences.

4.4.6 Concatenation

$\|:S^*,S^* \to S^*$ is defined:

$(t\|u)(i) = t(i)$ for $1 \le i \le n$ where $t = [x_1,...,x_n] = u(i-n)$ for $n < i$

A length operator len,|_| or #, where $len:S^* \to N$ is defined:

$$len\ t = n$$

Some obvious observations can be made:

$$len\ (t\|u) = len\ t + len\ u$$
$$len\ tl\ t = len\ t\text{-}1$$
$$t(i) = (tl\ t)(i\text{-}1)\ \text{for}\ i > 1$$
$$t\|[] = t = []\|t$$
$$len[] = 0$$

All these operators, and hence sequences themselves, can be defined in an axiomatic style.

Composite sets constructed using the various set operations can be used to define abstractions of the many different program language data types such as arrays, records, files, etc.

4.5 Relations

A relation R between two sets A, B is a subset of the Cartesian product $A \times B$. Thus any such relation is a set of pairs (a,b) with $a \in A$, $b \in B$.

A relation is thus, in general, a many-many correspondence. It can be used to capture the possession of attributes by individuals. The database for a telephone accounts system, for example, could indicate the possession of various facilities by subscribers by means of a relation between the set of subscribers and the set of facilities.

Another intuitively immediate example is the various relationships between members of a population. The relation 'is a cousin of' is a many-many relation from the set of members of the population to itself. A relation R from a set S to the same set S is said to be 'on' S.

Functions are, as already stated, closely associated with their graphs. For a function $f: A \rightarrow B$, the graph of f is indeed a set of pairs and is a relation:

$$\text{graph } f \subseteq A \times B$$

For this reason, in some disciplines (Z for example) functions are regarded as special cases of relations.

We normally write aRb for $(a,b) \in R$.

4.5.1 Properties of relations

There are a number of special properties and classes of relations on a set. A relation R on a set S is defined to be:

1. *Symmetric* if, for all $a, b \in S$, $aRb \Rightarrow bRa$.

2. *Reflexive* if, for all $a \in S$, aRa.

3. *Transitive* if for all $a, b, c \in S$, $aRb \wedge bRc \Rightarrow aRc$.

4. *Antisymmetric* if, for all distinct $a, b \in S$, $aRb \Rightarrow \neg bRa$.

5. *Irreflexive* if, for all $a \in S$, $\neg aRa$.

4.5.2 Equivalence relations

A relation R on a set S is called an 'equivalence relation' if R is reflexive, transitive, and symmetric.

Such a relation conveniently captures ideas of equivalence, or possessing the same properties. For example, in a database of subscribers for a telephone system, there is an equivalence relation relating subscribers who have the same facilities. There is an equivalence relation between terms in an algebra which evaluate to the same value, or between computer programs which calculate the same function.

Two degenerate equivalence relations on a set S can be distinguished. The maximal relation relates each member of S to every other:

$$R1 = \{(a,b) \mid a,b \in S\}$$

The other degenerate relation is the minimal equivalence relation in which each member of S is related only to itself:

$$R2 = \{(a,a) \mid a \in S\}$$

4.5.3 Equivalence classes

Every equivalence relation R on a set S induces a set of 'equivalence classes', which comprise a partition of S. That is, each equivalence class is a subset of S, they are pair-wise disjoint, and every member of S belongs to some equivalence class. Each equivalence class is such that all the members of the equivalence class are related to each other by R. Thus the definition of the equivalence classes induced by R on S is:

$$\{ SS \mid SS \subseteq S \wedge \forall a \in SS. \forall b \in S. aRb \Leftrightarrow b \in SS \}$$

Transitivity of the equivalence relation R ensures that the equivalence classes are pair-wise disjoint.

An example is the relation of equality modulo n for some number n, over the integers. This partitions the integers into n equivalence classes. The numbers in each class will give the same remainder when divided by n.

A common notation for the unique equivalence class to which an element a belongs is [a].

4.5.4   Partial orders

A relation which is reflexive, transitive, and antisymmetric is called a 'partial order'. A set S with a partial order R is called a 'partially ordered set' or 'poset', and written (S,R).

Many examples of partially ordered sets exist: for example, $(\mathscr{P}S, \subseteq)$ for any set S, $(\mathbb{N}, <), (\mathbb{R}, <), (\mathbb{R}, <)$.

Given a poset $(S, \sqsubseteq)$, the relation $\sqsubseteq$ can be extended to subsets of S thus:

$$x \sqsubseteq T$$
$$P \sqsubseteq y$$

where P, T $\subseteq$ S, means that:

$$\forall z \in T . x \sqsubseteq z$$
$$\forall z \in P . z \sqsubseteq y$$

respectively. In those cases, x is a lower bound of T, and y is an upper bound of P.

The greatest lower bound (glb) written $\sqcap$ T and least upper bound (lub) written $\sqcup$ T of a subset T of S are defined:

$$(\sqcap T) \sqsubseteq T \wedge \forall x \in S . x \sqsubseteq T \Rightarrow x \sqsubseteq (\sqcap T)$$
$$T \sqsubseteq (\sqcup T) \wedge \forall x \in S . T \sqsubseteq x \Rightarrow (\sqcup T) \sqsubseteq x$$

The lub $\sqcup \{x,y\}$ of a pair of elements x,y can be written as an operator $x \sqcup y$. Likewise the glb can be written $x \sqcap y$. These are called the 'join' and 'meet' respectively. These operators can easily be proved to be commutative and associative, i.e.:

$$x \sqcup y = y \sqcup x$$
$$x \sqcap y = y \sqcap x$$
$$x \sqcup (y \sqcup z) = (x \sqcup y) \sqcup z$$
$$x \sqcap (y \sqcap z) = (x \sqcap y) \sqcap z$$

The operations can be defined by axioms. Axioms for the Booleans (not the usual ones) could be expressed:

A poset in which every pair of elements has a meet and a join is called a 'lattice'. It follows by induction that in a lattice every finite subset has a lub and a glb.

A lattice can be defined in terms of the meet and join operators, in which case:

$$x \sqsubseteq y \Leftrightarrow x \sqcap y = x \wedge x \sqcup y = y$$

A set of propositions closed under $\wedge$ and $\vee$, forms such a lattice with $\sqcap$ corresponding to $\wedge$, $\sqcup$ corresponding to $\vee$, and $\sqsubseteq$ corresponding to $\Rightarrow$.

A lattice in which every subset has a lub and a glb is called a 'complete lattice'.

If $(S, \sqsubseteq)$ is such a lattice, then $\sqcup S$ is written T, and $\sqcap S$ is written $\bot$, the top and bottom elements respectively. Thus $\bot \sqsubseteq S$, $S \sqsubseteq T$.

An example of a complete lattice is the set of all functions of type $A \rightarrow B$ where A is any set and where $\sqsubseteq$ is defined:

$$f \sqsubseteq g \Leftrightarrow \forall x \in A. f(x) \Rightarrow g(x)$$

Then $f \sqcap g$ is:

$$(f \sqcap g)(x) = f(x) \wedge g(x)$$
$$(f \sqcup g)(x) = f(x) \vee g(x)$$

Further, for a set of functions $F \subseteq A \rightarrow \mathbf{B}$:

$$\sqcap F(x) = \forall f \in F. f(x)$$
$$\sqcup F(x) = \exists f \in F. f(x)$$

Lattices are fundamental to domain theory, which forms the theory of denotational semantics.

4.5   Algebras

An algebra consists of a finite number of sets (its carriers) together with a finite number of functions or (synonymously) operations defined on those sets. Constants can be considered as operations with no arguments.

Examples

1.   The Boolean algebra consisting of the set B with constants true, false, and operations:

$$\neg : \mathbf{B} \rightarrow \mathbf{B}$$
$$\wedge : \mathbf{B}, \mathbf{B} \rightarrow \mathbf{B}$$
$$\vee : \mathbf{B}, \mathbf{B} \rightarrow \mathbf{B}$$
$$\Rightarrow : \mathbf{B}, \mathbf{B} \rightarrow \mathbf{B}$$
$$\Leftrightarrow : \mathbf{B}, \mathbf{B} \rightarrow \mathbf{B}$$

The operations can be defined by axioms. Axioms for the Booleans (not the usual ones) could be expressed:

$\neg$true = false
$\neg$false = true

For $x \in \mathbf{B}$:

true $\wedge x = x$
false $\wedge x =$ false
true $\vee x =$ true
false $\vee x = x$
true $\Rightarrow x = x$
false $\Rightarrow x =$ true

2. The Natural numbers consisting of the set N with constants 0, 1 and operations +, *.

3. The above two algebras can be combined together. Axioms for N may be expressed:

$$x + 0 = x$$
$$x + (y + 1) = (x + y) + 1$$
$$x \times 0 = 0$$
$$x \times (y + 1) = (x \times y) + x$$

We can then define additional operators:

$$\geq : N, N \rightarrow \mathbf{B}$$
$$\leq : N, N \rightarrow \mathbf{B}$$
$$> : N, N \rightarrow \mathbf{B}$$
$$< : N, N \rightarrow \mathbf{B}$$

with axioms:

$$x \geq x = \text{true}$$
$$(x + 1) \geq x = \text{true}$$
$$x > y = \text{true} \land y \geq z = \text{true} \Rightarrow x \geq z = \text{true}$$
$$x \leq y = y \geq x$$
$$x < y = \neg x \geq x$$
$$x > y = y < x$$

4. A classical example of an algebra is a Group. A group has a carrier S, operations +:S, SÆS, -:SÆS, and a constant 0: S. The axioms are:

$$x, y, z \in S$$
$$0 + x = x$$
$$x = x + 0$$
$$x + (y + z) = (x + y) + z$$
$$x + (-x) = 0$$
$$(-x) + x = 0$$

In fact the above does not specify a single algebra, but a whole class of algebras, all of which are groups. For example, the integers with +, - and 0; the strictly positive Real numbers with *, reciprocal and 1; the integers modulo n with +, - (defined as $-x = n - x$), 0; and numerous others.

If one is given the symbols for operations and carrier sets, and axioms, but the carriers themselves are not specified, one has an 'algebraic specification'. In general many algebras conform to such a specification, and the specification can be used as a specification for a program.

If, on the other hand, the carriers are specified precisely and the operations defined either by axioms or more constructively, then the algebra can stand as a so-called 'model-based' specification for a program. The techniques VDM and Z use such model-based approaches.

4.6 Mathematical models and specification languages

Specifications provide the criterion for the acceptability of a piece of software to perform a particular task. The specification should be precisely stated in terms that the client can accept as representing their requirements and that the system designers can use as a definitive starting point for their design task. This means that specifications will be stated at a higher level of abstraction than the design or its implementation, but also in a form that is more precise than the original statement of the requirements. In common with other engineering disciplines, specification can be seen as the result of a process involving the presentation and synthesis of mathematically precise descriptions.

In software terms, a model-based specification is a description of the functionality of a software system presented in terms of a particular state space, together with a collection of operations and functions that act on it. These operations and functions are expressed in terms of a standard collection of basic data types and other type constructors.

Two commonly used specification languages, Z and VDM, share a common model-based approach to specification. Specifications in either notation introduce functions, types and predicates whose structure is intended to convey the semantics of a particular system. The most interesting general point of similarity is that they have the same view of what a software system consists of. This shared view says that a software system is a state space together with a series of operations and functions that act upon it. Software specifications express a relation upon the state space, and the intrinsic properties of the operations that are to be implemented. In some sense, a software system is considered to be a kind of state machine in which operations are applied successively one after another to produce outputs in response to input choices. The BSI/VDM and Z notations have both been given formal semantics (see Larsen et al (1989) and Spivey (1988)) and represent different trade-offs, in specification language design.

4.6.1 Z

Z originated in the paper 'Specification Language' by Abrial, Schumann and Meyer (1980). In 1980 Abrial, Tim Clement and Ib Sørensen, all of the Programming Reserach Group (PRG), started work on a project to specify formally and implement the 'Caviar' (Computer-aided Visitor Information and Reception) system. During this project the notation went through a re-design and the expressive power of classes was developed a little further through the introduction of a class-conjunction operator (which today would be recognized as schema conjunction). Towards the end of the project Abrial (1981) outlined a proof system for the mathematical sub language (a rudimentary proof system for classes appears in the same document, but was felt at the time to be a little obscure). The language which emerged from the redesign was essentially the same as the mathematical sub-language of Z, but the concrete syntax employed was very much more verbose. It was under the impact of Dana Scott's verdict on the notation 'too long-winded', that the Z group decided to revert to standard mathematical notation.

It was at this point that Cliff Jones and Lockwood Morris joined the PRG. Both were to play an important role in the development of Z; in Morris's case through the constructive criticism of the work of the Z group, and in Cliff Jones's case through the form of competitive collaboration. Impetus for the further development of schemas came from the realization that the standard mathematical forms of extending states and promoting the operations on them were too unwieldy for use in the specification of large-scale systems.

What was wanted was a formalism in which extension and promotion were as simply expressible as they were in the VDM metalanguage but for which proof rules could be given directly. The nucleus of what later became known as the schema calculus emerged from this effort, and it was Morris's critique of the early attempts to explain conjunction of schemas that forced the first serious attempt at formalizing a proof rule for schema conjunction. It was also in this phase of the development that the idea that a state should contain as little redundancy as possible, then advocated by the VDM school, was rejected (Sufrin, 1983).

The next important step in the development of Z coincided with the arrival of Carroll Morgan at the PRG in 1982. He and Sufrin worked together on a description of the Unix file system (1984) and it was here that, for the first time, the schema calculus was fully employed. Schemas were used to describe operations as well as describing state and schema disjunction, piping and hiding (all invented by Morgan) were used for the first time.

Further development in Z were due to Spivey (1988) with a semantic model and Hayes (1987) through his active development of case studies. In addition a Z Reference Manual was produced which provides a concise specification of the language (Spivey 1989).

4.6.2   VDM

The origins of VDM lie in the IBM Laboratory in Vienna. The IBM Laboratory originated in a group which Heinz Zemanek brought from the Technische Hochschule, (now the Technische Universitat Wien). The group initially worked on hardware projects. A compiler for Algol 60 followed. The recognition that language definition was a crucial issue for the future safe application of computers was emphasized by IBM's creation of the PL/1 language. The Vienna group built on the ideas of Elgot, Landin and McCarthy to create an operational semantics approach capable of defining the whole of PL/1 including its tasking features which involved parallelism. These massive reports were known as the 'Universal Language Document 3' and appeared in three more or less complete versions. The meta-language used was dubbed by outsiders the 'Vienna Definition Language' or VDL. These descriptions were used as the basis for research into compiler design in 1968/70.

The English VDM school, inspired by the publication of Jones (1980), resulted in further development impetus for the VDM language. In 1982 ITT IDEC, later to become STC IDEC, evaluated VDM for use in the development of an office automation product. The evaluation report (Hudson, 1982; Jackson et al., 1985) commented favourably on VDM and recommended its use on the project. Amongst its observations were that VDM, as expressed in Jones (1980), was not suitable for large-scale industrial applications as it lacked effective means for structuring specifications, facilities for specifying exceptions, an appropriate pseudo-code into which specifications could be refined and appropriate support tools. Two initiatives sprung from this report. Firstly, a VDM-like language called GREEN was developed along with a syntax and type-checker (Shaw et al., 1984). GREEN was based on a similar language (Beichter et al., 1982) produced by the IBM Laboratory in Boeblingen, Germany.

In with the development of GREEN, a separate activity was initiated to develop formally and specify an enhanced version of VDM based on Jones (1980 and 1981). This work resulted in the production of a concrete syntax, an abstract syntax, context conditions, proof obligations, type model (Monohan, 1987) and denotational semantics (Monohan, 1995) for the language. Amongst the new language features developed were means for structuring specifications including the idea of quotation, means for specifying exceptions, higher-order functions (with a restricted form of polymorphism) and 'not yet defined' types and functions. The STC Reference Language (STC-RL), as it was called, became the starting point for the BSI VDM initiative.

4.7 References and bibliography

Abrial, J.-R., Schuman, S. A. and Meyer, B. (1980) Specification language. In *On the Construction of Programs: An Advanced Course* (R. McKeag and A. Macnaghten, eds), Cambridge University Press

Barringer, H., Cheng, J. H. and Jones, C. B. (1984) *A logic covering undefinedness in program proofs.* At-la Informatica, 21, 251 269

Barwise, J. (I 989) *Mathematical proofs of computer system correctness.* Notices of the American Malhematical Society, 36, 844-851

Bear, S. (1988) *Structuring for the VDM specification language.* In VDM'88: VDM — The Way Ahead (Bloomfield et al., eds), pp 2-25

Bjorner, D. and Jones, C. (1978) *The Vienna Development Method — The Meta Language LNCS 61*, Springer-Verlag

Bjorner, D. and Jones, C. B. (1982) *Formal Specification and Software Development*, Prentice Hall International

Bjorner, D., Hoare, C. A. R. and Langmaack, H. (eds) (1990) *VDM'90. VDM and Z Formal Methods in Software Development, Lecture Notes in Computer Science 428*, Springer-Verlag

Bjorner, D., Jones, C. B., Mac an Airchinnigh, M. and Neuhold, E. J. (eds) (1987) *VDM'87: VDM A Formal Method at Work, Lecture Notes in Computer Science 252*, Springer-Verlag

Bloomfield, R., Marshall, L. and Jones, R. (eds) (1988) *VDM'88: VDM The Way Ahead, Lecture Notes in Computer Science 328*, Springer-Verlag

Blyth, T. S. (1986) *Categories*, Longman

Dijkstra, E. W. (1976) *A Discipline of Programming*, Prentice-Hall

Diller, A. (1990) *Z: An Introduction to Formal Methods*, John Wiley

Ehrig, H. and Mahr, B. (1985) *Fundamentals of Algebraic Specification Volume 1, EATCS Monographs 6*, Springer Verlag

Ehrig, H. (ed.) (1985) *Formal Methods and Software Development, Lecture Notes in Computer Science 186*, Springer-Verlag

Enderton, H. (1975) *Elements of Set Theory*, Academic Press

Fitzgerald, J. and Jones, C. B. (1990) *Modularizing the Formal Description of a Database System, Technical Report UMCS-90-1-1*, Department of Computer Science, University of Manchester

Gordon, M. J. C. (1979) *The Denotational Description of Programming Languages*, Springer Verlag

Gries, D. (1981) *The Science of Programming*, Springer Verlag

Hall, J. A. (1990) *Using Z as a specification calculus for object oriented systems. In VDM'90. VDM and Z Formal Methods in Software Development* (Bjorner et al., eds), Springer-Verlag

Halmos, P. R. (1960) *Naive Set Theory*, Van Nostrand

Hayes, I. (1987) *Specification Case Studies*, Prentice Hall International

Hayes, I. J. and Jones, C. B. (1989) *Specifications are not (necessarily) executable. Software Engineering Journal*, 4, 320-338

Hoare, C. A. R. (1969) *The axiomatic basis of computer programming, Communications of ACM*, 12, 576-583

Hoare, C. A. R. (1985) *The Mathematics of Programming*, lecture, Clarendon Press, Oxford

Hoare, C. A. R. and Sanders, J. W. (1986) *Data refinement refined. In Lecture Notes in Computer Science 213, pp 187-196*, Springer-Verlag

Hudson, P. (1982) *Evaluation of VDM, Technical Report 244 00004-AA*, ITT IDEC

Jackson, M. I., Denvir, B. T. and Shaw, R. C. (1985) *Experience of introducing the Vienna Development Method into an industrial organisation. In Formal Methods and Software Development* (H. Ehrig, ed.), Springer-Verlag

Jones, C. B. (1973) *Formal Development of Programs, Technical Report TR12.117*, IBM Hursley

Jones, C. B. (1980) *Software Development, A Rigorous Approach*, Prentice Hall

Jones, C. B. (1986) *Systematic Software Development Using VDM*, Prentice Hall

Jones, C. B. (1990) *Systematic Software Development Using VDM,* (2nd edn), Prentice Hall

Jones, C. B. and Shaw, R. C. (1990) *Case Studies in Systematic Software Development*, Prentice Hall

King, S. (1990) *Z and the refinement calculus. In VDM '90. VDM and Z Formal Methods in Software Development* (Bjorner et al., eds), Springer-Verlag

King, S. and Sorensen, I. H. (1989) *From secification, through design to code: a case study in refinement. In Formal Methods: Theory and Practice* (P. N. Scharbach, ed.), Blackwell Scientific

Kyburg, H. E. (1984) *Theory, and Measurement*, Cambridge University Press

Lakatos, I. (1978) *The Methodology of Scientific Research Programmes*, Cambridge University Press

Larsen, P. G., Arentoft, M. M., Monohan, B. Q. and Bear, S. (1989) *Towards a formal semantics of the BSI/VDM specification language. In Information Processing '89* (G. X. Ritter, ed.), Elsevier Science Publishers B.V. (North-Holland), pp 95-100

Manna, Z. and Weldinger, R. (1985) *The Logical Basis for Computer Programming*, Addison Wesley

McMorran, M. A. and Nicholls, J. E. (1990) *Z User Manual, Technical Report TR12.274*, IBM United Kingdom Laboratories Ltd

Middleburg, C. A. (1989) *VVSL: A language for structured VDM specifications. Formal Aspects of computing*, 1, 115-135

Monohan, B. Q. (1985) *A Semantic Definition for the STC VDM Reference Language, Technical Report*, STC IDEC Ltd

Monohan, B. Q. (1987) *A type model for VDM. In VDM '87: VDM A Formal Method at Work* (Bjorner et al., eds), Springer-Verlag

Morgan, C. (1990) *Deriving Programs from Specifications*, Prentice Hall International

Morgan, C. and Sufrin, B. (1984) *A formal specification of the Unix file system*. IEEE Software Engineering, SE-10

Popper, K. (1972) *Conjectures and Refutations*, Routledge and Kegan Paul

Rydeheard, D. and Burstall, R. (1988) *Computational Category Theory*, Prentice Hall

Schmidt, D. (1986) *Denotational Semantics*, Allyn & Bacon, Newton, Mass., USA

Schonfinkel, M. (1924) *Uber die Vausteine der Mathematischen Logik*, Math. Anal., 92, 305

Spivey, J. M. (1988) *Understanding Z, Cambridge Tracts in Theoretical Computer Science*, Cambridge University Press

Spivey, J. M. (1989) *The Z Notation, A Reference Manual*, Prentice Hall

Stoy, J. (1977) *Denotational Semantics*, MIT Press, Cambridge. Mass,, USA

Thatcher, J., Wagner, F. and Wright, J. (1979) *An initial algebra approach to the specification, correctness and implementation of abstract data types. In Current Trends in Programming Methodology, Vol. 4* (ed. R. T. Yeh), Prentice Hall, pp. 80-149

Turski, W. M. and Maibaum, T. S. E. (1987) *The Specification of Computer Programs*, Addison-Wesley

Wittgenstein, L. (1969) *On Certainty*, Blackwell, Oxford

Woodcock, J. (1989a) *Calculating properties of Z specifications. ACM Sigsoft Software Engineering Notes, 15*

Woodcock, J. (1989b) *Structuring specifications in Z. IEE Software Engineering Journal, 4*

Woodcock, J. and Loomes, M. (1988) *Software Engineering Mathematics,* Pitman

Wordsworth, J. B. (1987) *A Z Development Method, Technical Report,* IBM United Kingdom Laboratories Ltd

Chapter 5
Numerical computation

5.1   Introduction

A very wide variety of different kinds of computer arithmetic is currently available. For example, virtually all computers offer integer arithmetic, while one or more floating-point systems (such as single and double-length floating-point arithmetic) are frequently featured. There are also more specialized forms of computer arithmetic, such as interval computation (discussed later), and numerous experimental arithmetic systems. In general, a particular arithmetic system can be supported by hardware, software, or some software/hardware combination. So a computer arithmetic system can be any specific combination of the hardware or software for the arithmetic operations and the associated scheme for representing numbers as bit strings within the machine.

Virtually all computers support the four basic integer arithmetic operations, if only because these are required for indexing and addressing. Computer integer arithmetic is typically exact, with two exceptions. First, the range of integers that can be represented is not infinite but is bounded above and below. Second, the result of an integer division is usually given as a quotient and remainder, since fractions are not representable within a scheme for integers only. Note that as only a finite range of integers can be represented, the product of two integers may be too large for the representation scheme. In such cases an overflow condition is usually signalled. Integer arithmetic is adequate for many computing applications, provided care is taken to keep the integer quantities concerned within the available range. Furthermore, any rounding or inaccuracies that do arise must be handled carefully in a consistent way. For example, calculations involving currencies can be handled using integer arithmetic and working in terms of the smallest unit involved, provided rounding errors like those involved in currency conversions and interest calculations are properly handled. Suitable methods for rounding and for keeping the integer quantities concerned within the representable range are generally quite easily devised once the problems are fully appreciated, and integer arithmetic is perfectly satisfactory for many software engineering applications.

The handling of currency quantities in terms of multiples of the smallest unit involved suggests a variant of integer arithmetic, in which quantities are still represented as integers but with an implied decimal (binary) point at some fixed place within them. For example, a length in metres might be represented as an integer number of millimetres, with an implied point in the appropriate position. This type of working is known as fixed-point arithmetic, with the fixed point most frequently being taken to be at the leftmost end of the representable integers, so all fixed-point quantities lie between 0 and 1.

Fixed point addition and subtraction are exactly like their integer counterparts, but multiplication and division are different. In fixed-point multiplication the most significant half of the double-length product is retained, instead of the least significant half. This means that overflow is impossible but underflow (the returning of a zero result to indicate a quantity too small to represent) is a possibility. In fixed-point division, overflow occurs unless the divisor is greater in magnitude than the dividend.

Fixed-point arithmetic has been used successfully for many numerical computations, but the constant need for the scaling of results to avoid overflow and underflow makes its use tedious and error-prone.

It is rarely used for numerical computation, except in special cases, e.g. for the few computers that do not offer floating-point instructions. The use of floating-point arithmetic, in which the operations themselves take care of scaling within the available range and accuracy of representable numbers, is far simpler, and floating-point arithmetic is the preferred choice for the vast majority of contemporary numerical computations. For this reason, the following sections of this chapter are concerned exclusively with floating-point arithmetic.

It is important at this point to note one major difference between integer arithmetic on the one hand, and fixed and floating-point arithmetic on the other.

In integer arithmetic, all the basic arithmetic operations are accurate, in the sense that they all deliver exactly the same result as the corresponding mathematical operations, provided only that the operands and the result of the operation are within the range of representable integers. Further, there are no representation errors involved in integer arithmetic. For integers within the representable range there is no possible loss of accuracy in conversions between an integer quantity on an external medium and its representation as a bit string within a computer.

Any particular floating point representation is charaterised by the base, precision and exponent range. In other words the basic parameters of all integers are:

1. The base, b
2. The precision, p
3. The maximum exponent, e_{max}
4. The minimum exponent, e_{min}

These define a system of floating-point numbers consistsing of zero and all numbers of the form:

$$x = f.b^e$$

where: $f = \pm(f_p b^{-1} + ... + f_p b^{-p})$

with: $f_1 = 1..., b-1$

$$f_2, ..., f_p = 0, ..., b-1$$

$$e_{min} \le e \le e_{max}$$

Fixed and floating-point arithmetic support fixed numbers of significant digits of accuracy. Thus they are typically prone both to representation errors and to errors associated with the basic arithmetic operations. Such errors can be avoided in special cases for example. many floating-point systems incorporate accurate arithmetic for small integers but in general they are unavoidable. These basic facts about inaccuracy are at the heart of most, if not all, of the problems of numerical computation, and will be discussed further in the following sections.

Having introduced numerical computation and computer arithmetic systems in general, much more detailed consideration of floating-point arithmetic follows, as it is of central importance for numerical computations. Floating-point arithmetic is introduced in detail, both in general terms and in terms of typical implementations. Subsequently the problems of error control in numerical computation are addressed.

5.2 Floating-point arithmetic

This section describes the basic properties of floating-point arithmetic as it is commonly implemented on computers. An idealised view is given, removed from the details of the implementation of floating-point arithmetic or any particular machine, in an endeavour to show how errors in numerical computation may arise at the level of the basic arithmetic operations themselves.

Starting with the way floating-point numbers are represented, this idea should be familiar from the 'scientific' notation for numbers in terms of a mantissa and an exponent. The idea of a floating-point number representation as used within computers is just the same, a quantity n being represented by the pair of quantities (f,e) where:

$$n = f.b.^e$$

and b is a machine-dependent constant called the base of the representation.

Here f is called the fraction part (or mantissa) of the representation and e is an integer called the exponent of the representation.

For a given machine, the floating-point base, b, is fixed (some typical values being 2, 10 or 16). Also fixed are the number of base-b digits of f and the range of possible values of e; these last quantities determine the range and accuracy of the arithmetic offered. The range of representable numbers is given by the range of values of e, an overflow condition arising if e_{max} is exceeded and an underflow condition resulting if e takes a smaller value than e_{min} These parameters for a floating-point number system are summarised on page 180 and some representative parameter values for different floating-point arithmetic systems are given in Table 5.1.

System	Base, b	Precision p (number of base b digits)	Minimum Exponent (e_{min})	Maximum Exponent (e_{max})
IBM 370/168				
Single	16	6	-64	63
Double	16	14	-64	63
DEC VAX				
Single	2	24	-127	127
Double	2	56	-127	127
Honeywell 6000				
Single	2	27	-128	127
Double	2	63	-128	127
IEEE binary standard				
Single	2	24	-126	127
Single extended	2	≥32	≤1022	≥1023
Double	2	53	-1022	1023
Double extended	2	≥64	≤16382	≥16383

Table 5.1: **Characteristics of some floating-point systems**

A characteristic of the scientific notation for numbers is that a given number may be represented in more than one way for example:

$$3.14159E0 = 0.314159E1 = 0.0314159E2 = 3.14159$$

In floating-point number representations used on computers, the representation satisfying:

$$b^{-1} < |f| < 1$$

is generally taken to be standard, f being represented as a string of base-b digits with an implicit radix point at the left-most end. Floating-point representations satisfying this condition (giving a unique representation for each number) are said to be normalized. So if we use base-10 and the conventional notation for scientific numbers, the normalized representation of 3.14159 is 0.314159E1, while that of 27000 is 0.27E5.

Most of the floating-point arithmetic operations offered on current computers give their results in normalized form, so it is usual for all floating-point quantities arising within a computation to be held in that form. However, unnormalized arithmetic is occasionally useful and some machines offer it, although this is always in addition to the conventional normalized operations. Unnormalized arithmetic extends the range of representable numbers, albeit with some loss of accuracy. Also, it may be possible to use unnormalized arithmetic to provide an indication of the amount of accuracy in a floating-point result, although this is exceedingly difficult in general.

The previous remarks about errors in numerical computation may be amplified in the case of floating-point computation by making it clear that an extremely important characteristic of floating-point numbers, from the programmer's point of view, is that they should always be regarded as potentially inaccurate. This inaccuracy has several sources. It may stem initially from the fact that the floating-point representation used in the computer cannot match the known accuracy of the input data, or the input data may not be exactly representable as a floating point number within the computer. For example, the decimal constant 0.1 is not exactly representable as a floating-point number unless the base b has 10 as a factor. This excludes the common cases $b = 2$ and $b = 16$. A further frequent source of error is rounding. A number of different rounding methods have been implemented with some floating-point units offering a choice of rounding method. Note that additional errors may be introduced during floating-point computations as a result of roundings and cancellations during the execution of the individual arithmetic operations.

Consider purely as an example a decimal floating-point system with five significant digits of accuracy. Rounding errors in addition are unavoidable. In fact, if the quantities being added are too different in magnitude the smaller may be treated as if it were zero.

Example

$$0.50000E1 + 0.10000E-7 = 0.50000E1$$

Cancellation may lead to loss of accuracy in addition or subtraction.

Example

$$0.50000E1 - 0.49999E1 = 0.10000E-3$$

Further comment on this example may be helpful. If the two operands represent exact floating-point quantities, then the result of the operation reflects the difference between them and no further comment is necessary. However, bearing in mind the earlier remark that floating-point quantities should always be regarded as potentially inaccurate, if the operands represent approximate values, the loss of significance is serious since it greatly decreases the number of significant digits (i.e. increases the rounding error) in the result of the operation. Cancellation in the calculation of a sum $u + v$ reveals previous errors in the computation of u and v.

Having illustrated very briefly the kinds of errors that may result from the naive use of the basic floating-point arithmetic operations, it remains to consider how their effects may be minimized by the use of careful programming.

5.2.1 *Machine floating-point arithmetic*

A wide range of floating-point number formats have been used in different computers; some idea of the variability can be gained from Table 5.1. For example, the overall length of a floating-point number (which governs both the exponent range and the accuracy offered) ranges at least from 32 to 128 bits. Further, there is no standardization of the base, b, of the representation used. Values of 2, 10 and 16 are found among contemporary systems, with decimal ($b = 10$) floating-point arithmetic featured on many calculators, and hexadecimal ($b = 16$) floating-point arithmetic offered on the IBM System/ 360 and its subsequent developments. Precise details of the signalling of overflow vary, as do those of the occurrence of underflow, which may be signalled or ignored, with some machines simply replacing underflowed quantities with zero without informing the programmer. Normalized arithmetic is generally offered, but sometimes unnormalized arithmetic is available too, if only for the provision of gradual underflow' in which quantities slightly smaller in modulus than the smallest attainable normalized floating-point number are stored with diminished accuracy.

Overflow and underflow are major problem areas with portability. The following considerations apply:

1. If the machine has an asymmetric range, the statement *y: = x* may cause overflow or underflow.

2. On some machines the statement *y := x/x* may cause overflow or underflow.

3. If *x* is very small, the statement *y := 1.0*x* may cause underflow on an attempted normalization, and the statement **if** (*x≠0*) **then** *y:=1/x* may cause division by zero, *x* being regarded as non-zero by the comparison but not by the division! This example illustrates the general principle that comparisons for the equality or inequality of floating-point numbers should not be used because of the inherent inaccuracy of all floating-point quantities.

Further variations between different floating-point hardware units may be found in the areas of the accuracy of arithmetic operations (some units improve accuracy by the use of extended-precision registers internal to the floating-point unit), or in details of the rounding conventions used.

Besides such variations in the arithmetic offered, there are other problems, possibly caused by design errors in the floating-point hardware concerned. For example, on some computers there are small,

representable and computable floating-point numbers x satisfying:

$x \neq 0$

which also satisfy one of the identities:

$1.0*x = 0$ or $x + x = 0$

This means, for example, that a parameter representing the underflow threshold (the smallest representable and computable floating-point number supported by the machine) can be seriously misleading, in that this quantity does not behave in the way the programmer might feel entitled to expect. Further examples of unexpected machine behaviour can also be given. For example, some floating-point hardware units contain an error that sets the least significant bit of a floating-point number to 0 when multiplying it by 1.0.

An important response to the wide variation and numerous shortcomings of floating-point units was the development of the IEEE standards for floating-point arithmetic. These standards were designed with great care by experts in the field and have been implemented for a number of different machines. Features include guaranteed accuracy for arithmetic operations, a variety of rounding modes and a selection of traps and other exceptional conditions. As intended, these standards are becoming widespread and their general use should do much to raise standards in floating-point programming.

5.2.2 Portability of floating-point arithmetic

In the absence of similar universal (i.e. universally applied) standards, writers of portable numerical software need a way to write floating-point programs that provide equivalent numerical performance on different floating-point units. An approach that has been widely tried is to write programs using a set of parameters that characterizes the available floating-point arithmetic. However, as already briefly illustrated, the disadvantage of this approach is that there is no way of avoiding machine-dependent irregularities in the arithmetic.

A more comprehensive approach to this problem is manifested by the idea of 'model' floating-point arithmetic. The basic idea is to introduce a regular and realistic model of floating-point arithmetic that can be fitted to existing floating-point units in such a way as to minimize the effects of any machine-dependent irregularities in the arithmetic. This is done by identifying for each floating-point unit a subset of the arithmetic capabilities offered by the floating-point hardware, typically identified by reduced range and/or accuracy, for which the arithmetic performance is guaranteed to be sufficiently regular for the application of conventional error analyses. In other words, machines exhibiting unsatisfactory behaviour are 'penalized' by reductions in the range and/or accuracy for which conventionally regular behaviour is obtained.

Brown's 'model' of floating point arithmetic (1981) is an excellent quantitative description of the reliability of floating-point arithmetic on many different machines, the 'penalization' associated with it being an effective way of masking machine-dependent irregularities. Unfortunately, the model is difficult to apply correctly as the programmer receives no help from the computer hardware in keeping within the model boundaries. For example, the model overflow and underflow thresholds frequently differ from those detected by the machine hardware, so the user must test to see that they are not violated.

It is worth noting that Brown's 'model' was used as the basis for the floating-point arithmetic incorporated in the Ada programming language. The design of the Ada language broke new ground in addressing questions of floating-point portability.

5.2.3 Floating-point arithmetic and formal specification

The detailed characteristics of any floating-point system are far from straightforward, which militates against the prospect of being able to use such arithmetic in any software that is formally specified in a reasonably straightforward way. However, if one discounts floating-point units exhibiting machine-dependent irregularities, there is no reason in principle why floating-point arithmetic should not be used in a rigorous way. The complexities involved make this rather a daunting prospect.

5.3 Floating-point programming techniques

Enough has been written already to indicate that floating-point programming is full of pitfalls for the unwary, and that specialized techniques may be necessary to get the most accurate results from a given combination of problem and floating-point unit. The purpose of this section is to give a few examples of the kinds of programming techniques that are sometimes used. Only the very briefest of surveys can be given.

5.3.1 Some tricks of the trade

Sometimes special measures are needed because of the characteristics of the floating-point arithmetic in use. An example is the avoidance of machine-dependent irregularities in arithmetic of the kinds mentioned earlier. Another example concerns a multiplication by $\pi/2$ in a trigonometric functional routine. On hexadecimal machines, the normalized representation of $\pi/2$ starts with three zeros, whereas that of $2/\pi$ does not. The result is that division by $2/\pi$ is almost one significant decimal digit more accurate than multiplication by $\pi/2$ on such a machine.

A related problem is that of range reduction for functions such as $\sin(x)$ with arguments in radians. The requirement is to reduce the argument modulo 2π, which must be done with great care, especially for large arguments. The solution involves holding an appropriate constant to extended precision, and also raising an error condition if the argument given is too large for the range reduction, as programmed, to deliver acceptable accuracy in the final result.

Sometimes rearrangement of expressions or scaling of intermediate results is necessary to avoid loss of information by cancellation, or termination of a calculation due to overflow or underflow. As an example, consider the evaluation of the roots of a quadratic equation:

$$ax^2 + bx + c = 0$$

using the familiar formula:

$$x = \frac{-b \pm \sqrt{(b^2 - 4ac)}}{2a}$$

Some of the hazards that may attend a naive evaluation of this formula are;

1. If b is very large, overflow may occur during evaluation of b^2.

2. If $b^2 = 4ac$, there may be an unacceptable loss of accuracy in forming the discriminant ($b^2 - 4ac$).

3. If $b^2 > 4ac$ there may be unacceptable loss of accuracy in forming one of the roots.

This list is not exhaustive, simply serving as an illustration of the kinds of programming problems that may arise.

The types of technique which might be brought to bear on such problems depend both on the computer arithmetic in use and the precise circumstances of a particular case, but typical responses might comprise such suggestions as:

1. Use of alternative arithmetic (e.g. double-length floating-point) for evaluation of the discriminant.

2. Radical rearrangement of the formula, for example as a rational approximation or a power series.

3. Reformulation of the whole problem (of which the solution of the quadratic equation formed one small step) to avoid the need to solve the equation explicitly.

Numerous other examples of these kinds of rearrangement can be quoted. For example, if we have evaluated $f(x)$ and $f(a + \varepsilon)$ for given f, x and small ε, cancellation will frequently occur when evaluating ($f(x + \varepsilon) - f(x)$). Such cancellation may often be avoided by the device of finding symbolically an expression for $g(x) = (f(x+\varepsilon) - f(x))/\varepsilon$ and then calculating $\varepsilon * g(x)$. This is a simple example of how the symbolic rearrangement of an expression can help in its accurate computation.

5.3.2 Alternatives to floating-point arithmetic

Because of the difficulties of accurate floating-point programming, it is natural to ask whether alternatives to the conventional floating-point operations can be devised to provide better performance in terms of error propagation.

Since all floating-point quantities are inherently inaccurate, it is possible to represent such quantities not as single numbers but as intervals within which their true values lie. Then an algorithm delivering a single numerical result would instead produce an interval within which its result is known to lie, a technique sometimes called 'guaranteed inclusion' of results. This is obviously a very attractive idea, but straightforward replacement of all floating-point operations by their interval equivalents rarely produces satisfactory results.

Another alternative to conventional floating-point arithmetic, and in fact one that can be used to implement the basic operations of interval arithmetic, is the Karlsruhe Accurate Arithmetic (KAA). The idea here is that the basic conventional float-

ing-point operations with good error behaviour are augmented
with a new operation that allows scalar products to be calculated
with a single rounding error. Improved error behaviour of many
algorithms can result if the method is properly used, but again
naive use of the technique may well not produce any significant
improvement in the accuracy of the delivered results of complete
algorithms.

5.3.3 Error control

Extended numerical computations comprise long sequences
of floating-point arithmetic operations, each of which is subject to
the types of error discussed already. The study of error propagation in such calculations is an important aspect of numerical
analysis, the discipline concerned with the development of effective numerical algorithms for various mathematically formulated
problems. A detailed discussion of numerical analysis lies outside
the scope of this chapter, but the way error propagation is typically
handled by numerical analysts is discussed here briefly.

An alarming phenomenon in numerical analysis is the existence of so called ill-conditioned problems, which are exceedingly
sensitive to small changes in the input data. Ill-conditioning is
instructive, if only to serve as a reminder of how important error
analysis can be if any reliance at all is to be placed on the results
of a computation. An example of ill-conditioning is given below.
Finally, the section looks briefly at the scope for error control in
extended computations afforded by various alternatives to conventional floating-point arithmetic.

5.3.4 Error analysis

Any discussion of the error behaviour of algorithms resulting
from the basic shortcomings of floating-point arithmetic should
certainly be related to conventional error analysis.

If a quantity x approximates the value of an exact quantity x,
it is common to define the terms absolute error, referring to
quantity:

$$n = x - \hat{x}$$

and the relative error given by:

$$\hat{x} = x(1 + e)$$

Conventional error analysis is usually formulated in terms of
the relative error, taking as basic the equation:

$$Xofy = (xoy)(1 + \delta)$$

where o denotes any of the basic arithmetic operators (+, -, x,
/) and of denotes the corresponding floating-point arithmetic
operation. The error term, δ, is then assumed to reflect satisfactory
rounding behaviour; in terms of the quantities defined in Figure
5.1, the term δ is given by the equation:

$$|\delta| < \varepsilon$$

where

$$\varepsilon = b^{1-p}$$

represents a 'unit in the last place' (ulp) of the fraction part of the floating-point representation used.

Starting from this point, the conventional treatment of errors in numerical analysis follows a well-defined path expounded in many introductory numerical analysis texts. A distinction is drawn between forward and backward error analysis. In forward analysis, an equation equivalent to the relative error equation above is applied repeatedly to the steps of a calculation, bounding the accumulated error at each step and hence eventually the error of the final result. Backward analysis, on the other hand, starts with the computed solution and works backwards to reconstruct the perturbed problem of which it is an exact solution. Backward analyses are usually easier to perform than forward ones, and generally lead to more useful evaluations of the numerical methods in use.

5.4 References and bibliography

Alefeld, G. and Herzerberger, J. (1983) *Introduction to Interval Computation*, Academic Press, New York, USA

Barrett, G. (1987) *Formal methods applied to a floating point system. Programming Research Group Technical Monograph PRG-58*, Computing Laboratory, Oxford University

Brown, W. S. (1981) *A simple but realistic model of floating point computation. ACM Transactions on Mathematical Software*, 7, 445-480

Brown, W. S. and Feldman, S. I. (1980) *Environment parameters and basic functions for floating-point computation. ACM Transactions on Mathematical Software*, 6, 510-523

Cody, W. J. (1982) *Floating point parameters, models and standards. In The Relationship Between Numerical Computation and Programming Languages* (ed. J. K. Reid) North-Holland, pp 50-67

Cody, W. J. and Waite, W. M. (1980) *Software Manual for the Elementary Functions*, Prentice-Hall

Cody, W. J., Coonen, J. T., Gay, D. M. et al. (1984) *A proposed radix and wordlength-independent standard for floating point arithmetic*. IEEE Micro, 8, 86-99

IEEE P754:1985 *Standard for Binary Floating-point Arithmetic*, IEEE Inc., New York

Knuth, D. E. (1981) *The Art of Computer Programming, Vol. 2, Seminumeral Algorithms*, Addison-Wesley, (i) p 233 (ii) pp 213-223 (iii) p 574 (iv) pp 205-207

Kulisch, U. and Miranker, W. L. (1981) *Computer Arithmetic in Theory and Practice*, Academic Press, New York

Moore, R. (1966) *Interval Analysis*, Prentice-Hall

Ullrich, C. and Wolff von Gudenberg (eds) (1989) *Accurate Numerical Algorithms*, Research Report ESPRIT, Project 107, DIAMOND, Vol. 1, Springer-Verlag

Wallis, P. J. L. (ed.) (1990) *Improving Floating-Point Programming*, J. Wiley, Chichester (i) Chapter 2

Wichman, B. A. (1989) *Towards a formal specification of floating point*. Computer Journal, 32, 432-436

Wilkinson, J. H. (1963) *Rounding Errors in Algebraic Processes*, HMSO, London and Prentice Hall, USA

Wilkinson, J. H. (1965) *The Algebraic Eigenvalue Problem*, Clarendon Press

Chapter 6
Data structures and algorithms

6.1   Introduction

The design and analysis of data structures and algorithms play a very important role in software engineering. If the first two main goals in software development are reliability and maintainability, the third one is definitely efficiency. It is well known that in several applications, such as real-time systems and defence, efficiency is a critical issue. But it is worth stressing that efficiency is also a key issue in several other areas where users need fast and powerful interaction with complex systems (very large databases, expert systems, computer-aided design (CAD) and computer-aided software engineering (CASE) systems etc.). This chapter is describes the design of efficient algorithms and data structures.

According to the most widespread view of software design, based on the principles of modularity and abstraction, a software system can be viewed as a collection of data types, each one composed of a set of data items together with operations on such items. This approach has several advantages, the main one being the provision of a certain degree of independence between the logical specification of the operations and their physical implementation by means of different data structures. This allows the adoption of the particular implementation of a data type that is most suited to meeting the efficiency requirements.

Starting from this point of view, efficiency considerations should not be seen as being in contrast to other design principles. No clear difference can be established between designing algorithms and designing data structures. On the one hand, the efficient performance of an algorithm may derive from the appropriate choice of the implementation of the supporting data type, while on the other, ingenious algorithm design techniques may be exploited to provide efficient implementation complex operations on a data structure.

This chapter provides an overview of the basic techniques for analysing and designing algorithms and data structures with application to searching and sorting.

6.2   Analysis techniques

To evaluate the performance of algorithms various aspects have to be defined: the machine model on which the algorithm is supposed to run, the complexity measure to evaluate, and the type of analysis to be performed.

6.2.1 Machine models and complexity measures

Turing machines are mostly used for studying abstract properes of computations (such as space-time trade-offs or intrinsic ower of time and space bounded computations). As a machine mdel for analysing the complexity of algorithms, Turing machines and related kinds of automata are essentially applied in the analysis of string algorithms (recognition and syntax analysis of formal languages, pattern matching etc.).

In other areas of algorithms different types of machine models are used, ranging from natural (computer-like) models, such as the register machines (also called random access machines (RAMs)), to ad hoc models, defined with the specific aim of udying particular classes of algorithms, such as directed acyclic graphs (DAGs), which are applied in the study of compilers for describing code optimization techniques.

In its simplest version a RAM consists of a control unit, capable of performing the instructions of a very simple machine language, and of an unlimited set of registers (memory cells), each one containing an arbitrarily large non-negative integer. Additionally, the machine has a few special registers:

(a) *Accumulator*, which contains data processed by the instructions.

(b) *Input and output* registers.

(c) *Program counter*, which contains the address of the instruction to be performed next by the machine.

A schematic representation of a RAM is shown in Figure 6.1.

The instructions of a RAM are performed on various kinds of operands:

1. *Integers*. The integer n is denoted $= n$ and the operation is directly performed on the integer n.

2. *Registers*. The ith register is denoted R_i and the operation involves the content of register R_i

3. *Indirectly accessed registers*. The operand is denoted $[R_i.]$ and the operation involves the content of the register addressed by the content of register $R_i..$

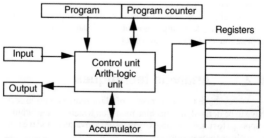

Figure 6.1   *Schematic representation of a RAM.*

We will call data an operand of type (1), (2) and (3) and register an operand of type (2) and (3). A label is simply an integer denoting the (progressive) number of an instruction (that is the instruction whose label is n is the nth instruction of a program). All registers that have not yet been accessed are set to 0. The basic instructions of a RAM are:

1. I/O instructions

READ <register>	read from input into register
PRINT <register>	print output from register

2. Copy from/to accumulator and registers:

LOAD <data>	load data into accumulator
STORE <register>	save content of accumulator into register

3. Arithmetic operations

ADD <data>	add data to content of accumulator
SUB <data>	subtract data from contet of accumulator
MULT <data>	multiply content of accumulator by data

4. Flow control instructions

JZERO <label>	jump to label if content of accumulator equal to zero
JGTZ <label>	jump to label if content of accumulator greater than zero
JUMP <label>	jump to label unconditionally
HALT	execution of the programstops

A program stops either when it comes to a HALT instruction or when it would otherwise jump to a non-existent instruction. When an algorithm is described by a RAM program its performance may be measured in two different ways:

1. *Uniform costs.* The cost of any instruction that is performed is equal to I and the overall cost of the execution of the algorithm is equal to the number of instructions that are performed; this way of evaluating computation costs is simple but leads to rather unnatural effects since it allows access to an arbitrarily large memory and the manipulation of arbitrarily large integers with unitary costs.

2. *Logarithmic costs.* The cost of an instruction depends upon the size of the accessed storage and the size of processed data (content of accumulator and content of registers). Since we imagine all integers expressed in binary notation the 'size' of an integer corresponds to its logarithm in base 2. For example, if the content of the ith register is n and the content of the accumulator is m, the

cost of the instruction 'ADD R_i' is: $\log i + \log n + \log m$. Though more complex, this cost measure is more accurate and realistic since it takes into account the physical limitations of the abstract model.

Example

Let us consider the simple algorithm for the sum of n integers $a_1, a_2, ..., a_n$, given in Figure 6.2. Let us suppose that the integers are stored in the registers R4, R5,...,R(3 + n) and that register R1 contains a pointer to such registers. In addition, register R2 contains the sum of the n integers and register R3 contains the integer n.

1	LOAD	= 3
2	STORE	R1
3	LOAD	R1
4	ADD	= 1
5	STORE	R1
6	LOAD	[R1]
7	ADD	R2
8	STORE	R2
9	LOAD	R3
10	SUB	= 1
11	STORE	R3
12	JGTZ	3
13	HALT	

Figure 6.2   RAM program for the sum of n integers

If we use the uniform cost criterion, since the loop is repeated n times, the program takes time a $n + b$ to be performed, where a and b are constants depending respectively on the length of the loop (10) and on the number of instructions (3) of the initialization and termination phases. If we use the logarithmic cost criterion instead, we have to consider that the sums at instruction 7 have a cost depending on the largest among the n integers (say a_{MAX}) and that the number of registers that have to be accessed is dependent on n. Hence the overall cost determined in this more precise way will be $c n (\log n + \log a_{MAX}) + d$ where again c and d are suitable values which depend on all other constant costs.

Its realism and accuracy mean that the RAM model also provides a good point of departure for the analysis of algorithms expressed in a high-level language or even in natural language. In this case the analysis is based on finding a dominant operation (that is, an operation whose contribution to the overall cost of the algorithm is at least of the same order of magnitude as the cost of all other operations) and in determining the cost of the algorithm in terms of this operation, as a function of some meaningful parameter of the input. For example, a sorting algorithm may quite reasonably be evaluated in terms of the number of comparisons executed as a function of the number of elements to be sorted. For these reasons, the analysis of an algorithm is often performed starting from a high-level description of the algorithm and only when one needs a very precise estimate of cost is it necessary to refer to a specific machine model.

6.2.2 Asymptotic analysis

The performance evaluation of algorithms and programs is usually based on an asymptotic analysis of the time (more rarely, space) execution costs as the size of the input tends to infinity. This means that, in an example such as the preceding one, we might have avoided determining the precise values of the constants (a b and c, d) and have simply said that the cost grows like n according to the first cost criterion, and like $n \log n$ according to the second, as n tends to infinity.

The drawback of asymptotic analysis is that in several practical cases we are not interested in the limit behaviour of an algorithm so much as in the behaviour for instances with small size. In these cases ignoring the constants may not be correct. For example, in comparing two algorithms for small-size data we may prefer using an algorithm which takes time $2n2$ than one that takes time $10000 \ n \log n$. Still asymptotic analysis provides a first approximate evaluation of the efficiency of an algorithm.

To express asymptotic analysis a specific notation has been introduced, called 'big-oh' notation. If two positive functions $t(n)$ and $g(n)$ are given we say that:

$t(n)$ is $O(g(n))$

if there are two positive constants c and n_0 such that, for all

$n \geq n_o$:

$t(n) \geq c \ g(n)$

For example, the function $t(n) = a \ n \log n + bn + c$ is $O \ (n \log n)$ The big-oh notation is usually applied for expressing both the worst-case behaviour of an algorithm and the average-case behaviour.

Let us denote by $t_A(x)$ the cost of executing algorithm A on input x . Let:

$t_A(n) = \max \ \{t_A(x) \ / \ \text{size} \ (x) = n\}$

In the worst-case asymptotic analysis we are interested in determining the asymptotic growth of $t_A(n)$.

In several cases, when we do not have severe efficiency constraints, we may use average-case asymptotic analysis instead of worst case. In this case we examine the growth of the function:

$t_A(n) = E \ \{t_A(x) \ / \ \text{size} \ (x) = n\}$

where $E\{t_A(x0) \ | \ \text{size} \ (x) = n \ \}$ denotes the expected cost of executing the algorithm on an instance x of size n, assuming that we know the probability distribution of the instances of size n.

Example

Let us consider two algorithms for sorting an array of *n* elements: SELECTION-SORT and INSERTION-SORT, respectively shown in Figures 11.3 and 11.4.

```
procedure SelectionSort (var vect: array [I . . N] of
integer);

var i, j, index to min, tmp: integer;

begin { SelectionSort }
    for i:= I to N—I do
        begin
            index to_min := i;
            for j : = i + I to N do
                if vect[j] < vect[index_to_min] then
index
                to min: = j;
            tmp := vect[index_to_min];
            vect[index_to_min] := vect[i];
            vect[i] := tmp
end
end; { SelectionSort }
```

Figure 11.3   *SELECTION-SORT*

```
var i, j, tmp: integer;

begin { InsertionSort }
    for i :=2 to N do
        begin
        tmp := vect[i];
        j :=i-1;
        while (j > = I) and (tmp < vect[j]) do
            begin
                vect[j + 1]: = vect[j];
                j := j-1;
            end;
        vect[j + 1]: = tmp
    end
end; { InsertionSort }
```

Figure 11.4   *INSERTION_SORT*

In the case of SELECTION-SORT both the worst-case and the average-case analysis are very simple. Since the algorithm essentially consists of determining the smallest key among *n*, *n-1*,..., *2* keys, the overall number of comparisons to sort the elements of the array is:

$$\sum_{i=2}^{n} (i-1) = n(n-1)/2$$

that is, $O(n^2)$, whatever the previous ordering of the array. This means that in all cases, and hence also in the average case, the execution cost of the algorithm is the same.

The situation with the INSERTION-SORT algorithm is quite different. In this algorithm the second, third, ... , *n*th keys are checked against the preceding ones in the array until the proper place is found. The cost is hence determined by (actually exactly equal to) the number of inversions in the array, that is, the number of pairs A[*i*], A[*j*] in the array such that *i*<*j* while A[*i*]>A[*j*]. Let us denote by inv(*j*) the number of inversions with respect to element A[*j*]. Then the overall number of inversions is:

$$\text{INV}(n) = \sum_{j=2}^{n} \text{inv}(j)$$

Clearly in the best case (the array is already sorted) the number of inversions is 0, while in the worst case it will be $n(n-1)/2$. It turns out that in the worst case the algorithm again takes time $O(n^2)$. The analysis of the average case complexity shows instead a better performance. To derive such an analysis we have to make some reasonable hypothesis about the distribution of the possible permutations of an array with n elements and compute the average number of inversions according to such a distribution. If we assume that all permutations are equally likely we have that for every element j:

$\text{Prob}\{\text{inv}(j)=1\} = \text{Prob}\{\text{inv}(j)=2\} = ...$
$= \text{Prob}\{\text{inv}(j) = j-1\} = 1/j$

Hence, if we denote $E(\text{inv}(j))$ the expected value of $\text{inv}(j)$ we have: $E(\text{inv}(j)) = (j-1)/2$ and consequently:

$$E(\text{INV}(n)) = \sum_{j=2}^{n}(\text{inv}(j)) = 1/2 \sum_{j=2}^{n}(j-1) = n(n-1)/4$$

This means that, while being still $O(n^2)$, the average cost of INSERTION-SORT is one half the worst case cost.

6.2.3 Analysis based on recurrence relations

Several problems may be efficiently solved by making use of a design technique consisting of decomposing the problem into subproblems and then recombining the solutions to obtain the solution to the original problem. This technique is called divide et impera (divide and rule).

Beside being important for algorithm design, this technique is also useful in the analysis phase because its inherent recursion allows the derivation of cost equations in the form of recurrence relations. A recurrence relation is an equation in which a function is recursively defined in terms of the values that the function itself takes for smaller values of the argument.

Example

Let us consider again the problem of sorting an array. A classical method based on divide and conquer is the algorithm MERGE-SORT, shown in Figure 6.5.

Suppose we are given an array with $2n$ elements. To determine the number $T(2n)$ of comparisons needed to sort the array we may simply observe that such a number is given by the solution of the following equation:

$$T(2n) = 2T(n) + n$$

since to sort the array of size $2n$ we have to sort two arrays of size n and we need n comparisons to merge the two sorted arrays. The solution of the equation gives:

$$T(n) = \log n$$

This shows that the MERGE-SORT algorithm is asymptotically more efficient than the two algorithms that were presented before.

```
procedure Merge (v1, v2: array [1..N] of integer;
                 i1. j1, i2, j2: integer;
                 var v_out: array [1..N] of integer;
                 i_out: integer);

    { merges v1[i1 .. j1] and v2[i2 .. j2] into: v_out
[i_out . (j1 + j2 - i2 + 1 + i_out)] }

var i: integer;

begin { Merge }
    while (i1 < = j1 ) and (i2 < = j2) do
        begin
            if v1[i1] < = v2[i2]
                then begin
                    v_out[i_out] := v1[i1];
                    i1 := i1 + 1
                end
                else begin
                    v_out[i out]: = v2[i2];
                    i2 : = i2 + 1
                end;
            i_out = i_out + 1
        end
    if i1 > j1
        then for i := i2 to j2 do
            begin
                v_out[i_out]: = v2[i];
                i out:=i out+1
            end
        else for i := i1 to j1 do
            begin
                v_out[i_out]:=v1[i];
                i_out: = i out + 1
            end
end
end; { Merge }

procedure MergeSort1 ( var vect: array [1..N] of
integer; i, j: integer);

var half: integer;

begin { MergeSort1 }
    if i < j then
        begin
            half: = (i + j) div 2;
            MergeSort1(vect, i, half);
            MergeSort1(vect,half+ 1,j);
            Merge(vect, vect, i, half, half + 1, j,
                                                vect, i)
        end
end; { MergeSort1 }

procedure MergeSort (var vect: array [1..N] of integer);

begin { MergeSort }
    MergeSort 1 (vect, 1, N)
end; { MergeSort }
```

Figure 11.5   MERGE-SORT

The divide and rule technique has been widely used to derive efficient algorithms in various fields of computer science, such as algebraic algorithms and computational geometry. As a design technique it is particularly advantageous under suitable conditions: not too many sub-problems, balanced decomposition, low cost of recombining the partial solutions. A very important result that has been achieved by a careful application of the technique is the famous Strassen's matrix multiplication algorithm the first matrix multiplication algorithm with a less than cubic (O($n2.81$)) running time.

A fairly general class of algorithms based on the divide and rule paradigm consists in decomposing a problem of size n into subproblems of size n/c. In many cases the cost of recombining the result of the given problem from the partial solutions of the subproblems is linear. In all these cases the recurrence relations have the following general form:

$$T(n)= \begin{cases} b \text{ if } n = 1 \\ a\, T(n/c)+bn \text{ if } n>1 \end{cases}$$

By solving the equation we may determine the computational cost of the solution in the various cases:

1. If $a < c$ then T(n) is O(n).

2. If $a = c$ then T(n) is O($n \log n$).

3. If $a > c$ then T(n) is O($n^{\log_c a}$).

The second case is the MERGE-SORT case where we have $a=c=2$.

In the case of the matrix multiplication algorithm the problem of computing the product of two $n \times n$ matrices may be reduced to the problem of computing seven products of matrices of size $n/2 \times n/2$. This corresponds to the third case and leads to a running time O($n^{\log_2 7}$)

Recurrence relations with the same structure arise in the analysis of many other algorithms. In several other cases the application of the divide and rule technique leads to more complex recurrence relations whose algebraic solution requires sophisticated mathematical tools.

6.2.4 *Analysis of lower bounds*

Beside giving information on the running time of a particular algorithm for the solution of a given problem, the formal asymptotic worst-case analysis also provides an upper bound on the complexity of the given problem, that is, with information on the amount of resource (time, space) that is sufficient to solve the problem.

The notation that is currently used to express a complexity upper bound is again the big-oh. When we say that 'a problem P has a complexity O($g(n)$)' this means that there exists at least one algorithm A for solving problem P whose running time $t_A(n)$ is O($g(n)$).

In order to assess the intrinsic complexity of a problem a second item of information is needed: the amount of resource that is necessary to solve it, no matter what algorithm we choose. This information is called the complexity lower bound.

To express a complexity lower bound a specific notation has been introduced, called omega notation. If two positive functions $t(n)$ and $g(n)$ are given we say that:

$$t(n) \text{ is } \Omega(g(n))$$

if there are two positive constants c and nO such that, for all $n \geq n_o$: $t(n) \geq c\, g(n)$

For example, the function $t(n) = a\, n \log n + b\, n + c$ is $\Omega(n)$ and also $\Omega(n \log n)$.

The omega notation is usually applied for expressing the amount of resource that is necessary to solve a problem. We say that the complexity of a given problem P is $\Omega(g(n))$ if any algorithm A for solving problem P has a running time $t_A(n)$ which is $\Omega(g(n))$, that is asymptotically as large as $g(n)$.

The difficulty of determining a complexity lower bound derives from the fact that it is a characteristic property of the problem and hence it does not depend on a specific algorithm used for the solution. In other words, it is related to the intrinsic computational nature of the problem. This means that the techniques that are used for proving complexity lower bounds (which may be algebraic, geometric, combinatorial, information theoretic techniques etc.) have to be chosen depending on the nature of the given problem.

A technique commonly used for searching and sorting problems, where the complexity is often measured in terms of number of comparisons, is the information theoretic technique. If we are given a problem such that for an input of size n the number of possible outcomes is $h(n)$, by means of a simple information theoretic argument we may state that the complexity of such problem is $\Omega(\log h(n))$. In fact, since identifying an object in a set containing $h(n)$ objects requires $\log h(n)$ bits of information and since any comparison provides a yes-or-no answer (corresponding to one bit of information), no algorithm based on comparisons can solve the given problem with less than $\log h(n)$ comparisons.

Example

By means of the information theoretic argument we can prove that searching for a key in a structure with n keys has a complexity lower bound $\Omega(\log n)$ comparisons.

When the complexity of a problem is neatly characterized by means of an upper bound $O(g(n))$ and a lower bound $\Omega(g(n))$ that are assymptotically coincident, we may say that we have an asymptotically optimal solution of the problem. In this case we use again a specific notation, the theta notation and we say that the complexity of the problem is $\theta(g(n))$.

Example

Since the well-known binary search method (see next section) provides an O(log n) algorithm for searching for a key in an array with n keys we may say that searching has a complexity $\theta(\log n)$

Example

Sorting an array with n keys has a complexity $\theta(n \log n)$. In fact we have seen that the MERGE-SORT algorithm gives an O($n \log n$) upper bound for sorting. Alternatively, using the information theoretic argument, we may derive that sorting takes $\Omega(n \log n)$ comparisons. In fact since the possible outcomes of a sorting algorithm are the $n!$ permutations of the array, the number of comparisons needed by any sorting algorithm are $\Omega(\log n!)$, that is $\Omega(n \log n)$ by Stirling's approximation. Since the upper bound and the lower bound coincide, this means that the complexity of sorting is precisely characterized and is $\theta(n \log n)$ and that MERGE-SORT is an (asymptotically) optimal algorithm.

6.3 Design of efficient data structures and algorithms

In this section fundamental data structures for the implementation of two data types with wide application in software systems will be considered: dictionaries (both in the static and in the dynamic case) and priority queues.

6.3.1 Dictionaries

Let us consider a collection of items (or records), each one consisting of two parts: the key (consisting of that data that characterizes the item, e.g. name and birth date in an employee information system) and the information (consisting of all supplementary data, e.g. the salary). The data type dictionary is a collection of items on which we want to perform the following operations:

1. *insert* (item).

2. *delete* (item).

3. *search* (key), in order to retrieve the associated information.

To implement a dictionary we may use various data structures. Their efficiency depends on the frequency of update operations (insert, delete) with respect to queries (search). If the latter are more frequent we speak of a static case, otherwise we speak of a dynamic case. This describes some of the most relevant data structures both for the static and for the dynamic case.

To make the exposition simpler the items will be considered as consisting only of an integer key and, unless otherwise specified, the way the associated information is stored will not be considered.

6.3.2 Static case

The typical structure used for implementing a dictionary in the static case is the array. If the array is maintained as sorted the well-known binary search method allows the search to be achieved for a key with a logarithmic number of comparisons. The drawback of this implementation, which makes it convenient only in the static case, is the high cost of maintaining the ordering under insertion and deletions.

A second possible implementation is based on lists. It is slightly more convenient for updating but its poor searching performance makes it useful only for small collections of items.

The table in Figure 6.6 shows the costs of the dictionary operations on an array (both in the sorted and in the unordered case) and on a list (the ordering does not affect the efficiency in this case). Note that the costs of insertion and deletion do not include the cost of first searching for the item.

	Insert	Delete	Search
Sorted array	O(n)	O(n)	O(log n)
Unordered array	O(1)	O(1)	O(n)
List	O(1)	O(1)	O(n)

Figure 6.6 *Execution cost of dictionary operations on tables and lists*

When the keys in the array are uniformly distributed the so-called interpolation search' technique may provide a better average access time (O(log log n)) but in the worst case (that is if the uniform distribution hypothesis is not satisfied) the access time is O(n).

A different table based approach to static dictionary management is the direct access method known as 'hashing'.

Let K be the set of possible keys and V the set of addresses in the table. A hash function is a mapping h:K->V. In an ideal situation this would allow access to a key with a single operation. Since, in general, the size of K is much larger than the size of V, the mapping cannot be injective. Hence for two different keys k_1,k_2 we may have $h(k_1) = h(k_2)$. Such a situation is called a collision. Colliding keys may be treated in two ways (see Figure 6.7):

(a) In open hashing, they are put in overflow buckets.

(b) In closed hashing they have to be reallocated in the table.

In both cases insertion and search for a key may require several accesses and this may cause a performance degradation.

The performance of hashing techniques mainly depends on the following two aspects:

1. Quality of the randomization performed by the hash function over the keys (keys should be uniformly distributed over the physical addresses to reduce collision probability).

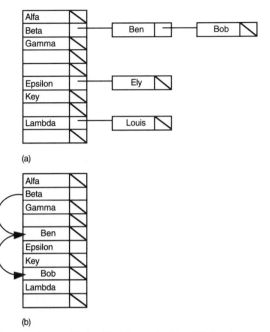

(a)

(b)

Figure 6.7 **Hash table (a) open hashing (b) closed hashing**

2. Efficient management of collisions and (in the case of closed hashing) of reallocation of colliding keys (reallocated keys should not increase the probability of collisions too much).

Let $B(k)$ be the binary string corresponding to the key k and let $|V| = 2^v$ be the size (number of rows) of the table. The most typical hash functions are obtained in the following ways:

1. Cut $B(k)$ in substrings $B_1, B_2, \ldots$ of v bits each and sum over all B_is mod 2^v.

2. Compute $B(k)^2$ and extract v bits from the middle of the result.

3. Compute the remainder of $B(k)/|V|$ (note that in this case $|V|$ should be odd).

The reallocation strategies in closed hashing are based on various probing techniques:

1. *Linear probing,* with constant step d: after collision in position $h(k)$ key is allocated in the first empty position among $h(k) + d, h(k) + 2d, \ldots, h(k) + n$ d. This technique

has the inconvenience of causing what is called 'primary clustering': two keys k_1 and k_2 such that $h(k_2) = h(k_1) + n\,d$ will have the same probing sequence, and hence a high collision probability.

2. *Quadratic probing*. The probing sequence is $h(k) + d$, $h(k) + d + (d + 1)$, ... , $h(k) + n\,d + n(n-1)/2$. Primary clustering is eliminated but secondary clustering still happens: two keys k_1, and k_2 such that $h(k_1) = h(k_2)$ still have the same probing sequence.

3. *Rehashing*. At each step the value of a new hash function is computed depending on the key and on the number of previous collisions. In this way both primary and secondary clustering are eliminated.

6.3.3   Dynamic case

When the frequency of updates is high the table-based implementations of a dictionary are unsatisfactory, especially if operations on secondary storage are required. In this case the most widely used implementations are based on various kinds of trees.

To use trees in the efficient implementation of dictionaries in the dynamic case two conditions have to be satisfied. First, keys have to be associated with nodes in such a way that searching for a key requires access at most nodes from the root to the leaves. Since it is well known that the depth of a complete binary (mary) tree is

$O(\log_2 n)$ $(O(\log_m n))$ where n is the number of nodes of the tree (see Figure 6.8) this condition would guarantee a logarithmic search time.

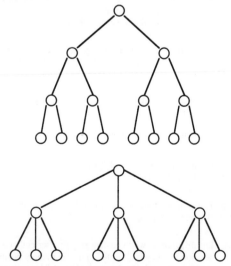

Figure 6.8   *Complete binary and ternary trees*

On the other hand, under insertions and deletions, the tree structure cannot be maintained complete but has, at least, to be maintained in a balanced way, that is, the subtrees branching from a node should contain 'approximately' the same number of keys. If this condition is satisfied logarithmic access time may still be guaranteed.

The main differences between tree implementations of dictionaries depend on how these two conditions are satisfied.

Let us first consider the binary case. A binary search tree is a tree where the key associated with an internal node is smaller than all keys in the right subtree branching from the node and larger than all keys associated with the left subtree (see Figure 6.9).

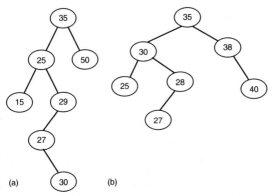

Figure 6.9   *Binary tree searches (a) unbalanced (b) balanced*

Historically the first tree structure that has been proposed for implementing dictionaries are AVL-trees. AVL-trees are binary search trees that are maintained balanced according to the following condition: at any internal node the absolute value of the difference between the depth of the right and of the left subtrees is at most one (see Figure 6.9b)).

If the balancing condition is satisfied it turns out that the minimum number of nodes $N(h)$ in a tree of depth h is given by the following recurrence relation:

$$N(1) = 1$$
$$N(2) = 2$$
$$N(h) = N(h-1) + N(h-2) + 1 \text{ for } h \geq 3$$

By solving the relation it can be shown that in a balanced tree with n nodes the depth is $O(\log n)$ and hence the number of comparisons needed to search for a key is also $O(\log n)$.

To maintain balanced AVL-trees we proceed as follows. When as a consequence of an insert or delete operation the balance condition is violated, a rotation is performed, that is, the nodes in the tree and their associated keys are reorganized in such a way that the balance is recovered. In Figure 6.10 two different trivial cases are considered in which an insert(3) operation might unbalance the tree and rotations are required to recover the balance.

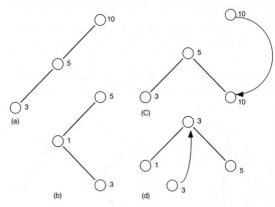

Figure 6.10 *(a) (b) Two unbalanced trees determined by insert(3), (c) (d) the balanced trees resulting from rotation*

To deal with more complex cases a balancing factor equal to -1, 0, 1 and corresponding to the difference between the depth of the left subtree and the depth of the right subtree is associated with all nodes in an AVL-tree. A suitable use of the balance factors allows the maintenance of balance, while performing insertion and deletion of keys, with a number of node accesses and (possibly) of rotations that is proportional to the depth of the tree and, hence, O(log n) again.

In conclusion we may assert that AVL-trees allow the management of all operations on a dictionary of n items in time O(log n).

A simple application of AVL-trees in sorting derives from the observation that visiting an AVL-tree in symmetric order accesses all keys in ascending order. To sort an array A[1...n] the algorithm, named TREE-SORT, performs the following two steps:

1. For all i = 1 to n in the array do insert A[i] on an AVL-tree.

2. Visit the tree in symmetric order and return all accessed keys.

Since both steps take time O(n log n) TREE-SORT is asymptotically optimal.

Despite the fact that AVL-trees allow a complete implementation of dictionaries in the dynamic case in logarithmic time, their performance is still rather poor if implementations on secondary storage are considered. A better performance is obtained by means of a widely adopted structure; the B-tree.

A B-tree is an mary search tree that satisfies the following properties (let us assume m even for sake of clarity:

1. Every internal node (except the root) has d subtrees with $m/2 \geq d \geq m$.

2. The root has at least 2 subtrees.

3. Starting from the root all branches have the same length.

4. To an internal node with d subtrees $T_1, T_2, ..., T_d$, $d-1$ keys $k_1, k_2, ..., k_{d-1}$, are associated, with the property that for all $i(i=1,...,d-1)$ k_i is larger than all keys associated with T_i and smaller than all keys associated with T_{i+1}

5. No keys are associated with the leaves.

Figure 6.11 is an example of quaternary B-tree.

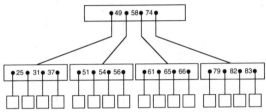

Figure 6.11   Quaternary B-tree

In contrast to the case of AVL-trees, where balance among subtrees is obtained by introducing a condition on their depth, with B-trees balance is based on a condition on the degree d of the nodes. If the condition is maintained the time to search for a key on a B-tree is determined by the number of nodes accessed (bounded by $O(\log_{m/2} n)$) and the cost of searching inside a node (bounded by $O(\log m)$). The overall search cost is therefore $O(\log_{m/2} n \log m)$.

To maintain the balance condition under insertions and deletions, when an attempt is made to insert a new key in a node that already contains $m-1$ keys (that is a node with m subtrees), the node is split into two sub-nodes one containing the $m/2$ smaller keys and the other one containing the $m/21$ larger keys. The intermediate key is moved to the superior node (see Figure 6.12). If the superior node is also already full the splitting is repeated until either a non-full node is reached or, eventually, the root of the B-tree is also split.

Using the node splitting technique, an insertion in a B-tree can be made without violating the balance condition, in time proportional to the depth of the tree.

The case of the deletion operation is treated in a similar way. When we attempt to delete a key from a node with the minimum allowed number of subtrees (m/2), a recombination of the node together with the other adjacent nodes takes place and may lead to a decrease by one level in the depth of the tree. This operation may be performed in logarithmic time.

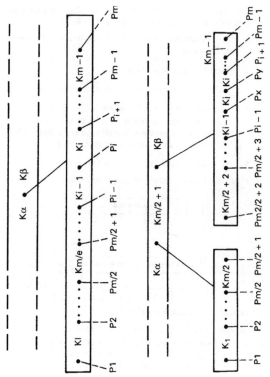

Figure 6.12   Node splitting in a B-tree

In conclusion, a B-tree provides an efficient implementation of a dictionary, allowing the performance of all operations in the dynamic case with a cost:

$$O(\log_{m/2} n \log m)$$

Several variants of B-trees exist (B*-trees, B*-trees etc.) and are frequently used for file management on secondary storage.

In real applications there is a need to keep the number of node accesses as small as possible (that is, m as large as possible, e.g. equal to 100) because node accesses correspond to disk accesses and are the most expensive contribution to the above indicated overall search cost. Besides, it is often the case that the information associated with keys is kept on secondary storage while the B-tree structure (or variants of it) are used as a directory in main storage.

A last class of tree structures for implementing dictionaries are variants of hashing (known as a 'dynamic hashing') which are suitable for dynamic data management on secondary storage.

In dynamic hashing overflow buckets are organized as leaves in a tree structure and keys are distributed among them on the basis of randomization (see Figure 6.13). When a new insertion means that a bucket is going to overflow, it is split in two and keys are randomly distributed in the two twin buckets. In case of underflow two twin buckets may be recombined into one.

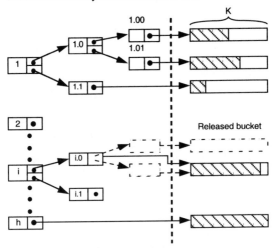

Figure 6.13   Dynamic hashing structure

Various implementations of dynamic hashing are based on different techniques for randomizing the keys and for managing the directory in main storage.

6.3.4   Priority queues

In several combinatorial problems such as job scheduling, shortest paths in graphs, and partial ordering the concept of pnority has to be efficiently managed. A priority queue is a collection of items characterized by a property (priority) consisting of an integer value ranging over a suitable interval. The operations that we want to perform on a priority queue are:

1.   insert (item).

2.   find-max.

3.   delete-max.

If the cardinality of the collection is small a priority queue may be implemented by means of naive structures such as arrays and lists. As in dictionary management, such implementations are rather poor (that is, linear) in terms of the efficiency of maintaining the arrays and sorting lists, and so we keep them unordered

Both AVL-trees and B-trees, the tree structures that efficiently implement dictionaries, may be used for implementing priority queues with logarithmic costs for every operation. In fact

	Insert	Del-: max	Find - max
Sorted array	O(n)	O(1)	O(1)
Unordered array	O(1)	O(n)	O(n)
Sorted list	O(n)	O(1)	O(1)

Figure 6.14   Execution costs of priority queue operations on lists and arrays

we already know that insertions and deletions can be performed in logarithmic time; at the same time the find-max (or find-min) operations can both be performed in logarithmic time because the largest (or the smallest) keys in the dictionary are located at the extreme left (or at the extreme right) in the tree.

Unfortunately, for both AVL-trees and B-trees the management of the tree structures is expensive in time (even though optimal from the asymptotic point of view) and, since explicit tree structures need pointers, costly in terms of space. A data structure that provides an efficient and, in both time and space, optimal implementation of a priority queue, is based on an implicit tree organization and is known as a 'heap'.

A heap of n elements is an array $A[1 \ldots n]$ satisfying the property that for every i:

1. If $2i \geq n$ then $A[i] \geq A[2i]$.
2. If $2i+1 \leq n$ then $A[i] \geq A[2i + 1]$

A heap may be considered to be the level-by-level representation of a binary tree in which all levels are complete except, at most, the lowest one and in which the integer associated with a node is always greater than or equal to the integers associated with both sons. In Figure 6.15 a heap and its corresponding tree representation are shown.

Since, in a heap, the root element has the largest priority, the find-max operation may be performed in constant time O(1). The programs for executing the other two operations are given in Figures 6.16 and 6.17.

Both operations may be performed by simply proceeding along one branch from the root to the leaf in the case of extractmax, or vice versa in the case of insert. Since a heap is an almost complete binary tree (where at most the lowest level is incomplete) and hence its depth is logarithmic with respect to the number of nodes, it follows that both operations require a number of comparisons O(log n).

As well as its applications in the implementation of priority queues, a heap may be applied to derive yet another asymptotically optimal sorting algorithm HEAP-SORT. Given an array $A[1 \ldots n]$, to sort it the algorithm proceeds in the following way.

First, the given array is transformed into a heap by repeatedly applying the insert procedure. Subsequently, by repeatedly applying the extract-max procedure the heap is transformed into a sorted array. By making use of the primitive operations defined above the HEAP-SORT algorithm may easily be expressed (see Figure 6.18).

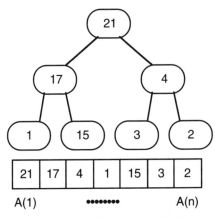

Figure 6.15 **A heap and its corresponding tree representation**

```
procedure InsertIntoHeap
                ( var vect: array [1..N] of integer;
                  k, dim:  integer);

{ dim is the dimension of the heap after inserting the
new value }

var father, son, tmp: integer;
    end_flag: boolean;

begin { InsertIntoHeap }
    vect[dim] := k;
    son: = dim; end_flag := false;
    while (son > I) and not end_flag do
        begin
            father := son div 2;
            if vect[son] > vect[father]
                then begin
                    tmp := vect[son];
                    vect[son]: = vect[father];
                    vect[father]: = tmp;
                    son := father
                    end
                else end_flag: = true
            end
end; { InsertIntoHeap }

procedure CreateHeap (var vect: array [1. . N] of
integer

var i: integer;

begin { CreateHeap }
    for i := 2 to N do InsertIntoHeap(vect, vect[i], i);
end; { CreateHeap }
```

Figure 6.16 **Procedure Insert-into-heap and Create-heap**

```
procedure ExtractMax (var vect: array [1..N] of integer:
            var max integer; dim: integer);

{ dim is the dimension of the heap before extracting the
max }

var left son, right_son, max son, father, tmp: integer;
end_flag: boolean:

begin { ExtractMax }
max := vect[l]:
vect[1] := vect[dim]:
end_flag: = false:
father := 1
    while (father * 2 < dim) and not end_flag do
        begin
            left_son := 2 * father;
            if left_son < dim - 1
                then right_son := left_son + 1
            else right_son := 0; { it does not exist! }
            if right_son > 0
            then if vect[right_son] > vect[left_son]
                then max_son := right_son
                else max_son := left_son
            else max_son := left_son:
            if vect[father] < vect[max_son]
                then begin
                    tmp := vect[father];
                    vect[father] := vect[max_son];
                    vect[max_son] := tmp;
                    father := max_son
                    end
                else end_flag := true
        end
end; { ExtractMax }
```

Figure 6.17   Procedure Extract-max

```
procedure HeapSort (var vect: array [1..N] of integer);

var  i, max: integer:
begin { HeapSort }
    CreateHeap(vect):
    for i := N down to 2 do
        begin
            ExtractMax(vect, max, i);
            vect[i] := max
        end
end; { HeapSort }
```

Figure 6.18   Procedure Heap Sort

6.4   References and bibliography

Adelson Velskii, G. M. and Landis, Y. M. (1962) *An algorithm for the organization of information.* Dokl. Akad. Nauk., 146, 263-266

Aho, A. V., Hopcroft, J. E. and Ullman, J. D. (1974) *The Design and Analysis of Computer Algorithms*, Addison-Wesley

Bayer, R. and McCreight, E. (1972) *Organization and maintenance of large ordered indexes. Acta Informatica*, 1, 173-189

Booch, G. (1987) *Software Components with Ada*, Benjamin Cummings

Ehrigh, H. and Mahr, B. (1985) *Fundamentals of Algebraic Specifications*, Springer-Verlag

Fagin, R., Nievergelt, J., Pippenger, N. and Strong, H. R. (1978) *Extendible hashing. A fast access method for dynamic files*, IBM Res. Rep. RJ2305

Ghezzi, C. and Jazayeri, M. (1987) *Programming Language Concepts, 2nd Edition*, John Wiley & Sons

Greene, D. H. and Knuth, D. E. (1981) *Mathematics for the Analysis of Algorithms*, Birkhauser

Hopcroft, J. E. and Ullman, J. D. (1979) *Introduction to Automata Theory, Languages and Computation*, Addison Wesley

Horowitz, F and Sahni, S. (1976) *Fundamentals of Data Structures*, Computer Science Press, Potomac

Knuth, D. E. (1973a) *The Art of Computer programming, Vol 1, Fundamental Algorithms*, Addison-Wesley

Knuth, D. E. (1973b) *The Art of Computer Programming, Vol 3, Sorting and Searching*, Addison-Wesley

Larson, P. (1978) *Dynamic hashing. Bit*, 18, 184-201

Litwin, W. (1978) *Virtual hashing. A dynamically changing hashing. In Proceedings of Symposium on Very Large Databases*

Maurer, W. and Lewis, T. (1975) *Hash table methods ACM Computing Surveys*, 7, 5-20

Mehlhorn, K. (1984) *Data Structures and Algorithms 3: Multidimensional Searching and Computational Geometry*, Springer Verlag

Sedgewick, R. (1989) *Algorithms, 2nd edition*, Addison-Wesley

Smith, P. D. and Barnes, G. M. (1987) *Files and Databases. An Introduction*, Addison-Wesley

Appendix A
Standards

Introduction

Standards are important in the regulation of the production of software and its deployment. They may be used:

(a) In the procurement of individual items of software, to help ensure that they are fit for the purposes that are intended.

(b) Across areas of technology to ensure the successful interoperation of independent pieces of equipment, as in communication standards.

(c) Within markets to ensure a free market for third party suppliers, as in operating systems and support environments.

(d) Within a company to regulate its development of software.

Standards-making and promulgation are generally associated with official bodies, ranging from the quality assurance (QA) department within a company to national and international bodies. The most prominent of these is the International Organization for Standardization (ISO), but there are many other transnational and regional standardization bodies, both military and civil, as well as national bodies in most countries.

Standards may arise as part of common industrial practice, when they are termed de facto. De facto standards are usually associated with a dominant commercial interest that determines the structure of a market such as the use of the MS-DOS or PC-DOS operating system on IBM PCs and compatibles. This form of standard will not be addressed here, though it must be recognized that de facto standards frequently themselves become the subject of standardization, as has happened in the transition from Unix to Posix.

Standards can take a variety of forms including:

1. Reference models. Some 'standards' do not prescribe particular practices, but instead lay down a framework within which other standards will be formulated (the best known of these is ISO 7498, the Open Systems Interconnection Reference Model).

2. Process standards (sometimes called method standards) are primarily concerned with the process whereby a software product is developed. Process standards deal with the overall regulation of the development process, such as ISO 9000, or with particular parts of the process such as design (e.g. BS6224) or testing (e.g. IEEE 829).

3. Product standards are concerned with specific software products, such as compilers and communications equipment. Within product standards one sometimes distinguishes interface standards, which determine purely what happens at the interface and not what happens within the product as a whole. Most communication protocol standards would be viewed as interfaces, while programming language standards would be viewed as product standards since the language semantics determines what should happen within the compiler.

3. Codes of practice, guidelines, and specifications. Under the general term of 'standard' a number of levels of enforcement are distinguished, though often these do not seem to be officially defined (codes of practice are normally 'self-imposed' within the developer's organisation). Broadly speaking, codes of practice and guidelines indicate desirable good practice to which conformance cannot be precisely determined, whereas specifications are precise and conformance is determinable by appropriate tests or analyses.

4. Functional standards ('profiles'). Groups of interrelated standards which together service a user need (function), for example standards for all layers in Open Systems Interconnection, e.g. MAP and TOP.

Timing of standards

There is a strong debate concerning the appropriate time to determine standards. If standardization is undertaken too early, then the technology may not have advanced enough, and standardization may fix on practices which arc not adequate, whereas if standardization were undertaken once the technology is advanced, then several incompatible practices may have become established so that the cost of change to conform to a single standard is prohibitive.

Standardization activities always face this dilemma, which is further exacerbated by the very long time it can take to formulate a standard. Thus it may be appropriate to develop a standard along with the development of the technology by the industrial concerns involved. The Open Systems Interconnection (OSI) standards are a pre-eminent example of these prospective standards. Alternatively a standard may be drafted but not fully developed, but still be published as an intercept standard, termed by the BSI a 'draft for development'. Such publication usually arises because insufficient agreement about the standard can be reached due to the immaturity of the technology, or sometimes because the various parties have irreconcilable interests which might be resolved through the passage of time.

Certification

The consumer's interest in standards is in the quality (fitness for purpose) of the software products that he or she wishes to purchase or use. As such, it is prospective product specification standards that are the concern. All other standards are secondary, a means to an end. Process standards only appear to be of value when there arc no product standards or insufficient product standards to enable the proper assessment of the quality of a product. For bespoke development of software, process standards are currently the only way to ensure quality. Of course, the process standards would include processes for specifying the intended software and assessing the successful attainment of these intentions.

Standards, particularly specification standards, bring with them the need to be able to prove conformance with the standard. This proof could be furnished in response to some dispute concerning claims of conformance (labelling a product with the number of a standard would be deemed to be such a claim), but could be furnished independently of any dispute through some certification procedure. Certification requires the participation of some independent organization, which itself will have to be licensed or certified as competent to make certifications. Certification procedures and agencies will be addressed later in this chapter.

Standards bodies

Standards making today is dominated by the international standards organizations, reflecting the international nature of trade. The most significant of these organizations are:

1. ISO, the International Organization for Standardization, founded in 1947, having the national standards bodies of 73 countries as members, with 14 other countries as corresponding members.

2. IEC, the International Electrotechnical Commission, founded in 1906, now constituted from the national equivalents of 43 countries. ISO and IEC have established a formal agreement that their activities should be complementary, so that together they should provide a comprehensive standardization service.

3. CCITT, the Comite Consultatif International de Telegraphie et Telephonie, a sub-agency of the United Nations International Telecommunications Union.

4. CEN, Comite European de Normalisation, and CENELEC, the electrotechnical counterpart of CEN, cover the European Economic Community (EEC) and the European Free Trade Association (EFTA). CEN was founded in 1961 from the national standards bodies of 16 countries of the EEC and EFTA, plus Spain, which was

not a member of either of these at that time. CENELEC was founded in 1971 from other groups known as CENEL and CENELCOM.

5. ASMO, the Arab standardization and Metrology Organization founded in 1965 by the Arab League.

There are also regional organizations for Africa (ARSO), Eastern Europe and the Commonwealth of Independent States (CMEA), the Americas (COPANT), and the Pacific area (PASC).

ISO/IEC have made explicit recommendations that appropriate standards should be cited in law, so that legislative work can be simplified and accelerated, barriers to trade can be eliminated, and technical regulations can be updated easily in the face of technological advance.

ISO, IEC and international standardization

Both ISO and IEC have their headquarters in Geneva. The IEC was established in 1906 to standardize developments in the electrotechnical industries. The technical work of ISO is carried out by Technical Committees (TC) which are each responsible for an area of technology. These committees are established by the ISO Council, but thereafter determine their own programme of work. Standardization in the area of information technology is carried out by a joint ISO and IEC committee established in 1987. This is JTC1 Information Technology, which integrates the work of the previous ISO committee TC97 Information Processing Systems and IEC Technical Committee Information Technology Equipment and sub-committee IEC/SC 47B Microprocessor systems. JTC1 is responsible for standardization in the field of information technology systems (including microprocessor hardware and software) and equipment, but does not cover specific applications in areas like banking, industrial automation, and process control.

The Technical Committees in turn establish sub-committees (SC) and working groups (WG) to cover different aspects of their work. Each Technical Committee and sub-committee has a secretariat assigned to an ISO member body by the ISO Council for Technical Committees or the parent Technical Committee for sub-committees. Each working group has a convenor appointed by the parent Technical Committee. There is some national advantage in having the secretariat of committee, and in consequence there can be competition for these roles. The member bodies that are actively involved in a particular committee are designated participating bodies, and have an obligation to attend meetings and vote.

Most of the sub-committees and working groups of JTC1 are of concern to software engineers.

Altogether there were 164 technical committees in ISO at the end of 1987, some of which do work of interest to the software engineering community. Principal among these are:

1. ISO/TC46 - Information and documentation - concerned with the standardization of practices relating to libraries, documentation and information centres, indexing and abstracting services, archives, information science and publishing. Of particular interest are SC4/WG1 on character sets, and SC4/WG6 on electronic publishing.

2. ISO/TC176 - Quality management and quality assurance - concerned with standardization of generic quality management, including quality systems, quality assurance, and generic supporting technologies, including standards which provide guidance on the selection and use of these standards. All work of this committee is of concern in software engineering, and particularly SC2/WG5 on software quality assurance.

3. ISO/TC184 - Industrial automation systems - concerned with standardization in the field of industrial automation systems encompassing the application of multiple technologies such as information systems, machines and equipment, and telecommunications. Of particular interest here are SC4 on external representations of product data, including IGES, the Initial Graphical Exchange Specification, for engineering drawings, and MMS, the Manufacturing Message Service, that is part of the MAP system of communication standards.

Most national standards-making bodies 'shadow' these committees, arranging their internal committee structures so as to relate to them easily.

ISO standards are prepared through a number of stages. A new area of concern is identified and a new work item (NWI) is proposed and agreed at some level within ISO, usually at the Technical Committee level. Usually this work item will propose the development of an international standard, although sometimes it will lead to a number of studies to clarify the area before specific standards-making activities can be begun.

An example of this preliminary study activity is seen in the Special Working Group (SWG) on Systems Software Interfaces (SSI) attached to the Advisory Group of JTC1. This Working Group debates the need for generic interfaces to operating systems and related services, and has to take into account concerns such as attempts to standardize Job Control Languages, and the needs for application portability.

Once a work item has been agreed and assigned to a particular sub-committee (or a new sub-committee raised to handle it), then its first step towards an international standard is to create a draft proposal (DP) for circulation and study within the Technical Committee. This DP may be written from scratch, but more typically would start with some existing document. This could be a national standard, as happened with ISO 9000 which started from BS5750, and ISO 646 which started from the better known ANSI ASCII standard. Alternatively it could start from some industry standard as has happened with Posix, working from

Unix. The DP is debated and modified a number of times until as wide an agreement as possible has been reached (ideally a consensus) and the Technical Committee feels it is suitable to become an official standard of ISO.

At this point the draft proposal is forwarded to the secretariat for registration as a Draft International Standard (DIS). The DIS is circulated to all member bodies for voting. If 75% of the votes cast are in favour of the DIS, it is sent to the ISO Council for acceptance as an international standard. While a consensus is not necessary, it is important that no major disagreements remain, and all issues raised should be answered. The vote in ISO Council provides a final check on this. If the DIS fails in its membership vote, it may have to continue through more draft proposals, although it may also be issued as an intercept standard.

Under special circumstances, standards that have been prepared in organizations other than ISO may be adopted without technical change (but of course with formatting changes to conform to ISO requirements). These procedures are referred to as the abbreviated procedures; the standard effectively enters the ISO procedures at the DIS stage, going straight into voting for acceptance.

All ISO standards are subject to a periodic review at not more than five yearly intervals, when they could be confirmed for a further period, be withdrawn, or be revised. In a rapidly changing technology like computing, such frequent review and revision is essential. In citing standards it is important to indicate which revision of the standard is being referred to. This is done by indicating the year of the revision, as in 'ISO 4057: 1986'.

Functional standards and profiles are handled in a similar manner, with a proposed draft International Standard Profile (pdlSP) subject to voting within JTC1, leading to the promulgation of the ISP.

For further details of ISO procedures, the required format of standards, and the various forms used within ISO procedures, the ISO Directives should be consulted.

Standardization in the UK

Information technology standards in the UK are largely produced through the British Standards Institute (BSI). The BSI originated in 1901 as the Engineering Standards Committee, set up by various professional bodies, and later became the British Engineering Standards Association. A Royal Charter was granted in 1929, and in 1931 the body adopted its present name. It is an independent organization, charged in its charter to draw up standards by voluntary agreement among interested parties, and to promote the adoption of standards once they have been drawn up. The BSI also operates a certification service, particularly well known for its award of 'kitemarks' of quality.

The BSI's standards work is funded largely by sales of standards, the running of specialized information services concerning standards, and by subscription from member organiza-

Reference	Secretariat	Title
AG	ANSI	Advisory group
WG2	BSI	Instrumentation magnetic tape
SWG	ANSI	Procedures
SWG	SCC	Strategic planning
SWG	SNV	Registration authorities
SWG	IISC	Systems software interface
SC1	AFNOR	Vocabulary
WG1	SCC	Advisory group for SC 1
WG4	ANSI	Fundamental terms and omce systems
WG5	DIN	Software
WG6	SCC	Hardware, services and operations
WG7	SCC	Communication
SC2	AFNOR	Character sets and information coding
WG1	SNV	Code extension techniques
WG2	ANSI	Multiple-octet coded character set
WG3	SNV	7-bit and 8-bit codes
WG6		Control functions
WG7		Coded representation of picture and audio information
SC6	ANSI	Telecommunications and information exchange between systems
WG1	ANSI	Data link layer
WG2	BSI	Network layer
WG3	DIN	Physical layer
WG4	AFNOR	Transport layer
SC7	SCC	Software development and system documentation
WG1	ANSI	Symbols, charts, and diagrams
WG2	BSI	Software system documentation
WG3	SCC	Program design
WG5	SCC	Reference model for software development
SC11	ANSI	Flexible magnetic media for digital data interchange
SC13	DIN	Interconnection of equipment
WG3	DIN	Lower-level interface functional requirements and lower-level interfaces
SC14	SIS	Representation of data elements
WG1	SIS	Standardization guidelines for the representation of data elements
WG3	SIS	Terminology
WG4	ANSI	Coordination of data element standardization
SC15	SNV	Labelling and file structure
SC17	BSI	Identification and credit cards
WG1	DIN	Physical characteristics and test methods for ID cards
WG4	AFNOR	Integrated circuit card
WG5	ANSI	Registration Management Group
WG7	BSI	Data content, tracks I and 2
SC18	ANSI	Test and office systems
WG1		User requirements and SC18 management support
AG	ANSI	Advisory group
WG3	BSI	Document architecture
WG4	AFNOR	Procedures for test interchange

Table A.1   **Principal sub-committees and working groups of JTC1 Information Technology. Secretariat of JTC1 is ANSI.**

Reference	Secretariat	Title
WG5	SCC	Content architectures
WG8	ANSI	Text description and processing languages
WG9	ANSI	User/systems interfaces and symbols
SC20	DIN	Data cryptographic techniques
WG1	BSI	Secret key algorithms and applications
WG2	AFNOR	Public key cryptosystem and mode of use
WG3	ANSI	Use of enciphertnent techniques in communication architectures
SC21	ANSI	Information retrieval, transfer and management for open systems interconnection (OSI)
WG1	AFNOR	OSI architecture
WG3	SCC	Database
WG4	JISC	OSI management
WG5	BSI	Specific application services
WG6	ANSI	OSI session, presentation and common application services
SC22	SCC	Languages
WG2	BSI	Pascal
WG3	SCC	APL
WG4	ANSI	COBOL
WG5	ANSI	FORTRAN
WG8	SNV	Basic
WG9	ANSI	Ada
WG11	ANSI	Binding techniques
WG12	AFNOR	Language conformity validation
WG13	BSI	Modula 2
WG14	ANSI	C
SC23	JISC	Optical digital data discs
SC24	DIN	Computer graphics
SC47B	JISC	Microprocessor systems
WG1		Definitions of microprocessor instructions and their mnemonic representation
WG3		Bus connector pic assignments
WG4		. Architecture
WG5		Guidelines for the technical details
WG6		Revision of Publication 821
WG7		Microprocessor systems quality management
SC83	DKE	Information technology equipment
WG1		Home electronic systems
WG2		Fibre optic connections for local area networks
P&R		Planning and requirements

Table A.1   Continued.

tions, such as firms, trade associations, local authorities, and professional organizations, plus a government grant. Certification work is financed separately through the services provided. The BSI organizes itself in a manner that more or less 'shadows' the ISO structure, so that it is clear which parts of the BSI liaise with the Technical Committees, sub-committees and Working Groups of ISO.

There are six Councils responsible for the standards-making programme. Some 60 Standards Committees are responsible to these councils for authorizing work on standards. The actual work

Reference	Title	ISO liaison
IST/-	Office and information systems	JTCI
IST/-/1	Management panel for IST	
IST/-/2	European Harmonisation Panel	
IST/-/3	IEC/TC83 monitoring panel	
IST/1	Computer glossary	SCI
IST/2	Coding	SC2
IST/3	Office machines	
IST/3/-/1	Steering committee	
IST/3/1	Typewriter	
IST/3/9	Ribbons and spools	
IST/4	Magnetic tape and magnetic disc packs	
IST/5	Programming languages	SCZ2
IST/5/3	COBOL	
IST/5/4	Pascal	
	Prolog	
	C	
	Modula-2	
IST/5/	VDM Vienna Development Method	
IST/6	Data communications	SC6
IST/6/1	Data link layer	
IST/6/2	Network layer	
IST/6/3	Physical layer	
IST/6/4	Transport layer	
IST/6/6	LAN/PABX interfaces	
IST/8	Instrumentation magnetic tape	
IST/9	Punched cards	
IST/10	Paper tape for ADP	
IST/11	Labelling and file structure	SC15
IST/12	Banking procedures	
IST/13	Interconnection of units of DP equipment	SC13
IST/14	Representation of data elements	SC14
IST/14/-	Dial maintenance advisory panel	
IST/14/1	Guidelines	
IST/14/2	Check character systems	
IST/14/3	Dates and times (drafting)	
IST/15	Software development and documentation of computer-based systems	SC7
IST/15/2	Documentation of computer-based systems	
IST/15/3	Program design	
IST/15/5	Computer systems testing	
IST/15/6	Achievement of quality in software	
IST/17	Identification and credit cards	
IST/17/1	Credit card identifiers	
IST/18	Text preparation and interchange	SC18
IST/18/-/1	User requirementslmanagement support	
IST/18/3	Document structure (NDF)	
IST/18/4	Message transfer (electronic mail)	
IST/18/7	Keyboard layouts for omce machines and DP equipment	
IST/20	Sarety of DP and omce machines	
IST/20/1	Electrical safety of DPE	
IST/20/2	Electrical safety of ofnce equipment	
IST/20/3	Mechanical safety of DP and OE	
IST/20/4	Acoustic safety	
IST/20/5	Safety from fire in DP installation	
IST/20/6	Information technology equipment (drafting)	

Table A.2   **BSI standards committees.**

Reference	Title	ISO liaison
IST/21	Information retrieval, transfer and management for	
	open systems interconnection	SC21
IST/21/-/1	Co-ordination panel	
IST/21/1	OSI architecture	SC7/WGI
IST/21/1/1	Security architecture	
IST/21/1/2	Naming and addressmg	
IST/21/1/3	Formal description techniques	
IST/2 1/1/4	Conformance testing	
	Connectionless mode	
	Multi-peer transmission	
	Distributed application work	
IST/2 1/2	Graphics	
IST/21/2/1	Metafiles and interfaces	
IST/21/2/2	Language bindings	
IST/21/2/3	3D, GKS-3D and PHIGS	
IST/21/3	Database	SC7/WG3
	Database management reference model	
	Database languages	
	Information resource dictionary system	
	Remote database access	
IST/21/4	OSI management	SC7/WG4
	Management framework	
	Management information systems	
	Directory access	
IST/21/5	Specific application services	SC7/WG5
	File transfer, access and management	
	Virtual terminal	
	Job transfer and manipulation	
	OSCRL	
	Transaction mode	
	Management of distributed applications	
IST/21/6	Session, presentation	
	and common application services	SC7/WG8
IST/2 1/6/1	Session	
IST/2 1/6/2	Presentation	
IST/2 1/6/3	ASN.1	
IST/21/6/4	CASE association control	
IST/21/6/5	Commitment, concurrency and recovery	
	Upper layer architecture	
IST/23	Optical character and mark recognition	
IST/24	Continuous stationery for ADP	
IST/28	Drawing office equipment	

Table A.2   Continued

Reference	Title	ISO liaison
QMS/2	Quality Management Systems	
QMS/2/1	Quality Terminology	
QMS/2/2	Quality Management Procedures	
QMS/2/2/7	Software Quality Management Systems	TC176/ SC2/WG:
QMS/2/3	Reliability Systems	
QMS/2/4	Metrology Terms	
QMS/2/5	Quality Auditing	

Table A.3   BSI Coordinating and Advisory Committees of the Quality Management Systems Standards Committee QMS/2

on standards is undertaken by the numerous Technical Committees. These Technical Committees carry out their detailed work through panels, equivalent to the ISO working groups.

It is the Information Systems Council, designated S/- and its IST standards committee that is responsible for the standards of concern in software engineering. The technical committees and panels responsible to IST are shown in Table A.2. BSI reorganized its committees around 1980, to align these partially with the corresponding ISO committees, and the numbering of committees within IST were made to correspond to those of TC97. With the creation of JTC1 in 1987, some renumbering of committees of the former TC97 took place, but no changes were reflected into the BSI committees of IST. The ISO committees corresponding to the BSI committees are also given in Table A.2.

Standards for advanced manufacturing technology (AMT) are developed by the AMT Technical Committee, which corresponds to the ISO TC/184. It thus looks after the higher levels of the MAP communications protocols.

Generic engineering standards are the concern of the Quality Management Systems Standards Committee (QMS). QMS has a series of Coordinating and Advisory Committees, of which QMS/ 2 is responsible for Quality Management Systems through its panels shown in Table A.3. It is the QMS/2/2 Committee that is responsible for BS 5750, the UK equivalent of ISO 9000.

The work on BSI standards is initiated within a Technical Committee, but the initial drafting should preferably be done by a 'responsible body' and not the committee. Existing de facto standards, or documents produced by professional or trade associations, may form a suitable starting point. The Technical Committee, and particularly its BSI secretary, would be responsible for final drafting of the standard in the correct format, ready for public comment. Drafts are circulated for public comment, normally allowing eight weeks. This is usually done once only. All comments must be properly taken into account leading to consensus in the Technical Committee before the standard is published. Note that there is no voting procedure within BSI, unlike the approach taken in ISO and other standards making bodies.

When guidance is required urgently, but it is judged to be too early for satisfactory formulation of a standard, then a Draft for Development (an intercept standard) might be prepared instead.

Standardization in the USA

Standards-making in the USA follows quite a different pattern. The official standards body in the USA is ANSI, the American National Standards Institute. ANSI represents the USA in international standards bodies.

However, the actual formulation of standards is carried out by a number of accredited agencies. Accreditation is given only if the body can show that all interested parties are permitted to participate unrestricted by membership or financial constraints, and that an appropriate mechanism exists to reach consensus.

ANSI policy in the software engineering area is determined by the Information Systems Standards Board (ISSB). ANSI recognizes two major bodies in this area:

1. IEEE, the Institution of Electrical and Electronic Engineers, Computer Society, which covers the JTC1 areas of work of SC7, SC83, SC47, Posix, and LAN.

2. The X3 committee, with secretariat CBEMA (the Computer and Business Equipment Manufacturers Association), which covers all other areas of ISO JTC1 work.

The IEEE works through the raising of projects charged with preparing standards and guidelines in their particular area. The IEEE projects active in the software engineering area are shown in Table A.4. As projects complete their standard they are closed down, while new projects are raised regularly. The IEEE is very active in standards making, particularly in the development process and communications areas.

The X3 committee has a number of sub-committees charged with standardization in particular areas, and thus is similar in its approach to ISO or BSI. The most relevant sub-committees are shown in Table A.5.

Another important organization is the National Institute for Standards and Technology (NIST) formerly known as the National Bureau of Standards (NBS) which through its Institute of Computer Science and Technology (ICST), is charged with developing standards, providing technical assistance and conducting research for computers and related systems. It formulates Federal Information Processing Standards (FIPS) and issues these for conformance in US federal government work. The NIST also represents the US government in other public standards making activity, chairing the activity if the standardization is seen as critical to the US government.

Military standards

Military systems are very large and complex, typically either custom-built for a particular defence force, or built in relatively small numbers. Military systems frequently have very long lives, continuing in service for perhaps 25 years or more, with later systems being functionally compatible but built on a vastly different technological base.

Quality is a very important issue in military procurement, and most of the concerns about quality systems and project management began in military procurement. A major mechanism in the control of procurement has been the use of standards. The market forces that play an important role in ensuring quality in the civil sector are rarely present in the military sector.

Thus military administrations have established standards making and enforcement mechanisms. All too frequently the separate branches of the armed forces land, sea, and air have proceeded independently and duplicated each other's work, though clearly they do have major areas of interest that do not overlap. However, in the area of software they do overlap.

Over many years there has been a strong move to harmonize work on standardization, to bring the separate armed forces within a single defence force together, and to bring separate forces within a military alliance together.

There is no global or international effort in military standardization, but the military alliance NATO (North Atlantic Treaty Organisation) generates standards for use by member countries. Authority for all standards derives from the North Atlantic Council through either the Military Agency for Standardisation (MAS) or the Conference of National Armaments Directors (CNAD).

Standards are published as Allied Publications (APs) and the nature of the AP is indicated by its short title, e.g. Allied Quality Assurance Publications (AQAP), Allied Reliability and maintainability Publication (ARMP). Agreement to use APs by some or all of the member countries is recorded in the NATO Standardization Agreement (STANAG).

A key committee in relation to software is the AC/250 Main Group with its sub-groups:

1. SG VIII – review and development of AQAPs.

2. SC IX – reliability and maintainability assurance.

3. SG X – quality assurance of software.

The AC/250 group is responsible for AQAP 1, NATO requirements for Industrial Quality Control Systems and AQAP 13, NATO Software Quality Control System Requirements. Defence suppliers in the software industry are contractually required to comply with these standards. Both AQAP 1 and AQAP 13 are under review, firstly to consider the absorption of AQAP 13 requirements into AQAP 1, and secondly to consider the inclusion of aspects of the international civil quality systems standard ISO 9001 into a revised AQAP 1. In the longer term, a convergence between the military and civil standards is sought with perhaps the acceptance by defence procuring agencies of certification to the international civil standards.

In the UK, the senior Ministry of Defence (MOD) committee on standardization is the Defence Material Standardization Policy Committee, which operates largely through the Defence Engineering and Equipment Standardization Committee (DEESC) and the Defence Electrical and Electronic Standardisation Committee (DELSC). These committees in turn have specialist sub-committees dealing with specific technical topics.

The Directorate of Standardisation (D Stan) is responsible for coordinating and publishing the output of these committees. D Stan also maintains a register of MOD representation of BSI committees, over 400 of which are supported by MOD staff.

MOD standards are published in a variety of guises, the most well-known being Defence Standards (Def Stans), Joint Services Publications (JSPs) and Naval Engineering Standards (NES).

Reference	*Title*
P610	Computer dictionary, see 729, P1084 1089
P729	Software engineering terminology
T755	Extended hi-level language implementations
P770	Extended Pascal
P802	Local area networks
P802.1	High ievel interface working group ('Hi Li')
P802.3	CSMA/CD
P802.2	Logical link control
P802.4	Token bus
P802.5	Token ring
P802.6	Metropolitan area network (a slotted ring)
P802.7	Broadband TAG
P802.8	Fibre optics TAG
P828	Software configuration management plans
P829	Software test documentation
T855	Micro operating systems interface
P982	Standard dictionary for measures to produce reliable software
P1003.0	Guide to Posix-based open system architecture
T1003.1	Portable operating system — Posix
P1003.2	Shell and utility application interface
P1003.3	Test methods: measuring conformance to Posix
P1003.4	Real-time Posix extensions
P1003.5	Ada language binding for Posix
P1003.6	Security interface standards for Posix
P1016.2	Guide to software design descriptions
P1028	Software reviews and audits
P1044	Classification of software errors, faults, and failures
P1045	Software productivity metrics
P1059	A guide for software verification and validation
P1061	Software quality metrics methodology
P1062	Software certification
P1074	Software life cycle process
P1077	A recommended practice for design management
P1078	Information model description language
P1084-9	Computer terminology
P1141	FORTH: a microcomputer language standard
P1151	Modula-2
P1152	Object-oriented programming language

Table A.4 IEEE projects in software engineering

Reference	*Title*
X3H4	Information resources dictionary systems
X3H33	Virtual device interface and virtual device metafile
X3J3	FORTRAN
X3J4	COBOL
X3J11	C
X3L2	Character sets and coding
X3S3	Data communications
X3S3.4	Data link control procedures
X3T5	Open systems interconnection
X3T9	Input/output interfaces
X3T9.3	Intelligent peripheral interfaces
X3T9.5	Fibre distributed interface
X3V1	Office systems
X3V1.3	Message body format
X3V1.4	Message heading format and message related protocols

Table A.5   **ANSI X3 sub-committees in software engineering area**

Appendix B
Abbreviations

The following abbreviations have been used throughout this book and most are in common usage within the fields of computing and software engineering:

4GL	Fourth Generation Language
AFL	Abstract Family of Languages
AI	Artificial Intelligence
ANC	Additive Noise Channel
ANSI	American National Standards Institute
APSE	Ada Programming Support Environment
APT	Automatically Programmed Tools
AQAP	Allied Quality Assurance Publication
ASCII	American Standard Code for Information Interchange
ASMO	Arab Standardization and Metrology Organization
ASN	Abstract Syntax Notation
ASRS	Automated Storage and Retrieval System
ATM	Automated Teller Machine
BDOS	Basic Disk Operating System
BIOS	Basic Input/Output System
BNF	Backus Naur Form
BS	British Standard
BSI	British Standards Institute
CAD	Computer Aided Design
CAM	Computer Aided Manufacturing
CAPM	Computer Aided Production Management
CAPP	Computer Aided Process Planning
CASE	Computer Aided Software Engineering
CCC	Change and Configuration Control
CCS	Calculus for Communicating Systems
CCTA	Central Computer and Communications Agency
CIM	Computer Integrated Manufacturing
CIP	Computer-aided Intuition-guided Programming
CISC	Complex Instruction Set Computer
CLOS	Common Lisp Object System
CMF	Configuration Management Facility
CMOS	Complementary Metal Oxide Semiconductor
CNC	Computer Numerical Control
COCOMO	Constructive Cost Model
CORE	Controlled Requirements Expression
CPM	Critical Path Method
CPU	Central Processing Unit
CSMA	Carrier Sense Multiple Access
CSMA-CD	Carried Sense Multiple Access with Collision Detection
CSP	Communicating Sequential Processes
DBMS	Database Management System
DIS	Draft International Standard
DMA	Direct Memory Access
DMAC	Direct Memory Access Controller
DNC	Direct Numerical Control
DP	Data Processing

DTI	Department of Trade and Industry
ERA	Entity-Relation-Attribute
ERAE	Entity-Relation-Attribute-Event
ETA	Event Tree Analysis
EVES	Environment for Verifying and Emulating Software
FAT	File Allocation Table
FDDI	Fibre Distributed Data Interface
FIFO	First-In First-Out
FMS	Flexible Manufacturing System
FSM	Finite State Machine
FTA	Fault Tree Analysis
FTLS	Formal Top-Level Specification
GKS	Graphical Kernel System
GSA	General Service Administration
GSM	Generalized Sequential Machine
GT	Group Technology
HCI	Human-computer interaction
HOL	Higher Order Logic
HOOD	Heirarchical Object Oriented Design
I/O	Input Output
IDA	Inter-communication Data Areas
IEC	International Electrotechnical Commission
IEEE	Institute of Electrical and Electronics Engineers
IKBS	Intelligent Knowledge-Based System
IPSE	Integrated Project Support Environment
ISAM	Indexed Sequential Access Method
ISDN	Integrated Services Digital Network
ISO	International Standards Organisation
JCL	Job Control Language
JIT	Just-In-Time
JSD	Jackson System Design
JSP	Jackson Structured Programming
KADS	Knowledge Acquisition and Documentation Structuring
KBRA	Knowledge-Based Requirements Assistant
LAN	Local Area Network
LBMS	Learmonth and Burchett Management Systems
LIM	Library Interconnection Language
LOC	Lines-Of-Code
LOOPS	Lisp Object-Oriented Programming System
MASCOT	Modular Approach to Software Construction Operation and Test
MIMD	Multiple-Instruction Multiple-Datastream
ML	MetaLanguage
MOD	Ministry of Defence
MPS	Master production Schedule
MRE	Magnitude of Relative Error
MRP	Manufacturing Resource Planning
MUX	Multiplexer
NAG	Numerical Algorithms Group
NATO	North Atlantic Treaty Organisation
NCC	National Computing Centre
NIST	National Institute for Standards and Technology
NSE	Network Software Environment
OBCS	Object Control Structure
OMS	Object Management System

OOD	Object-Oriented Design
OORA	Object-Oriented Requirements Analysis
OPCS	Operation Control Structure
PC	Personal Computer
PERT	Programme Evaluation and Review Techniqe
PES	Programmable Electronic Systems
PID	Personal Identification Device
PLC	Programmable Logic Controller
PMS	Problem Monitoring System
PSD	Process Structure Diagram
PSL	Problem Statement Language
PWB	Programmers Workbench
QA	Quality Assurance
QMS	Quality Management System
RAM	Random Access Memory
RCS	Revision Control System
RISC	Reduced Instruction Set Computer
RLP	Requirements Language Processor
RML	Requirements Modelling Language
ROM	Read-Only Memory
RPC	Remote Procedure Call
RSL	Requirements Specification Language
SA/RT	Structured Analysis/Real-Time
SA/SD	Structured Analysis/Structured Design
SCCS	Source Code Control System
SDLC	Synchronous Data Link Control
SEPT	Shortest Expected Processing Time
SFTA	Software Fault Tree Analysis
SI	Systeme Internationale
SID	Symbolic Interactive Debugger
SISD	Single-Instruction Single-Datastream
SLOC	Source Lines Of Code
SMA	Software Maintenance Association
SML	Standard MetaLanguage
SOW	Statement Of Work
SPC	Stored Program Controlled
SQL	Structured Query Language
SREM	Software Requirements Engineering Methodology
SSADM	Structured Systems Analysis and Design Method
TGM	Time grain marker
TMR	Triple Modular Redundant
TPA	Transient Processing Area
TSQM	Test Specification and Quality Management
UD	Uniquely Decodable
UIMS	User Interface Management System
V&V	Verification and Validation
VDM	Vienna Development Method
VDU	Visual Display Unit
VMCS	Version Management Common Service
VTFL	Variable-To-Fixed-Length
VTVL	Variable-To-Variable-Length
WAN	Wide Area Network
WBS	Work Breakdown Structure
WIMP	Window/Icon/Mouse/Pointer
WORM	Write Once/Read Many
WYSIWYG	What you see is what you get

Index